Organized Business and the New Global Order

Advances in Political Science: An International Series

Members of the editorial board: **Asher Arian** (general editor), **Luigi Graziano,
William Lafferty, Theodore Lowi** and **Carole Pateman**

As an expression of its commitment to global political science, the International
Political Science Association initiated this series to promote the publication of
rigorous scholarly research by its members and affiliated groups. Conceptual and
theoretical developments in the discipline, and their explication in various settings, represent the special focus of the series.

Titles include:

Christa Altenstetter and James Warner Björkman (*editors*)
HEALTH POLICY REFORM, NATIONAL VARIATIONS AND GLOBALIZATION

Dirk Berg-Schlosser and Jeremy Mitchell (*editors*)
CONDITIONS OF DEMOCRACY IN EUROPE, 1919–39
Systematic Case-Studies

Klaus von Beyme
PARLIAMENTARY DEMOCRACY
TRANSITION TO DEMOCRACY IN EASTERN EUROPE

Ofer Feldman
THE JAPANESE POLITICAL PERSONALITY

Justin Greenwood and Henry Jacek (*editors*)
ORGANIZED BUSINESS AND THE NEW GLOBAL ORDER

Asha Gupta
BEYOND PRIVATIZATION
A Global Perspective

Mino Vianello and Gwen Moore (*editors*)
GENDERING ELITES
Economic and Political Leadership in Industrialized Societies

Advances in Political Science
Series Standing Order ISBN 0–333–71458–X
(*outside North America only*)

You can receive future titles in this series as they are published by placing a standing order.
Please contact your bookseller or, in case of difficulty, write to us at the address below with
your name and address, the title of the series and the ISBN quoted above.

Customer Services Department, Macmillan Distribution Ltd, Houndmills, Basingstoke,
Hampshire RG21 6XS, England

Organized Business and the New Global Order

Edited by

Justin Greenwood
Jean Monnet Professor of European Public Policy
The Robert Gordon University
Aberdeen

and

Henry Jacek
Professor of Political Science
McMaster University
Ontario
Canada

Foreword by Philippe C. Schmitter
European University Institute

in association with
INTERNATIONAL POLITICAL SCIENCE ASSOCIATION

First published in Great Britain 2000 by
MACMILLAN PRESS LTD
Houndmills, Basingstoke, Hampshire RG21 6XS and London
Companies and representatives throughout the world

A catalogue record for this book is available from the British Library.

ISBN 0–333–78991–1

First published in the United States of America 2000 by
ST. MARTIN'S PRESS, INC.,
Scholarly and Reference Division,
175 Fifth Avenue, New York, N.Y. 10010

ISBN 0–312–22796–5

Library of Congress Cataloging-in-Publication Data
Organized business and the new global order / edited by Justin
Greenwood and Henry Jacek ; foreword by Philippe C. Schmitter.
p.   cm. — (Advances in political science)
"In association with International Political Science Association."
Includes bibliographical references and index.
ISBN 0–312–22796–5 (cloth)
1. Commercial associations.   2. International economic relations.
3. Competition, International.   I. Greenwood, Justin.   II. Jacek,
Henry J.   III. Series: Advances in political science (New York,
N.Y.)
HF294.O73   1999
658'.049—dc21   99–36940
                                                                        CIP

This book is printed on paper suitable for recycling and made from fully managed and sustained forest sources.

10   9   8   7   6   5   4   3   2   1
09   08   07   06   05   04   03   02   01   00

Printed and bound in Great Britain by
Antony Rowe Ltd, Chippenham, Wiltshire

Contents

List of Tables and Figures

Tables

Figures

Foreword

To those few scholars who have struggled to convince their respective disciplines and the public-at-large that 'organized business interests' are a significant and underestimated component of domestic and international political economy, this book will come as a particularly welcome contribution. It elevates the discussion to the level of the entire globe (even if the authors do not find a great deal of 'order' there); examines a wider range of political units (national-states, supra-national regions, and subnational provinces) than ever before in such collective efforts; and covers examples of virtually all economic sectors (industry, agriculture, commerce and finance).

To those out there in the realm of international relations who have insisted for so long that only states acting as unitary actors promoting their (alleged) national interests count, and to those out there in the realm of business administration/economics who have built their models exclusively on the competitive interaction of individual firms maximizing profits or market shares, this book may come as a bit of a shock. Collectively, its chapters make a strong (but not uniform) case for the importance of 'business interest associations' at various levels of aggregation and in various sectors of the economy in regulating markets organizing production and distribution, improving productivity and influencing public policies. These specialized intermediaries are shown not only to be significant players within their respective domestic economies, but also to have reconfigured their operations at the international level in ways that both indirectly affect the positions taken by national negotiators in international forums, and directly improve their capability to generate public goods across national borders.

I doubt that *Organized Business and the New Global Order* will be successful in compelling the practitioners of these disciplines to revise their respective paradigms. It is well-known that such deeply-rooted systems of thought are never defeated merely by the facts, but only by an alternative theory – and this multi-authored and multi-sited volume makes no effort to create such an alternative. It does, however, provide lots of 'food for thought' for those who would take up such a much needed task.

One place to start might be *'the paradox of liberalization'* – a point that is made in several essays in the book. Precisely as the dominant consensus in economic theory, neoliberalism, is put increasingly into practice at the international and even global level – previous barriers to the exchange of all factors of production are dismantled and market forces are unleashed from the constraints of national protection and regulation – the greater is the need for new policies of consumer protection and product regulation at the supranational level. The very increase in the scale and scope of exchange creates new asymmetries of information and potentialities for collusion, and these tend to destroy the mutual confidence of producers and consumers in the very market mechanisms that have been so dramatically liberated. Unless some new arrangements for market governance can be established, the neoliberal project risks becoming self-defeating rather than self-reinforcing.

However, because it is so difficult to reach agreement on these norms and standards among such a heterogeneous set of national interests, and because 'sovereign' states are so reluctant to endow formal international organisations with the authoritative/coercive means for implementing these rules, the burden of adjusting to the need tends to fall on associative forms of collective action. Initially, the response comes in the form of voluntaristic cooperation between national business associations, but increasingly (and, especially, where there exist supranational regional policy-making organizations, for example the European Union) the affected parties begin to establish more specialized, direct member associations across national borders and to endow them with a greater capacity to monitor and enforce the new regulatory norms and production standards.

Several of the contributions in the volume make use of a theoretical distinction that Wolfgang Streeck and I developed in the course of our Organization of Business Interests Project in the early 1980s. We found it useful to analyze the organizational properties of the national business associations we were studying in terms of two, often contradictory, sets of causal factors: 'the logic of membership' and the 'logic of influence'. At different points of time in the history of these organizations, and under the changing conditions of specific sectors and countries, these variables tended to push BIAs (as we called them) in different directions. It would seem that the same is true for supranational forms of business associability – even though the time frame is much shorter and the sectoral national circumstances are more varied. In a few cases – Karsten Ronit's account of the shipping industry is clearly the primary example – the emerging organizational structures are being generated 'from below' by prospective members with little or no encouragement, or subsidization from inter-governmental organizations. As hypothesized, the outcome is a more fragmented, specialized, voluntaristic set of BIAs or, in other words, an essentially pluralist system of weak governance. Elsewhere, there exist relatively powerful external sponsors in the form of supranational policy-makers – the chapter by Justin Greenwood captures this best – and the resulting organizational structure is much more concentrated, monopolistic and authoritative (specially at the sectoral level). Again, this is more-or-less what one would have expected on the basis of previous patterns emerging within national states.

Having observed these similarities, I hesitate to extrapolate further and claim that nothing new is going on at the global level as far as business associability is concerned. For one thing, enormous transformations have been occurring at the level of firms in terms of transnational operation and concentration of ownership. This has produced a subset of very large and very resourceful organizations of production/ distribution that are quite capable of acting alone, bypassing altogether the need for 'concerting' with smaller and medium-sized firms, and addressing their demands directly to the relevant authorities at whatever level of aggregation. One development that I personally found puzzling was the almost simultaneous emergence of 'clubs' composed of a restricted number of very large enterprise directors and dedicated to influencing the policy-processes of regional and global institutions. The model was, clearly, the American (national) Business Round Table, but such informal means of coordination have now been cloned in Europe (the European Round Table of Industrialists), Canada (Canadian Business Council on National Issues), Mexico (Consejo de Hombres de Negocios) and, to a much lesser extent, the Pacific Basin (Pacific Basin Economic Council and APEC Business Advisory Council). Only the ERT is explicitly transnational in its activities, but all of these 'clubs' have been active players on issues transcending their national borders. What we may be observing is a rupture in the previous pattern of organizational development that leads to more and more elaborate and formalized hierarchies of intersectoral or 'class' coordination towards more interpersonal and informal means of nevertheless comprehensive collective action – but one that quite deliberately segregates the 'business community' into units of different size. Whether this is related to the afore-mentioned trends toward globalization and regionalization, and whether it is being driven exclusively by 'the logic of membership' among large enterprises, has yet to be determined.

So I invite the reader to take a voyage into largely unchartered waters. The essays in this volume will lead him or her to almost every continent and into a wide range of economic activities. Most importantly, he or she will discover for the first time the rising importance of an archipelago of recently formed 'regional islands' whose functional tasks and organizational configurations have yet to be determined. Nevertheless, individual firms and organized business interests have quickly landed upon them and are busy trying to exploit them for their own purposes. Perhaps I am exaggerating, but my reading of these preliminary maps suggests that these regions may be even more susceptible to being transformed into political units colonized by 'executive committees for governing the common interests of the Bourgeoisie' than the much more established nation-states from whence they embarked.

European University Institute   PHILIPPE C. SCHMITTER

Acknowledgement

This book could not have been completed without the editorial assistance provided by Lara Stancich and Linda Strangward. We owe them a considerable 'thank you'.

J. G.
H. J.

Notes on the Contributors

William D. Coleman is Professor of Political Science and Director of the Institute of Globalization and the Human Condition at McMaster University. He is the author of *Financial Services, Globalization and Domestic Policy Change: A Comparison of North America and the European Union* (1996), *Business and Politics: A Study in Collective Action* (1988) and *The Independence Movement in Quebec, 1945–1980* (1984). He is also co-editor with Henry Jacek of *Regionalism, Business Interests and Public Policy* (1989).

Michelle Egan is Assistant Professor in the School of International Service at the American University in Washington DC. Her research focuses on comparative integration, comparative public policy and institutional analysis. She is currently working on a manuscript on interstate commerce, corporate strategy and regulatory boundaries in the EU.

Nicole Gallant is Research Intern at the Asia Pacific Foundation of Canada. She has recently been awarded an MA in Political Science from McMaster University. Forthcoming publications include 'Canada's Role in APEC', in *Canada Among Nations*, with Karen Minden and Paul Irwin, and 'Apec's Dilemmas: Institution-building around the Pacific Rim', in *Pacific Affairs*, with Richard Stubbs.

Rolf Gerritsen is Professor of Local Government and Applied Policy at the University of Canberra. His research interests lie in the area of national and regional economic development policy; agriculture and resources policy; and service delivery to remote and rural areas.

Justin Greenwood is Jean Monnet Professor of European Public Policy at the Robert Gordon University, Aberdeen. He is the author of *Representing Interests in the European Union* (1997), editor of the *European Casebook on Business Alliances* (1995), and co-editor of *Collective Action in the European Union: Interests and the New Politics of Associability* (1997), and *Organised Interests and the European Community* (1992).

Elisabetta Gualmini is a doctoral researcher in Political Science, working at the Centre of Public Policy Analysis at the University of

xiii

Bologna and collaborating with POLEIS – Centre for Comparative Political Research at the Bocconi University in Milan. Her main interest areas cover labour market policies and organised interest groups. She has written *La politica del lavoro in Italia*.

Henry Jacek is Professor of Political Science at McMaster University in Hamilton, Ontario, Canada. His main research interest centres on the public policy role of interest associations, especially organized business, in regional governance regimes such as NAFTA. His published work in recent years has dealt with subnational public policy processes as well. He is co-editor and co-author of *Regionalism, Business, International and Public Policy*. Although he is interested mainly in comprehensive business organizations, he has reported on developments in the chemical and agrifood sectors. Conceptually he is interested in modern corporatist practices, especially those that result in the establishment of private interest government regimes.

Martha Diaz de Landa is Director of the Research and Political Analysis Institute at the Universidad Católica de Córdoba. She has doctorate in Law and Social Science, and is director of the Instituto de Investigacion y Analisis Politico in the School of Political Science and International Relations at the Catholic University of Cordoba, Cordoba, Argentina. She is also Professor of Sociology in the Law School of the National University of Cordoba. Her current research centers on industrial policy in Brazil and Argentina, especially in the more dynamic sectors such as the automobile and food sectors.

Luca Lanzalaco is Associate Professor of Public Administration at the Bocconi University in Milan and acting Professor of Public Administration at the University of Bologna. He has written several articles and books about business interest associations, industrial relations and political theory. He recently published a book on the institutional analysis of politics entitled *Istituzioni, Organizzazioni, Potere* (1995).

Éric Montpetit is a PhD candidate in Political Science at McMaster University. His dissertation topic is 'Balancing Green and Brown: Institutions and the Politics of Sustainable Agriculture'. He is coauthor of 'Retrenchment in Agriculture: Analyzing Policy Change in France and the United States', published in *World Politics*. Eric has also written on the Canadian Constitutional Crisis and on Political Party Mandates and the Life-Cycle of Partisan Realignments.

Sergei Peregudov is Professor of Political Science at the Institute of World Economy and International Relations at the Russian Academy of Sciences, where his research interests and publications have centred on business interest groups in Russia.

Karsten Ronit is a lecturer at the University of Copenhagen. He is contributing editor of *Organized Interests and the European Community* (1992), and *Evolution of Interest Representation and Development of the Labour Market in Post-Socialist Countries* (1995). He has researched and published on business associability in national, European and global contexts.

Mariá Carola Sajem is a doctoral student at the Graduate Institute of International Studies in Geneva. She is a research associate at the Instituto de Investigacion y Analisis Politico in the School of Political Science and International Relations, Catholic University of Cordoba, Cordoba, Argentina, where she received her licenciature. Mariá is a specialist in regional integration processes which she also teaches as an Assistant Professor in international relations. In particular she is doing research on industrial policy and organized business in MERCOSUR.

Volker Schneider is Professor of Political Science at the University of Konstanz.

Richard Stubbs is a Professor in the Department of Political Science, McMaster University, and a research associate at the Joint Centre for Asia Pacific Studies, University of Toronto – York University. He is author of *Hearts and Minds in Guerrilla Warfare: The Malayan Emergency 1948–1960* (1989); co-editor of the following: with Geoffrey Underhill, *Political Economy and the Changing Global Order* (1994); with Amitav Acharya *New Challenges for ASEAN: Emerging Policy Issues* (1995); with Paul Rich *The Counter-Isurgent State: Guerrilla Warfare and State Building in the Twentieth Century* (1997).

Geoffrey R.D. Underhill is Lecturer in Politics and International Studies and Director of the MA programme in International Political Economy at the University of Warwick. He has published on the political economy of international trade, money and finance issues, including (ed. with Richard Stubbs) *Political Economy and the Changing Global Order* (1994); *The Single Market and Global Economic Integration*, special issue of *Journal of European Public Policy* (ed. with William Coleman), vol. 2, no. 3, 1995; *The New World Order in International Finance* (ed.) 1996. His recent book is *Industrial Crisis and the Open Economy: Politics, Global Trade and the Textile Industry in the Advanced Economies*.

Duncan R. Wood is Assistant Professor of International Relations at the Instituto Tecnologico Autonomo de Mexico (ITAM) in Mexico City, where he has taught since 1996. His areas of research interest are the politics of international money and finance, the political economy of financial crisis and financial reform in Mexico. He has published on the role of international financial institutions in South Africa, and is currently co-authoring, with George MacLean, an introductory text on political studies entitled *Introduction to Political Studies: Incorporating the Political Economy Approach*.

List of Abbreviations

ABAC	APEC Business Advisory Council
ABM	Mexican Bankers' Association
ACCI	ASEAN Chambers of Commerce and Industry
ADEFA	Motor Car Factories Association of Argentina
AENOR	(Fig. 13.1)
AFL-CIO	American Federation of Labor/Congress of Industrial Organizations
AFTA	ASEAN Free Trade Agreement
AIMI	American Textile Manufacturers Institute
AISI	American Iron and Steel Institute
AMCHAM-EU	The EU Committee of the American Chamber of Commerce
AMUE	Association for Monetary Union in Europe
ANCE	The National Association for Foreign Trade (Italy)
ANFAVEA	Automobiles Producers Brazilian Association
ANIMA	The National Association of Italian Mechanic Industry
ANSI	American National Standards Institute
APEC	Asia Pacific Economic Cooperation
API	Milan Association of Small- and Medium-sized Firms
APTA	Automotive Products Trade Agreement
ARB	Association of Russian Banks
ASEAN	Association of South east Asian Nations
Assolombarda	Milan association of industry
ATA	Admission Temporaire/Temporary Admission
AWE	Average Weekly Earnings
BCNI	Canadian Business Council on National Issues
BIAs	Business interest associations
BSI	British Standards Institute
BRT	American Business Round Table
CAFTA	Canadian–American Free Trade Agreement
CARICOM	Caribbean Common Market
CARIFTA	Caribbean Free Trade Association
CAOBISCO	Association of the Chocolate, Biscuit and Confectionary Industries in the EEC

CC	Chamber of Commerce
CCIAA	Chamber of Commerce, Industry, Artisanship and Agriculture (Italy)
CE	Council of Europe
CCHREI	Canadian Council for Human Resources in the Environment Industry
CECIMO	Comité Européen de Coopération des Industries de la Machine-Outil
CEEP	European Centre of Public Enterprises
CEFIC	European Chemical Industry Council
CEIA	Canadian Environmental Industry Association
CEN	Comité Européen de la Normalisation
CENELEC	Comité Européen de la Normalisation Electrotechnique
CEO	Chief Executive Officer
CEPT	Common Effective Preferential Tariff
CIF	Cost, Insurance and Freight
CIS	Commonwealth of Independant States
CLC	Canadian Labor Congress
CMC	Canadian Meat Council
CMI	Comité Maritime International
CNA	Milan Association of Artisan Firms
CNBV	Comision Nacional Bancaria y de Valores
COMPARMEX	Confederation of Employers of the Republic of Mexico
CONCANAC	Confederation of National Chambers of Commerce
CONCAMIN	Confederation of Chambers of Industry
Confcommercio	National Association of Commercial Firms
CPC	Canadian Pork Council
DIN	(Fig. 13.1)
DTI	Department of Trade and Industry
EAEC	East Asian Economic Caucus
ECOSOC	UN Economic and Social Council
EEC	European Economic Community
EEG	European Enterprise Group
EEP	Gerritsen's chapter
EFPIA	European Federation of Pharmaceutical Industry Associations
EFTA	European Free Trade Area
EICs	European Information Centres

EP	European Parliament
EPG	Eminent Persons Group
ERT	European Round Table of Industrialists
ETC	Electronic Trade Credits
ETSI	European Telecommunications Standards Institute
ETUC	European Trade Union Confederation
EU	European Union
EUROCHAMBRES	Association of European Chambers of Commerce and Industry
EUROPMI	European Committee for Small and Medium-sized Independent Companies
EWOS	European Workshop for Open Systems
FAO	Food and Agriculture Organization of the United Nations
FDI	Foreign Direct Investment
Federchimica	The National Association of Italian Chemistry
FIG	Financial–Industrial Groups
FITUR	Federation of Independent Trade Unions of Russia
FOB	Free on Board
FP	Federation of Producers
G7	Group of Seven
GATT	General Agreement on Tariffs and Trade
IBCC	International Bureau of Chambers of Commerce
ICC	International Chamber of Commerce
ICE	National Public Institute for Foreign Trade
ICMS	Tax on Goods and Services Circulation
ICS	International Chamber of Shipping
IIF	International Transport Workers' Federation
IFPMA	International Federation of Pharmaceutical Manufacturers Associations
ILO	International Labour Organization
IMCO	Intergovernmental Maritime Consultative Organization
IMF	International Monetary Fund
IMO	International Maritime Organization
IMO	International Maritime Organization
Incoterms	International Commercial Terms
Intertanko	International Association of Independent Tanker Owners

IPE	International Political Economy
ISA	Islamic Shipowners' Association
ISF	International Shipowners' Federation
ISO	International Organization for Standardization
ITF	International Transport Workers' Federation
JPAC	Joint Public Advisory Committee
L/C	Letters of Credit
LASA	Latin American Shipowners' Association
LDSE	League of Defence Sector Enterprises
Marisec	Maritime International Secretariat Services Ltd
MERCOSUR	Southern Cone Common Market
MNCs	Multinational Corporations
NAAEC	North American Agreement on Environmental Cooperation
NACE	North American Commission on the Environment
NAFTA	North American Free Trade Agreement
NAM	National Association of Manufacturers
NFF	National Farmers' Federation
NGO	Non-Governmental Organization
NIC	Newly Industrialized Countries
NDP	New Democratic Party
NPPC	National Pork Producers Council
OECD	Organization for Economic Cooperation and Development
PAFTAD	Pacific Trade and Development
PBEC	Pacific Basin Economic Council
PBF	Pacific Business Forum
PBQP	Quality and Productivity Program
PDTI	Industrial Technology Development Programs
PECC	Pacific Economic Cooperation Conference
PIPA	Pacific Islands Producers' Association
PTA	ASEAN Preferential Trading Arrangement
R&D	Research and Development
RBRT	Russian Business Round Table
RCCI	Russian Chamber of Commerce and Industry
RUIE	Russian Union of Industrialists and Entrepreneurs
SAGB	Senior Advisory Group on Biotechnology
SEA	Single European Act

SEBRAE	Small and Medium-sized Firm Support Brazilian Service
SMEs	Small and Medium-sized Firms
TABD	Trans-Atlantic Business Dialogue
TEN	Trans-European Network
TRIPS	Trade-Related Intellectual Property Systems
UCIMU	National Association for Italian Machine Tools
UEAPME	European Association of Craft, Small and Medium-sized Enterprises
UHT	Ultrahigh Temperature
UIA	Argentinian Industrial Union
UN	United Nations
UNCSD	UN Commission for Sustainable Development
UNCTAD	United Nations Conference on Trade and Development
UNEP	UN Environment Programme
UNICE	Union of Industrial and Employers Confederations of Europe
UNIDO	United Nations Industrial Development Organisation
USTR	United States Trade Representative
WICE	World Industry Council for the Environment
WIPO	World Intellectual Property Organisation
WTO	World Trade Organization

1
Introduction

Henry Jacek

The purpose of this volume is to describe the response of organized business to the growing globalization of markets and politics. The latter is scrambling to keep up with increasingly liberalized markets. For that reason, public policy, formerly confined to nation-states, is now being internationalized in various ways.

Front and center in this process is organized business. On the one hand, business is correctly seen as pushing along new global trading rules while specific business interest associations (BIAs) may resist this trend if their leadership calculates potential losses in the future. While sectoral BIAs may be seen as defensive at times, peak business groups, umbrella associations and associations of large firms are seen in the vanguard of promoting the new liberal world trading order. The European Round Table of Industrialists (ERT) has been decisive in moving Europe forward to greater depths of commercial compatibility (Cowles, 1995), the Canadian Business Council on National Issues (BCNI) led Canada into the Canadian–American Free Trade Agreement (CAFTA) in 1988 (Doern and Tomlin, 1991: 217–19), and the American Business Roundtable (BRT) was clearly responsible for pushing through the North American Free Trade Agreement (NAFTA) in November, 1993 (Jacek, 1994: 5–6).

This book will extend the business-politics literature by describing in detail business responses to the growing internationalization of public policy and the changing levels of trading and commercial regimes. The contributors will describe a number of regimes, the dimensions of the organization of business, the arrangements in a number of sectors and the impacts of international relations trends. These descriptions show how important organized business is as a form of economic and political coordination in the new global order. Specifically, the chapters in

1

this book address a number of key issues. First, they look at the extent to which organized business participation in policy-making and implementation in the various commercial regimes represents a disruption to national-level relationships (and regional-level in federal-type states) with state authorities (see for example, 'From National Corporatism to Transnational Pluralism', Streeck and Schmitter, 1991: 133), or whether public/private symbiosis in global and supranational regimes has disabled national and territorial organizations. Second, what types of 'regimes' have attracted symbiotic business/government relations and what are the properties of these relations?

On the basis of the business/politics literature we can expect some sectors to respond much faster to the extension of free market territories than would other sectors. Industries marked by the dominance of large transnational corporations, such as pharmaceuticals, the chemical industry and the oil industry, are one of the first places to look for a quick response (Hancher, 1990; Martinelli, 1991: 18–46; Eden and Hampson, 1997: 362–6). But there are other factors that account for variable responses. As some of our chapters will show, part of the answer also depends on the actions of national peak level, umbrella or comprehensive business associations to the internationalization of markets, politics and public policy.

The authors of the various chapters will thus describe the patterns of business collective action which are associated with responses to transnational functional and territorial regimes, and the alliances with non-business groups (including forward and backward linkages) present. In turn, our authors will analyze the organizational formats of business which have responded at different speeds to the extension of free market territories. Our authors are especially interested in the conditions that encourage or impede the transnational organization of interests as well as the impact of globalization on national-level organizations. Expanding markets and growing associational organization seem to interact and respond to each other despite Olson's dramatic challenge to this generalization (Coleman, 1997: 145; Olson, 1982: 38–41). Finally, the various authors uncover, at times, new forms of public policy-making in the expanded trade areas and the impact of these new forms on the various definitions of 'the public interest' and on the allocation of goods, labour, resources and services.

The aim of this introductory chapter is to describe the major issues addressed by the various chapter authors, especially the complex and reciprocal influences exerted between organized business interests and political and economic internationalization. The expression of the internationalization of commercial market regimes will lead us to understand the dialectic between organized business and regional political institutions . This chapter will primarily delineate the dimensions and possible answers to the questions and topics described above. The next section looks at business interest associations (BIAs) as agents of economic and political coordination, followed by examination of the development of transnational regions as trading regions and their relationship to global commercial governance. The chapter then focuses on what lessons can be learned from observed subnational regional practices and those in decentralized or collapsed nation-states such as the former Soviet Union (Chapter 8). In particular, what has been the impact in these situations on interest representation and domestic sectoral governance? What are the important properties of the provision of certain goods and services, in other words, what is the nature of sector-specific patterns? Finally, the chapter seeks to develop an explanation for the growing importance of business interest associations in the new global order.

Business interest associations (BIAs) as agents of economic and political coordination

Since the 1980s, business interest associations (BIAs) have often been important domestic state agents of political coordination for purposes of formulating, and most importantly, implementing public policies (Streeck and Schmitter, 1985; Grant, 1987 and Martinelli, 1991). Even in the absence of government support, BIAs have also been important in providing economic coordination. Over the last ten years the issue has been whether BIAs can perform the same tasks and with the same vigor at the interstate regional level?

The chaotic economic conditions that often mark interstate relations certainly need coordination. Nation-states seem either unable or disinterested in such 'low politics' as they try to cope with the 'high politics' of international and regional security regimes. Our book is an attempt to outline the important role that organized business plays in managing the 'low politics' of economic coordination. While there has been a great surge of energy in the 1990s to highlight the new importance of private governance systems (Young, 1989; Rosenau and Czempiel, 1992; Rittberger, 1995 and Risse-Kappen, 1995), the significant, if not primary, role of organized business continues to be neglected. Mainstream international relations does not significantly encapsulate the specfic role of organized business associations in the process of regional and global integration. In the world of capitalism, business is the key interest. In addition, the coordination of regional trading regimes in particular, indeed their very establishment and enhancement over the past 15 years, depended on organizing the large transnational corporations into business interest associations. On their own, transnational corporations, even the largest ones, do not seem able to initiate regional regime change (Cowles, 1995; Jacek, 1994).

Secondly, global considerations still seem to capture the imagination of scholars, especially the neorealists, despite the dramatic emergence of the 'new regionalism' (Hurrell, 1995: 344). The rules and the capacity to enforce these rules seem far more important at the emerging regional level than they do globally. This is not to minimize the importance of private non-state governance authority at the global level, where, as the chapters by Schneider (Chapter 14), Ronit (Chapter 12) and the concluding chapter by Greenwood (Chapter 15) demonstrate, global business interest associations have contributed significantly. But it is at the regional level where there is most evidence of the role of organized business in governance.

While there has been some speculation about the likely demise of interest associations in the transnational world, the contrary case, and in our view the correct case, is rarely put forward cogently and in great detail. One of the most significant examinations of arguments about the demise of interest associations and their lack of validity comes from one of our contributors, William Coleman (1997). One of this central tenets is that interest associations thrive in the complexity of the policy process. Multitiered regional governance systems only make this process more complex. In addition, interest associations offer the opportunity for political participation in an era when trading regimes seem to be ringing up increasing 'democratic deficits'. The expected decline of interest associations and their importance is certainly a premature generalization and there is every reason to believe organized interest groups will outlive their critics and will continue to have a growing influence at the transnational level.

Just as organized business reacts to changes of intergovernmental scale such as the development of regional trading regimes and growing global governance, so do BIAs as they interact with regionalism within nation-states (Coleman and Jacek, 1989: 2). Within nation-states and perhaps especially within federalist systems, the balance between central and subnational authority seems to be always dynamic. At times, centrifugal tendencies may destroy a federalist system as happened to the Soviet Union. What roles do BIAs play in the dynamic interaction between center and periphery? In turn, how do the changing political arrangements affect the maintenance, organization and resources of these BIAs? As Coleman and Montpetit (Chapter 10) and Peregudov (Chapter 8) show us in this volume, it is important to ask if there are parallels in the relationships between organized business and central/subnational authority in the nation-state on the one hand, and the relationships between national and supranational organized business within regional trading regimes and the emerging global order?

The relationship between organized business and multitiered government authorities is in principle similar whether located within a complex federalist or within a multinational regional trading regime as Coleman and Montpetit (Chapter 10) point out. In the case of NAFTA, the absence of institutional pulls upon business interest integration seems to help explain the lack of development of regional transnational business associations (Jacek, Chapter 3). Indeed, that 'institutions matter' is a clear contention of most of the contributions to this volume. However, what is surprising is the lack of clear, direct relationships between governmental structures within a multitiered system, and the organizational structures of BIAs. Rather, what is striking is the extent of the autonomy of interest associations from state structures which these associations sometimes exhibit. This is a challenge to the idea of institutional isomorphism as the dominant influence on interest association structure (DiMaggio and Powell, 1993: 147–60; Jacek, 1987: 52). This theory posits that as the public policy demands of the complex state increase, associational systems and associations themselves will be enveloped by a system that produces a convergence in state and association institutional structures.

At the same time, business sectoral characteristics seem to be of greater import. Industrial Fordist production systems seem indifferent to multitiered governmental organizations. As Stephen Gill (1990: 209–10) and Robert O'Brien (1997: 1) argue, transnational economic integration has moved much faster than the internationalization of political authority. Mass production and broad markets are far more important. On the other hand, business organizations of an older artisanal tradition (Streeck, 1989: 92) and the newer diversified quality production seem to be more affected by the organizational aspects of the state.

Another important distinction for understanding the impact of multitiered systems on associations is the difference between functional and jurisdictional divisions of political action. As Coleman and Montpetit (Chapter 10) point out, in a jurisdictional multitiered state system, responsibilities are divided between central and regional authorities. In a functional situation, public policy functions are divided between central and regional authorities. Policy design and formulation are found at the central level usually, while administration and implementation is the responsibility of the regional units. In a jurisdictional system, BIAs concentrate their activities on one particular level. In contrast, in a functional governmental setting, associations seem interested in all levels. Overall though, market structures and regulatory responsibilities seem to merge, however. In decentralized Canada, the Canadian Bankers Association is highly integrated, six out of a seven-point scale,[1] while in the United States the American Bankers Association is surprisingly decentralized, only scoring a two out of seven for a full unitary model. Thus, as Coleman and Montpetit show (Chapter 11), the American Bankers Association has affiliate only arrangements with state banking associations. In banking policy, Canadian regulation is national, while US directives are based in the American states.

In general, functional divisions within a multitiered governance system seem to have a salutary effect in problem-solving. The various state and association actors are propelled into a continual conversation about common policy problems. The technical merits of the policy problem tend to overshadow the political gamesmanship of jurisdictional politics. Finally, the very dynamism of the policy process rules aids in problem solving and the continuation of a virtuous cycle.

Philippe Schmitter (1997) has followed up on these insights to show how they apply to the European Union. His great counterintuitive insight is that '*attaining a less regulated internal market will require a great deal of regulation!*' (*ibid.*: 419). However, these regulatory efforts are dressed up as technical and not really political. As the EU continues to privilege functional policy-making at the regional level, the ground is prepared for a greater public policy role for organized business. Transnational European corporations need and demand consistent regulations and the basis for these regulations is the information that can be provided by European BIAs (*ibid.*: 420). As Michelle Egan (Chapter 13) shows in her contribution to our volume, there are other examples in the EU as well as in APEC.

Transnational regions and global trading regimes

The major fear among many enthusiastic analysts of the new globalization is that the new resurgent regionalism represents the rise of large trading blocs designed to privilege certain geographical areas. These regional arrangements are seen to enhance certain cultures, languages or value-homogeneous areas. Nation-states who are members of these new regions are seen as wanting to protect and enhance these non-economic factors at the expense of pure commercial and economic considerations. Within the regional bloc, preference in commercial transactions is often only given to the bloc members.

These regional blocs vary, though, a great deal among themselves along a scale of increasing commercial integration. The weakest form is a preferential trade agreement. Members have better access to each others markets than outsiders. The next step up is the free trade area. The major step here is to eliminate tariff barriers among members but each country maintains in an independent way tariffs against outsiders. The Canadian–American Free Trade Agreement (CAFTA), and the later NAFTA worked to create larger and larger free trade areas. But even with the 'free trade area', individual countries are likely to retain the right to enforce national dumping regulations and different definitions of subsidies; all these tax the dispute resolution mechanisms among the members. Differential national tariffs may remain.

The middle case is the customs union. Here the distinguishing characteristic is a common tariff policy that applies to all outsiders. Probably the most well-known historical example is the 1834 German Customs Union (*Deutscher Zollnerein*). A common market attempts to go further. The factors of production are given freedom of movement within the region. Finally, the highest level of commercial regionalism is the economic union. The latter is marked by common fiscal, monetary and social policies with a common currency. Some would say the EU is optimistically named in that it is attempting to move from the fourth to the fifth level. In contrast, it is questionable that APEC has even begun moving into the first step of the trading bloc arena.

What are the preferences of organized business with regard to region and regimes? It would seem that BIAs representing large business prefer to move in a steady, if not rapid, manner to higher and higher levels of integration. Medium-sized and small business in particular would appear to be more ambivalent to this trend. Their pro-market ideology propels them to favor increasingly higher levels of economic integration. However, they are cross-pressured because they realize that ever expanding and deepened markets means stronger and stronger competition from large transnational firms. Thus, business organizations are likely to be divided when calculations are made about the advantages of the changing scale of markets. Increased market competitiveness is likely to undermine regulatory arrangements that limit territorial boundary penetration by foreign firms. While many may see global regimes at the end of this process, others (Schmitter, 1997; Eden and Hampson, 1997) see the foreseeable future as one where regionalism is the dominant political/commercial form.

While many pro-free market globalists, especially economists, bemoan this trend, some do understand the growth of the new regionalism. The global process has moved along very slowly. The talks seem to drag on for long periods, it is difficult to make new global rules and implementation seems a long time coming, and even then there is no hegemony or strong world institution to prevent cheating (Schultz, 1996: 21).

Amongst other tasks, this volume examines the revival of regionalism or the 'new regionalism' as it is sometimes called. Why is regionalism so vigorous when many observers talk mainly about globalization? Certainly the prestige of the EU and NAFTA have been felt worldwide. Latin Americans and Asians would like to have similar, prestigious regional trade associations. Contributors to this volume examine not only the prestigious, first world regimes such as the EU (Chapter 5) and NAFTA (Chapter 3), but also at attempts by some developing regions, APEC (Chapter 6) and MERCOSUR (Chapter 7), to follow the lead of the advanced industrial economies. The EU, in particular, has influenced the attempt to develop regional organizations outside of the affluent OECD countries (Axline, 1994: 10). In the 1960s, especially, the third world was both reacting to and copying the principles that were seen to be embodied in the European Community of the time (Axline, 1994: 182).

The MERCOSUR (*Mercado del Cono Sur*) was founded much later, in 1991, by Argentina, Brazil, Paraguay and Uruguay, but its model was clearly the then EC (Schultz, 1996: 25). Like many regional associations progress has been slow. However, what progress that we have seen is more like that of Canada and the United States, not the EU. The response of both member governments and business has been sectorally-based. As in North America, automobile production including auto parts manufacturing has developed to rationalize production within the MERCOSUR common market while keeping outside-manufactured supplies out of the area. As Diaz de Landa and Sajem (Chapter 7) show, the leading proponent of this policy has been the Brazilian Association of Automobile Producers (ANFAVEA). Their intense lobbying has led to restrictions being placed on cars coming in from outside of the MERCOSUR area. This is part of Brazil's clearly defined industrial policy. Even when Brazilian auto manufacturers set up assembly plants in Argentina, Brazilian auto part suppliers are tied to the automobile assembly plants. In contrast, the Motor Car Factories Associations of Argentina (ADEFA) feels outgunned by its Brazilian counterpart and the managed automobile trade of MERCOSUR. ADEFA, like most Argentinean business, is now tied to free trade in the MERCOSUR area. This produces an asymmetry in trade relations between the two biggest countries in the MERCOSUR common market.

This is somewhat similar to the experience of the USA and Canada in the same industrial sector. In January 1965, the American and Canadian governments established the Automotive Products Trade Agreement (APTA). This managed trade Auto Pact has survived intact through both the Canadian–American Free Trade Agreement (CAFTA) and NAFTA negotiations. The Auto Pact has been especially beneficial to Canada despite some initial concerns by Canadian nationalists. The Canadian assembly plants are the most efficient in North America, producing cars with less defects than those in the United States, and they have produced conditions that were favorable to a major expansion of the Canadian Automobile parts manufacturing. All of these developments were supported by Canadian automobile BIAs. The APTA was never intended to remain unchanged forever, but over 30 years it has been resistant to any fundamental changes (Keeley, 1983: 281).

In looking at another developing regional trading area, that of the Asia Pacific Economic Cooperation (APEC), Gallant and Stubbs (Chapter 6) point out that organized business is more of a follower than a leader. It wasn't until 1993 that a Pacific Business Forum (PBF) was established to bolster political initiatives. Each of the 18 members appointed two people from the business sector, one representing the interests of large business and the other representing small to medium enterprises (SMEs). A subset of six APEC members plus Vietnam, the Association of Southeast Asian Nations (ASEAN), has spawned the ASEAN Chamber of Commerce and Industry (ACCI) which works with a number of ASEAN's committees.

In 1996 the APEC Business Advisory Council (ABAC) was formed as a successor to the PBF and an Eminent Persons Group. Their first report was 'APEC Means Business: Building Prosperity for our Community', and was presented to the APEC leaders in November of that year. Each APEC member appoints three private sector representatives, one of which is from a small or medium-sized enterprise. ABAC now meets several times a year, reports to the main APEC leaders once a year, and has so far identified five areas where it will focus its energy. ABAC sees as its role making it easier for business to do business in the APEC region. They see themselves as APEC's voice of the private sector. They are especially interested in the Small and Medium-sized Enterprise (SME) Policy Level Group which also deals with human resource development. The other four areas besides the SME and human resource one that are targetted for attention are cross-border trade flows, finance and investment, infrastructure, and economic and technical cooperation.[2]

National business organizations have often joined together to set up and speed up regional integration. In the 1980s the ASEAN Chamber of Commerce and Industry came together from their national associations to pump life into ASEAN (Association of South East Asian Nations), a regional organization founded in 1967. The result was a Basic Agreement on ASEAN Industrial Joint Ventures and another on Industrial Complementation (Thambipollai, 1994: 114, 132). This form of behaviour could be termed, like so much third world business and regional actions, as an exercise in defensive regionalism aimed at protecting these nations from the Europeans and North Americans. In one regional case not covered in our volume, we see similar regional state and regional business interaction for defensive purposes. The Caribbean Association of Industry and Commerce was instrumental in pushing forward the benefits of CARIFTA (the Caribbean Free Trade Association), the forerunner of CARICOM (the Caribbean Common Market) launched in 1973. There are similar patterns of comprehensive business involvement in the cases of the Canadian–American Free Trade Agreement (CAFTA), the NAFTA (Jacek, 1994), and the EU (Cowles, 1995).

Not only are regional efforts at economic and commercial cooperation in the third world vulnerable to the power of European and North American regional cooperation, but at times they must also consider dealing with foreign BIAs as if the latter possessed state sovereignty. In the South Pacific, the individual nations, the South Pacific Forum and the Pacific Islands Producers' Association (PIPA) have all had to contend with the American Tuna Boat Association (Axline, 1994). Thus, BIAs interact and are affected by regional developments impacting their home countries but they have the capacity to shape regional developments elsewhere, especially if the BIAs are based in the Organization of Economic Cooperation and Development (OECD) countries and the object of their attention is regional arrangements among less-developed countries.

Lessons from subnational regions and decentralized nation-states

The opportunities and problems facing BIAs in the transnational regional context are similar to the texture of associational life in regionalized nation states, especially highly decentralized ones such as Canada and Switzerland, and in the extreme case of national disintegration as was evident in the collapse of the Soviet Union. These experiences pose a number of questions:

1. How has the decentralized or collapsing nature of the nation-state affected business associations?
2. Did the organization of BIAs matter in terms of influencing the decentralized nature of the state structure or of accelerating or slowing down the political disintegration?
3. To what extent do these intra-state experiences provide us with a guide to learning about government–business relationships at the transnational regional level?

If we are to learn lessons from national experiences of the type described above, we need to recognize that how we select information is crucial to the development of knowledge. In particular, we need to understand and compare simultaneously the degree of integration in states, markets and interest associations over the same territory. Proper selection of relevant information in these three spheres of organization prepares us for a careful analysis of causes, concomitants and consequences. Through all of this analysis we have the opportunity to use time as an ally while fending off changing contingencies outside of these three dimensions (Rose, 1993: 147).

If we put together the governmental and market dimensions or contexts and then compare their configurations to associational structures, we can see the associational role more clearly.[3] The first clear case is the antithesis of the trends we talk about in this chapter, namely integrated markets coinciding with governmental authority structures. In this type of situation we expect BIAs to reinforce the general trend. Associations should be highly centralized. At the national level the Swedish unitary state and national market are reinforced by highly integrated associations. Conflicts across this space are sectoral, not territorially specific.

The second case becomes decidedly more interesting. Here a regionalized country contains national markets. Associational structures may follow one tendency or another. It could be expected in one scenario for the market to be reinforced especially along product-specific lines. The Swiss Confederation conforms to this pattern. But what if the decentralized and decentralizing state weakens the integration of BIAs? Even sectoral associations may find it hard to maintain a national focus as they get entrapped in disputes among strong subnational governments. Canada is a prime example here. Even though over the last generation Canada's markets have become more and more national, if not international as a result of CAFTA and NAFTA, the Canadian state has in effect become more and more decentralized as efforts are strained to keep Quebec in Canada. BIAs would like to respond to the market but they find themselves weakened by constant intergovernmental disputes in which Canada and the individual provinces use political authority to counteract market forces. Even the largest transnational firms are affected.[4]

The third case is the reverse of the second in that a strong central state contains within it regionalized markets which may be reinforced by historical memories, language and customs. The latter traditions may be so strong that even a powerful, central state must face regionalized interest associations in alliance with regional subunits it does not even want to recognize. Both Spain and the former Soviet Union seem to fit this pattern. On the other hand, the associational structures for various reasons may respond to the centralized state. France is the best example here.

The fourth possibility mirrors many transnational regional groups today, a highly autonomous decentralized state system with national markets but the hope is for more integration. As Gallant and Stubbs (Chapter 6) will indicate for APEC, and Diaz De Landa and Sajem (Chapter 7) will show for MERCOSUR, this scenario has some important applications. Overall in this situation the associational system generally mirrors the political-economic context. There is still the possibility, however, that interest associations could attempt to fight this general trend. While we have no clear case study of this situation in our volume, we have alluded already to such cases as the Caribbean Association of Industry and Commerce and the Pacific Islands Producers Association (PIPA) which have both sought to swim against the decentralized currents of both state and market.

One of the chapters in this collection considers the evolution of associational roles in the Soviet Union which was transformed into the Commonwealth of Independent States (CIS). We are fortunate to have the contribution of a Russian scholar of this dramatic transformation.

Sergei Peregudov shows in this volume (Chapter 8) and elsewhere (1997) that the collapse of the Soviet Union led to a collapse of the state corporatist interest association system itself. The former associational leaders are backward-looking, pessimistic and demoralized. Although they would like to counter the state and market disintegration, they are in no position to do so.

Sector-specific patterns

Much of the discussion of BIAs focuses on peak or comprehensive associations. Yet national, regional or international systems of capitalist production may privilege sector-specific associational life. Business associations may not only respond to the characteristics of specific products and services but may also be influenced by *how* these economic activities are produced. A great deal of the industrial production literature emphasizes Fordist production. Others, such as Streeck (1992), contrast this system of production with the system of diversified quality production. In fact, there are other possibilities as well, depending on how production characteristics are combined. Three of the most important dimensions of the production process include the volume of production, the speed at which adjustments in the production process are made in response to outside influences and the quality of goods and services produced. There is no reason to believe that these characteristics would not influence associations, their organization and transnational regions (Hollingsworth and Boyer, 1997: 22). Indeed, there is good reason to believe that these sector-specific qualities would lead to uneven regional developments. To be specific, a service such as those provided by financial institutions is now marked by high transaction speeds and stunning increases in volume (Millman, 1995: 4). Such characteristics should lead to international associational integration of a kind that is in the vanguard of global and regional integration (Coleman and Porter, 1994: 197–200). In our volume we can see this development in NAFTA and particularly its application to Mexico.

Duncan Wood's chapter (Chapter 4) on the *Asociatiòn de banqueros de México* (ABM), the Mexican Bankers' Association, shows how this domestic trade association and its business sector must respond to changes brought about by a country's entry into a regional trade system. Mexican manufacturing and its resource sectors have been able to maintain associational autonomy that is not available to the financial sector. The changes have not only greatly affected the

Mexican banking industry, but they have also altered the internal make-up and priorities of the ABM. As well, the new changed ABM is affecting the agenda and practices of Mexican state institutions themselves in the banking field. The adoption of NAFTA in 1994 produced within one year a massive devaluation of the Mexican currency and a major contraction of the world value of Mexican assets including those held by banks. This economic crisis uncovered the structural weaknesses of the Mexican banking system. The banks were greatly overvalued in previous sales and coupled with this was their weak loan portfolios. Probably most important of all, Mexican bankers were poorly educated in basic banking practices, especially risk management.

To deal with the peso crisis, Mexican banks needed new capital and new foreign partners, if not owners. But these foreign banks brought more than capital; more importantly they brought high levels of banking expertise. This expertise quickly moved into the internal deliberations of the ABM. Training programs and technical assistance as a result of the injection of foreign expertise has already taken place. Now the ABM, clearly influenced by the new foreign banks, is pushing the Mexican state authorities, especially the state banking regulator the *Comisiòn Nacional Bancaria y de Valores* (CNBV) to loosen up its control over the banking sector. It now argues for a system based on collective self-regulation which is based on a bedrock of industry self-knowledge and sector-specific technical expertise. Once again we see the familiar traits of private interest government (Grant, 1987: 12–13). In this system of production, state institutions are captured and transformed by the firms they are supposed to regulate through the increasing institutional capability of BIAs.

A somewhat different expectation arises with agricultural systems of production. Some commodities have high volume, but interchangeable units that cannot be differentiated by quality. And in sharp contrast to the financial sector, speed of adjustment is the last characteristic we would expect. Thus, the chapter on the Australian agricultural industry presented by Rolf Gerritsen (Chapter 9) comes as something of a surprise. While most national associations are attempting to shield their producer members from the impact of liberalized global trading rules, other members and regional trading blocs, the Australian associations pursue deregulation. Once again an important part of the answer is found in some unexpected sector-specific characteristics. Most intriguing is the development of a public interest position by the relevant interest groups. This was done by integrating the farm industry and rising above the typical interest group structure, namely commodity-based interest organization. These groups were able to pull together into a national peak council. Shortly after these developments, the national government agreed to restructure the relevant farm agencies so as to produce 'corporatist-like' policy sectors. This included policy in the functional areas of marketing, research as well as in general policy areas. The use of these 'corporatist' peak councils also involved trade unions and food processors.

The particular government proposal that allowed the institutional transformation of these interest groups was the government promise to significantly reduce input costs to the sector. The main components of this promise and subsequent state action was a reduction of tariffs on imported agricultural machinery as well as the reduction of other manufacturing tariffs, reform of transportation and communications services, more efficiencies in public utilities and other public services. All of these allowed significant reductions in input and handling costs and thus allowed the industry to be far more competitive in world trade.

Our volume provides a third case of a sector-specific economic activity, that of global shipping (Chapter 12), which although international in name, was European-focused for a long period. The most general sector-specific characteristics seem to mark this activity as high volume, with slow adjustment because of its bulk characteristics with virtually no quality differentiation. For that reason, the evolution of global shipping is a particularly interesting case. Because of the sector-specific characteristics of maritime shipping, early global organization was very useful. In this case business interest associations (BIAs) predate any political attempt to regulate this industry. As Karsten Ronit points out, organized global shipping was probably the first sector to develop a global policy sector. At the very beginning of this century, shipowners formed the International Shipowners Federation (ISF). A short time later, business producers founded the International Chamber of Shipping (ICS). On the employee side the International Transport Workers' Federation (IIF) organized after that.

This sector is known for its capacity to use private collective action to manage, among other things, safety issues. There are clearly parallels to the use of private interest governments at the domestic level (Grant, 1987; Martinelli, 1991). The function of private interest governments found at the national level are useful for understanding the development of inter-state regimes (Porter, 1997: 8). Just as interesting about this sector is the fact that the ISF and the ICS operate from the same premises in Britain. This is clearly a case of the highest level of the integration of horizontal relations among associations. In this situation of interassociational cooperation, BIAs either share their paid administrative bureaucracy, their elected unpaid officers or directors, or are serviced by a common secretariat (Schmitter and Streeck, 1981: 195–9; Jacek, 1986: 425–7). All of these characteristics have produced an interesting policy and institutional developmental pattern. The political legitimation for the system of associational governance emerged many years after the associations organized and became active themselves. The associations and the system of political support went formally from the national to the international level, pretending to bypass regional formations. As Ronit points out, only much later did regional associations emerge in a formal way, mainly as a response to the rise of regional trade agreements such as the EU.

There is certainly a great deal more work to be done on sector-specific businesses. How varying characteristics affect sector-specific associations and their relationships with comprehensive associations is still unclear. Equally, while there has been some work of the role of business wide associations at the global level (see, for instance, Schneider, Chapter 14, this volume), there has been little analysis of the role of sectoral business in interacting with global regimes in sectoral governance; Ronit's examination of shipping (Chapter 12) is a notable exception.

The growing importance of business interest associations in the new global order

The ultimate purpose of our volume is to foster study and research of one of the most intriguing issues of our age. That issue is the growing interrelationship between global trends in the world economy and the seemingly contradictory rise of the new regionalism of transnational cooperation and organization. The world trend of globalization affects the human condition by impacting on our environmental needs and desire for personal economic security in an increasingly changing commercial world. We are all vulnerable from the strongest to the weakest. But we all seek to *organize* in order to preserve and promote what we can of distinctive and cherished commercial, economic, environmental, labour and social policies that each interest has grown to be dependent on. If we cannot preserve our national autonomy and national programs and practices, then regionalism is a way to avoid being exposed to threats from anywhere from around the globe. Perhaps, no region more than Western Europe has taken these lessons to heart. The

European Union is the brave pioneer here. Canada and the United States, first in CAFTA and then joining Mexico in NAFTA, followed suit in the developing trend of defensive regionalism. For political scientists interested in understanding public policy processes, it is crucial to pay more attention to these new transnational, multitiered regional organizations. This is not easy since so many of us approach our understanding of politics from either a national comparative politics perspective, or one large world international relations viewpoint. Both types of scholars find it hard to move from their preferred level of analysis.

In addition, there is still another difficult scholarly problem. Mainstream international relations has long paid scant attention to the influence of business in world affairs and the interdependence of the world of money and markets, with that of states. Geoffrey Underhill, in the chapter following this one, seeks to redress this imbalance by focusing on the contribution which the growing literature in international political economy makes to the study of international relations by highlighting the distinctive influence of business on globalization and regionalization, arguing that any credible theory of transnational governance needs to focus on both states and transnational actors. As Justin Greenwood summises in the concluding chapter, the great strength of international political economy is its stress upon how market relations structures political activity, and the ways in which the political structures within which actors are embedded (institutions; regimes) structure and socialise the political responses of firms and organised business. Going some way beyond studies of 'lobbying' and 'influence' by business interests, comparative political economy, too, is strong in analysing the ways in which institutions and regimes structure the responses of business interests to their environment. This tradition has dominated the study of the behaviour of actors in the policy process, and therefore analysis of political action by, and organisation of, key business interests, including the construction of international regimes through 'private interest government'.

In the concluding chapter, Justin Greenwood uses insights from each of these perspectives in conjunction with the contributions to this volume, and beyond, to analyse the role of business in global and regional governance. At the global level, somewhat curiously, more analysis has been given to the role of non-business, non-governmental organizations (NGOs) in governance interactions with global regimes than has been paid to the role of business (O'Brien, *et al.*, 1998). Thus, our book should be seen as a first step to correct a major scholarly oversight, the lack of research on the most important of all NGOs in international affairs, the transnational firm and the BIAs that represent these firms.

The BIA as transnational NGO is likely even more important at the regional level. As national BIAs coalesce the opportunity costs, of course, are lower when there are fewer members involved. The development of the new second wave of regional reorganizations over the past 15 years is thus fertile territory for this new BIA. This development is aided by the weakening of security concerns and the growing importance of commercial and economic politics. Nations no longer try to defeat their rivals militarily, they attempt to outsell them by exploiting their comparative advantages in export markets. As firms reach out to transnationalize their production, BIAs either expand or are created to encompass the expanding borders of these markets. At the same time states, under pressure from domestic BIAs, attempt to organize, expand and empower transnational governance schemes.

As Andrew Hurrell (1995: 346) points out in a telling analysis of the resurgence of transnational regionalism, there are a number of functional needs associated with the thrust towards regionalism. These needs are particularly well-suited for organizational solutions in the form of transnational BIAs. BIAs contribute to global governance from the establishment of norms through to the more developed mechanisms of governance, such as self-regulation. World political integration calls for collective economic management, the expertise for which is just as, or more than, likely to be found in the BIA bureaucracy rather than in a national-state bureaucracy. The use of the BIA is especially important in standard setting. As Michelle Egan shows in her chapter (Chapter 13), standards are significant in international trade, and at the regional level both the EU and the copycat APEC members have looked to BIAs for leadership and information. Issues of enforcement and effective implementation are especially suited to BIAs as private interest governments. In addition to such properties, the leadership of the BIA is less intrusive than a public agent and may be more acceptable and legitimate to society, although private interest government always raises its own problems of accountability and legitimacy.

In all levels of political action, interest associations matter. They provide differential benefits, and because they have this capability, they influence the national calculations of members, non-members and governmental organizations alike. Perhaps their most unrecognized function is the way in which they define both the public interest and impute the interests of important stakeholders. When you couple that with their control over the provision of vital, technical information, we can see their ability to structure the meaning of politics. As Hurrell (1995: 358) so astutely recognizes, 'much greater attention needs to be given...[to the study of]..."state-society complexes" on which many examples of the new regionalism have come to rely'. Interstate interactions are only part of the story.

Perhaps it is appropriate to give the last word to one of the authors in this collection, William Coleman, who has written that 'many associations have survived as governance mechanisms in the present wave of globalization and neoliberal hostility' (1997: 128). There are a number of reasons for understanding this development. Most of them relate, however, to the complexity and variations of modern political life. To deal with this complexity and variation, the public policy process needs an ongoing technical orientation for effective policy solutions. This is true for national, regional and global governance.

Notes

1. Coleman and Montpetit use a seven-point scale, with seven being a unitary form of organization where there is no differentiation along territorial lines, to a one, a system of independent sub-territorial associations.
2. I am grateful to Nicole Gallant for this additional information.
3. The following analysis builds on 'Table 1 Associational roles and likely corresponding structural arrangements' in Coleman and Jacek, 1989: 8.
4. Perhaps the most stunning example is the pharmaceutical industry. Unlike most large firms, the branded pharmaceutical corporations are trapped into staying in Quebec by the obvious positive interest of the provincial government on the one hand, and the inducements, if not the outright bribery, of the Federal Government on the other, a case of defensive federalism. Additional market distortions occur in other large industries such as airline transport and airplane construction. 'Privatized' firms in these sectors are required by law to keep their headquarters and existing assets in the Province of Quebec by Federal legislation.

2

From Ships Passing in the Night to a Dialogue of the Deaf: the Contribution of International Relations Theory to Understanding Organized Business

Geoffrey R.D. Underhill

This chapter will assess the contribution of international relations theory to our understanding of organized business in the global era. If one simply puts the question, 'how much has IR theory enhanced our understanding of organized business?', the most immediate reaction might be, 'not much'. On the whole, traditional international relations theorists have been spectacularly unconcerned with business, its organizational characteristics, or the market setting, despite the intuitively obvious importance of these factors to the global system and relations among states. This chapter will argue, however, that on closer examination a more measured and equivocal response can be made. What could have been a remarkably short article can in fact run its course, rescued by the rise of International Political Economy (IPE) as a field with strong theoretical roots related to international relations and the wider body of social theory. Even so, IPE still has some way to go when it comes to integrating fully the role of organized business into its theoretical framework.

The first point to make is that traditional IR theorists have created a theoretical discourse which effectively precludes serious consideration of business interests and their organizations as important actors in the global system. Furthermore, traditional approaches to the study of international relations have largely precluded systematic discussion of the economic structures within which business interests are to be contextualized. This is not without some rationale: traditional international relations theory, with its emphasis on the crucial question of security, sees states as the principal actors of consequence in a setting characterized by a lack of overarching authority. In this sense, relations among states-as-actors leaves little room for non-state or sub-state actors in general and relegates them to 'second image' (Waltz, 1959) or 'unit' (domestic) level politics (Waltz, 1979: 81–8).

Secondly, therefore, much of postwar international relations theory has developed a peculiar view of states as autonomous and unitary actors making rational decisions for the maximization of security in a highly conflictual international system. There is little room in the model for a conceptualization of states as institutions based on an interdependence of public and private interests, wherein the international milieu is characterized by complex and cross-cutting patterns of conflict and cooperation amongst public and private. This rather arid view of the international system is emphasized more by some than others; the rich analyses of Hans Morgenthau (1956) or of Hedley Bull (1977) are hardly to be compared with the starkness of Waltz (1979) in this regard.

Thirdly, even approaches to international relations which deal explicitly with economic issues have often dealt organized private interests out of the equation, reducing the international system down to the choices of states defined as unitary rational decision-makers. In general, there is a failure among international relations specialists to consider states and the international system in their larger socioeconomic context, or to consider seriously in theoretical terms either the interaction between domestic political processes and those at the global level, including relations among states, or the interaction between public and private interests (or indeed how they might be differentiated) in a global context.

This chapter will be structured as follows. First it will analyse traditional theories of international relations, known as the realist school, demonstrating how the discipline arose so as to exclude many aspects of international politics which might have led to serious analysis of the role of organized business. Secondly, it will look at the rise of international political economy and the steady inclusion of issues related to the global market economy in the discipline of international relations. This section will argue that IR specialists coming to political economy were biased toward importing traditional conceptual models of the state, seeing states and market phenomena as contradictory principles (Gilpin, 1987: 11), and consequently theorizing the political and economic domains as separate realms or sectors with contrasting dynamics. The result was a stunted notion of international political economy, focusing on states as unitary rational actors maximizing self-interest in a world characterized by inherent competition among states. There was little real regard for the ways in which markets are part of an integrated pattern of political authority and governance in the contemporary political economy. There was little attempt to demonstrate the ways in which private interests might become integrated into the various institutional layers of global governance (Rosenau and Czempiel, 1992).

Finally, the chapter will draw attention to the limited body of literature which has emphasized the role of non-state actors, particularly international business, and the interrelationships between the interests of states and the interests of the socioeconomic coalitions underpinning the operation of the global market economy. This eclectic group of approaches to the subject includes the notable work of the late Susan Strange, some in the radical tradition, and some migrants to IPE from comparative political economy. The article will conclude by demonstrating that international relations theory represents a temporary side-track in social science, and that the more inclusive 'new international political economy' (Murphy and Tooze, 1991) represents a welcome return of at least some IR scholars to the mainstream and indeed best traditions of political economy in the social sciences. These perspectives, starting with Adam Smith and the Scottish Enlightenment via Marx and Polanyi to the contemporary period, have focused on the broader problematic of the 'state-society complex' (Cox, 1986: 205) at both domestic and global levels of analysis.

Crucial to this is a rejection of traditional IR models of the state, conceptualizing it instead as a set of institutionalized (or at least bargained) socioeconomic relationships. This set of relationships between private organized interests and the multiple agencies of political authority known as the state interact to produce historically-specific notions of the public good and public policy. The changing politics of society takes place in the interstices between what is sometimes identified as 'civil society' and the changing institutional forms of official authority in the modern state. State authority and the socioeconomic structures of the market are fused in a pattern of global governance which cuts across domestic and international levels of analysis.

Ships passing in the night: traditional international relations theory and the place of organized business

The discipline of international relations arose out of a European concern with war, diplomatic history, international law, and the practice of foreign relations among states and their governments. This concern with statecraft developed at a time when relations among states in Europe had been relatively conflictual and competitive over the centuries.

The birth of the modern state system is generally associated with the Thirty Years' War and the 1648 settlement known as the Treaty of Westphalia. Roughly speaking, the Thirty Years' War had been sparked by the Catholic Counter-Reformation, led by the then Holy Roman (Habsburg) empire against the Protestant German principalities, and had developed into a struggle for European domination between France and the Habsburg dynasty. An important aspect of the settlement was to enshrine in international law the principle of the sovereign equality of states. States would be defined as inviolable territorial units, and entirely independent in their internal affairs. In other words, no power had the right to determine the religious or other internal politics of any other.

Of course the Treaty was a legal fiction. As long as states might be powerful enough to abuse their position with respect to others, there was little guarantee they would not do so. But the Treaty did establish states as persistent and secular entities, and it severed the link between the Church in Rome and the system of governance in post-Reformation Europe, a considerable turnaround from the earlier medieval sociopolitical order (see Hinsley, 1963, especially chs. 8–9). As the emerging system of relations amongst these 'sovereign' units developed, their ambitious monarchs often sought advantage over their neighbors, where it could be had. Grabbing territory enhanced wealth, was often popular, and at least in the short term enhanced the security of a particular state against incursions by others. As this competitive game developed, weaker states seeing potential external threats to their domestic arrangements might seek pragmatic alliances to resist attempts at domination by others.

This situation of self-policing competitive behaviour came to be known as the European balance of power, which functioned on the basis of a relative plurality of relatively equal Great Powers (Hinsley, 1963: 175–7) The Napoleonic Wars gave the system a severe jolt as revolutionary France very nearly succeeded in absorbing most of the

European continent under a single hegemonic rule, but the balance of power system was consciously reestablished, with additional legal paraphernalia, by the Congress of Vienna of 1815. Limited Great Power concertation maintained the system until the Great War of 1914.

The Great War, followed by the instability of the interwar period, provided considerable impetus for scholars and foreign policy practitioners to think more systematically about the international system, if indeed it could be called a system. The tremendous loss of life and the accelerated progress of military technology focused minds. This combined with the increasing democratization of European politics to bring about an increased role for popular opinion. The catastrophe of World War Two, the onset of the Cold War, and the rise of nuclear weapons as a serious question of human survival rendered a systematic understanding of the world of international relations yet more urgent.

In view of the ongoing tragedy and increasing risks of war, it is not surprising that international relations specialists, including theorists, became centrally concerned with issues of war and peace, focusing on the behaviour of states as the key units in the international system. States, and the political and social forces which underpinned them, sought security from external threat, but in such a way as to avoid the competitive antagonisms of a raw balance of power system. International relations specialists began to develop a 'hierarchy of issues', wherein the politics of security were rated as 'high politics', with virtually everything else relegated to the second division (Viotti and Kauppi, 1987: 7). Some theorists explicitly separated the political dynamics of the international system from economic or legal dynamics (Morgenthau, 1956: 10). There were those who attempted to draw attention to the socioeconomic underpinnings of competition among states (Carr, 1939; Lenin, 1967) and economic issues in general (Gilpin, 1975), but on the whole the problem of war and peace was regarded as the main problem of relations among states-as-units.

This tradition of IR theory came to be regarded as the 'realist' approach to international relations (Dougherty and Pfaltzgraff, 1990). Realism in the past had been periodically challenged by various forms of liberal idealism which proposed a better mousetrap to lessen the chances of an abuse of state power leading to war. The League of Nations was a clear expression of this in the interwar period, just as the United Nations was a by-product of the liberal idealism of the Roosevelt administration. However, it was always easy to retort to the idealists that collective security mousetraps like the League had not worked, and that they failed seriously to address the realities of power management in international affairs, probably an invalid criticism (Claude, 1962: 106, 204). By the early Cold War period realism was established as the dominant school of thought, and the theoretical discourse of the postwar discipline of international relations revolved around these relatively pragmatic questions thrown up by historical tragedy.

Despite a rich and varied heritage (Carr, 1939; Morgenthau, 1956), realism became increasingly stripped of its philosophical and historiographical underpinnings. By the 1980s the conceptual problematic involved a model of the international system as populated not by peoples, nor societies, nor economic structures, nor even governmental bureaucracies, but instead by unitary rational actors called states which sought to maximize their individual security in a setting characterized by 'anarchy'. By anarchy was meant not necessarily chaos, but a decentralized and uncertain locus of political authority. Differences in the relative power (particularly military power, but this included some notion of the economic resources as well) among states in the system became the principal variable determining the responses of states to their external environment. This model, a reformulation of traditional realist principles which came to be known as 'neo-realism', was encapsulated in the particularly barren work of Kenneth Waltz (1979).

The Realist tradition as expressed in the neo-realist model had a sense of inevitability about it: unpleasant realities required often unpleasant decisions and actions. The chief object of statecraft in the nuclear era became one of avoiding the ubiquitous 'security dilemma': how to maximize security through economic and military power, but without causing potential adversaries to expect aggressive and expansionist ambitions. While the role of nuclear weapons in all of this is often disputed, it is not unreasonable to assume they had some restraining effects on the politics of the situation. International relations had succeeded in carving out a separate domain which had political dynamics quite distinct from those prevailing at the domestic level of analysis.

The neo-realist model (and Realist tradition on the whole) asserted that the inter-state politics of security would largely determine the pattern of economic relations in the larger international system. This is not an unreasonable assertion in some respects. It certainly makes more sense than economic liberal assertions that markets are natural and self-regulating, as well as being guaranteed to bring the greatest possible good to the greatest many (the notion of optimality). Realists at least understood that politics were omnipresent and that economic policies were bound to be influenced (many realists would argue determined) by so-called 'non-economic' objectives of state policy, especially national security. In this sense, firms and their representative organizations might have a role in statecraft, but in a purely derivative fashion as tools of state policy.

The earlier realist tradition was rich and adaptable in its analysis of the complexities of the international system. Over the postwar period many theorists steadily lost sight of this broad intellectual heritage stemming from Machiavelli and Hobbes, or even earlier. Where the Realist concept was weak (particularly in its neo-realist guise) is that it failed to see that national security had a function – the protection of the larger socioeconomic whole. States did not compete as units for the sake of competition itself, in an inane and endless game of one-upmanship. States, as institutionalized centers of political authority 'presiding' over particular socioeconomic structures (structures which were never, incidentally, wholly confined to domestic states themselves), were condemned to interacting with their domestic and international environments simultaneously (Gourevitch, 1978). This makes it difficult to assert, as the Realists continue to do, that there is some separate dynamic to politics at the international level of analysis, separated out from the more humdrum concerns of competing social groups, lobbyists, and the messy affairs of legislatures and political parties. Why should international politics have a different dynamic? Why should states at the international level suddenly become disinterested in domestic political legitimacy and socioeconomic management, especially when the success of domestic arrangements often includes considerable interdependence with state and non-state actors alike in the international domain? Why indeed should political dynamics operate according to a separate logic from the realm of society and the economy? Surely the principal objective of state security (internally *and* externally) is to preserve the balance of advantages and opportunities accruing to dominant coalitions of domestic social forces, just as the law is a domestic political instrument to ensure that outcomes in favor of some, whether broadly perceived as legitimate or not, are maintained?

The 1970s were generally associated with an intellectual questioning of realism. The nuclear stalemate, the rise of economic interdependence, and the apparent fragmentation of the bipolar order through East–West economic ties, it could be argued, was leading to the declining importance of security issues in the international system (Brown 1974). Despite these challenges, the assumptions of the Realist model reached a rigidified apogee in the 'neo-realist' theories of Kenneth Waltz, who but for his adoption by realists in a constant search of dogmatic reassurance would surely have gone unnoticed. Instead Waltz (1979) was greatly celebrated; while the more pragmatic models of traditional realism were undoubtedly anecdotal and inductivist, and hence of dubious theoretical merit in the formal sense of the term, they nonetheless proved adaptable as heuristic devices to guide one to a flexible and practical understanding of a number of historical and foreign policy questions. On the subject of this article, however, it should be clear that realism, the dominant trend in international relations theory, was neither adapted to nor focused on issues of organized business for reasons largely connected with its genealogy as a discipline.

The dialogue of the deaf: state centrism, the politics of international economic relations, and understanding organized business

There was a clear and urgent need for the discipline of international relations to research and indeed conceptualize the place of economic issues in relations among states. The pervasiveness of economic interdependence and its obvious effects upon relations among states raised the profile of economic questions in the study of international relations. The growing size and power of multinational corporations, the obvious tensions of the international trade regime and the relationship of trade to national resources and security, the collapse of the Bretton Woods fixed exchange rate system, and the OPEC oil crisis as well as the increase in East–West trade, heightened the sense that the discipline risked becoming unidimensional. Organized business clearly played a vital role in the policy processes we associate with states. These important, indeed seminal, events of the 1970s were hardly even on the research agenda of most international relations specialists. Paradoxically, the stalemate in the nuclear balance had put the security question on hold, except for the issue of arms control and the occasional attempt by one superpower or other, or usually both, to make a major addition to their already ridiculously large arsenals.

Even the realist tradition began to explore these uncharted waters. Quite sensibly, there was a conviction (against prevailing theories of the market economy) that states and state power had a lot to do with the evident transformation of the world economy and the apparent rise of economic interdependence (Gilpin, 1977). Confronting them were the ideas of liberal transnationalists, who saw interdependence as leading to a dissipation of rivalry among states as they became increasingly tied together (Morse, 1976). Realists countered this optimism based on idealism by pointing out that economic issues could be seen as a function of national security, and that interdependence is unlikely to yield harmony as the differing power capabilities of states would lead to its costs and benefits being unevenly distributed (Knorr and Trager, 1977).

A substantive attempt to synthesize realism and transnationalism was made by Robert Keohane and Joseph Nye in their 'complex interdependence' model (Keohane and Nye, 1977).[1] Without denying the importance of states and state power, Nye and Keohane nonetheless sensibly asserted that patterns of interdependence would vary across the issue-areas of foreign policy, and that this would to an extent attenuate the utility of raw military power in the international system. Even military superpowers like the United States would be constrained by the foreign policies of others, the customs and norms of international law and institutions, and the shared costs of interdependence. These ideas had appeared in another guise as the 'English School' (Buzan, 1993) which championed notions of 'international society' (Bull, 1977) as opposed to the raw anarchy and competition of more full-blooded realists.

Nye and Keohane among others went on to develop the concept of 'transnational relations' – the idea that relations among states could take place not just at an aggregated, 'state-as-unit' level, but also through subnational agencies with differentiated and varied interests in the different issue-areas of international bargaining processes. States could thus be 'disaggregated' as actors in international politics. This left room for conceptualizing the role of the wide array of interested socioeconomic coalitions and non-state actors which lay behind and indeed merged with the fragmented organs of state. The study of 'transnational relations' became a growth industry throughout the 1970s, with volumes appearing which reflected the central idea that the borders of sovereign states were not necessarily the most salient feature of international politics (Keohane and Nye, 1971; Rosenau, 1980); some of this even survived the 1980s to emerge in more sophisticated form (Rosenau, 1990).

In other words, Nye and Keohane opened the door to including organized business in models of international relations, although they did not explicitly do so themselves. Unfortunately, Nye and Keohane's efforts at synthesis fell on infertile ground. Realists had rallied to Waltz's colors, taking others in the growing field of international economic relations such as Robert Gilpin and Stephen Krasner with them (Gilpin, 1987; Krasner, 1979). Even Keohane himself became a partial convert to Waltz's neo-realism and its rational choice method-ologies (Keohane, 1984; 1989), which were in turn borrowed from liberal microeconomics.

The concern with economic issues did not diminish, but the search for alternative conceptualizations in mainstream international rela-tions did. The idea of disaggregating conceptual models of the state and injecting into them a notion of states composed of fragmented bureaucracies and non-state actors, competing coalitions of interest, and divided purposes in an interdependent world, was overshadowed. Waltz had developed a 'parsimonious' model of an international system characterized by the principle of anarchy (Waltz, 1979). This anarchy structured relations among the 'units' of the system, which were thus compelled to self-preservation and competition. In so doing they preserved (hopefully) themselves and the fundamental character-istics of the system, anarchy – a rather circular and static piece of rea-soning (Underhill, 1994: 29–33). The structural variable which gave the system its dynamism-within-stasis was differences in power among states, which served to structure their interactions as units. This model persisted in the stark identification of an international level of analysis with its own separate dynamics which worked on fundamentally dif-ferent principles from the realm of domestic affairs. It likewise per-sisted in separating political from economic dynamics. Anarchy led states to avoid entangling relationships of interdependence, and ulti-mately the systemic distribution of power would define the politics of security and economy alike in the realm of the international.

States would therefore behave as rational utility maximizers seeking security against other states as an end in itself. This model lent itself well to rational choice methodologies, game theoretic approaches, and so-called 'economic' theories of politics of which Waltz was so enam-ored. The crucial assumption was of the state as a unified rational actor operating in a system quite separate from the domestic domain, which was allegedly characterized by the state's capacity to impose outcomes within its territorial jurisdiction (for a critique of Waltz's assumptions see Milner, 1991).

This framework adapted itself easily if simplistically to economic questions. One could substitute any policy issue for the politics of global security. Thus international trade could be seen as a bargaining process among unitary utility maximizers, as could monetary relations, the politics of the environment, law of the sea, or whatever. These issues would still be subordinated to the imperatives of military power, to which economic resources remained a necessary adjunct. The ways in which domestic issues of political legitimacy or economic policy, and the messy political processes involved, might interact with this systemic realm, was clear: they did not (Aggarwal, 1985).

This approach at its extreme was clearly unsatisfactory for dealing successfully with the hurly-burly of economic issues, the particularistic interests and organizations involved, the state intermediation processes. At the very least, it could be pointed out, the anarchic environment in which these unitary states interacted was shaped by international norms, rules, decision-making procedures, and indeed formal institutions. These factors could be encapsulated in the concept of 'international regimes', the formal and informal patterns of institutionalized behaviour which shaped and constrained economic relations among states and affected their expectations as intervening variables (Krasner, 1983). There could be considerable debate about the actual nature and role of international regimes, but it seemed difficult to deny their overall importance, embedded as they were in the practice of states' foreign policies.

The problem was that the assumption of a unified rational actor state remained intact. Keohane and Nye's foray into disaggregating the state-as-actor and indeed bringing in non-state actors appeared a flash in the pan. International regimes remained conceptually the preserve of state bargains (Strange, 1983), and power relations among unitary states played the determinant role in deciding eventual outcomes (Krasner, 1983a).

To take an example, the concept of regimes could be applied to the policy issue of international trade. The 1970s saw a renewed threat of protectionist policies. The bargained outcomes which yielded a changing (more protectionist) international trade regime could be conceptualized as a function of changing patterns of state power. States sought outcomes in bargaining which would enhance their economic security and national comparative advantages as the costs of interdependence worked their way on state choices. States could form alliances in the negotiating process, but broadly speaking one could expect the preferences of the more powerful economies to prevail.

There is a hint here that a sound understanding of the negotiating preferences of states might require a dip into the realm of the domestic level of analysis and the realm of economic interest groups. Anyone familiar with comparative political economy would immediately invoke the role of interest groups (especially business), the institutions of interest intermediation, and the relationship between the politics of the domestic economy to the pressures of international competition. Not so in mainstream postwar international relations. These complex niceties were instead reduced to notions of 'state power' in the setting of international regimes.

The most popular model became the Theory of Hegemonic Stability, which provided the theoretical backdrop for an influential but flawed text in the realist tradition on international political economy (Gilpin, 1987). The theory argued that the crucial factor in the changing nature of international regimes was the relative decline of the United States as a superpower. As America declined, the incentives for it to act as a benevolent hegemon providing the 'public good' of a set of well-functioning liberal international economic regimes diminished. American economic and military decline led to a more aggressive and unilateralist policy on the part of US negotiators. The evidence used to substantiate this hypothesis was America's increasingly unilateralist trade policy, the unwillingness of the United States to underpin international monetary relations, and the increasingly conflictual relations between the US and its erstwhile Cold War allies. Economic structural variables and variables related to the policy process were not included.

A logical fallacy in the hypothesis should be immediately apparent: changes in power variables are not necessarily connected to changes in motivation. In this sense, observable American behaviour was not necessarily causally connected to changing international power relationships. There were also several sorts of empirical objections to the theory as well (Stubbs and Underhill, 1994a). This seemed to bother few of its proponents, and the hegemonic stability theory continues to infiltrate the unsuspecting minds of university students through the lectures of IR economic relations specialists who continue to find it intellectually satisfying.

Once again there was little room for a more sophisticated understanding of state policy processes, the coalitions of socioeconomic interests involved, and the changing nature of interstate bargains. Despite the ongoing attempts to develop the notion of transnational relations and alternative conceptions of international regimes, the regime approach championed by the inheritors of the realist mantle simply grafted realist assumptions onto a consideration of those economic issues of interest to states in the international context. International relations specialists continued to see states and markets as opposing organization principles (Schwartz, 1994), rather than understanding markets and their diverse institutionalized forms as interdependent with state policy, authority and governance.

As states wrestled with ongoing competition among private interests in the socioeconomic whole, this competition increasingly exceeded the jurisdictional boundaries of individual states themselves as market structures became more global. The IR discourse appeared to assume that 'levels of analysis' had some real existence in the material world, and that there was a firm barrier between the conceptualized worlds of anarchy and unitary states on the one hand, and domestic political processes and authority on the other. The fact that it was the same state acting at both levels seemed to have little impact on their fantasies.

Ending the dialogue of the deaf: bringing private interests back into international relations theory

Fortunately for international relations theory, there were always more competitors to the sterility of orthodoxy than the above rather manichean account has indicated. The honor of the discipline can be salvaged by the efforts of a heterodox (and essentially non-American) minority who have examined the wider social world of political economy in which international politics takes place, and who sought also to overcome the domestic/international divide. The particular focus of attention in terms of this wider perspective has varied, depending on the concerns of the scholars involved, but the 'wider social world' of course included business organizations and firms. While many approaches linking the political and economic domains neglect to integrate business organizations explicitly into the analysis – they assume it – these broader political economy approaches were the necessary starting point. A brief analysis of some examples of these theoretical approaches can lead us towards a better understanding as to how business organizations, and for that matter other constituents of the socioeconomic whole, might be included in theories of international relations.

The most notable contemporary proponent of a serious reconsideration of international relations theory with a view to including the role of non-state, especially market actors, was Susan Strange. Until her death in October 1998, Strange demonstrated a vitality and an irreverent capacity to upset the established icons of the discipline (Strange, 1994a; 1995a,b). While seldom formulating her critical insights in terms of rigorous theoretical constructs, she took seriously the scholar's mandate to engage in analysis overshadowed by skepticism about established ways of perceiving the world.

The first books in Strange's long publishing career were an analysis of the role of money in international relations (Strange, 1971, 1976). In her analysis of the collapse of the Bretton Woods fixed exchange rate regime, she drew attention to two factors with serious implications for theories of international relations. Firstly she demonstrated the extent to which the world of money and markets was interdependent with the world of states and that the political and economic domains were thus an integrated whole. The exchange rate system was a highly managed system, characterized by central bank cooperation and policy coordination. The domestic constraints of the countries involved, the differing interests behind the negotiators, and the uneven distribution of the benefits of the regime led to disagreement on what to do, and eventual collapse. These interstate bargaining processes were, then, rooted in economic structure, non-state actors, contrasting domestic constraints, a continuity of political processes across levels of analysis and across the 'economic' and 'political' domains.

Secondly, Strange drew attention to the key role played by off-shore financial markets in undermining the exchange rate regime. But Strange did not portray these market processes as autonomous, external constraints in opposition to the efforts and policies of states. She linked off-shore market development to state policies and understood the connection between the markets populated by market actors (banking and securities firms), and the policies of the states involved (particularly the US and the UK). State decisions and non-decisions contributed to the emergence of the Euromarkets (Strange, 1976: ch. 6; 1986). Furthermore, the ambivalent attitude of states, in particular the USA and the UK, towards the multinational firms involved and the consequences for national macroeconomic policies prevented any serious action being taken to constrain these market processes. States were finally overwhelmed and the interests of the private market actors prevailed, not from the *outside*, but from within the policy-making processes constituted by the agencies of official monetary control.

The role of non-state actors, particularly firms, was thus integral to the politics of monetary relations among states. The monetary regime could not be disaggregated into relations among states on the one hand, and market forces on the other. They were part of the same pattern of governance. Strange went on to examine the question of the politics of trade and its connection to the changing structure of production in the global economy (Strange, 1979) and eventually she focused squarely on the multinational corporation itself in tandem with a professor of international business (Stopford and Strange, 1991).

In this latter work she began more explicitly to conceptualize the role of business in the larger global order, challenging traditional accounts of IR or IPE and their state-centric failure to take firms-as-actors seriously. Stopford and Strange developed a model of 'triangular diplomacy', characterized by ongoing triangular bargaining state–state, state–firm, and firm–firm. This particular formulation has its difficulties (Sally, 1994), in that it does not conceptualize (although it does observe) how the business world merges with the state in the policy process, as specialists in interest intermediation or corporatism take for granted. Where state policy processes are concerned it is difficult to separate out the role of private market interests as one point of the triangle, the state as another. Firms operate within state processes, often through institutionalized arrangements such as corporatism where private interests manage a series of public responsibilities. Nonetheless, Strange remained untiring in her pursuit of the issue of non-state actors, with a volume on an array of the same appearing recently (Strange, 1996).

Radical approaches to the international system also drew attention to the role of business in international relations. This included a wide variety of literature drawing on an essentially Marxist heritage from traditional Marxism (Owen and Sutcliffe, 1972; Baran and Sweezy, 1966), through dependency theory (Cardoso and Faletto, 1969; Galtung, 1971), and through modern world systems theory (Wallerstein, 1979; Chase-Dunn, 1989). The accepted and perfectly reasonable shared assumption was that there was some intimate connection between the (capitalist) socioeconomic structures of states on the one hand, and the observed politics of the international system on the other. The structure of the economy was interdependent with the politics of international security and economy. The struggles among social groups were inherent in the politics of global economic and military rivalry, and these struggles spilled across borders as the structures of the market economy became transnationalized. The structural power of capitalist business interests was crucial to the equation.

While this seems an eminently sensible line of inquiry and gave birth to a wide variety of literature as such, radical approaches were regarded by the dominant realists as the 'beyond-the-pale' school of international relations theory. The recent cursory treatment of dependency approaches by Stephen Krasner, in an era characterized by growing inequalities and related tensions throughout much of the globe, is a case in point (Krasner, 1994: 15–17; critique in Strange, 1994b: 214–16).

The weakness of radical approaches may be more properly regarded (for those who remain unconvinced) as their overemphasis on class tensions and economic structural variables (Cerny, 1990: 12–18). Tensions between capital and labour are undoubtedly important in the politics of domestic and international levels of analysis, but they do not necessarily predominate and most social groups have ambiguous and indeterminate interests with regard to vital issues of political economy. More specifically, it was all too often assumed that because capital clearly dominated and owned the vital production process, it necessarily dominated in an instrumental fashion the politics of states and international relations as well. Radical theorists often did little to illustrate the concrete mechanisms and organizational setting through which this dominance of a particular coalition translated into control (often incomplete) of political institutions.

One of the most important mechanisms is of course organized business and its close, institutionalized relationships to state agencies. The ways in which states delegate public responsibilities to private, profit-seeking and organized market interests is a crucial mechanism of governance (Streeck and Schmitter, 1985), but many radical theorists avoided in-depth empirical investigation and conceptualization of this complex domain. The politics of big business is obviously crucial to the foreign economic policies of states, but business groups are not the only organized political actors and they do not always carry the day. How the competing coalitions of the social whole (of which organized business is but one albeit important element) across domestic and international levels of analysis come together in a pattern of governance might have dominated radical efforts, but on the whole did not.

Perhaps the most sophisticated of the more radical approaches is a branch of 'critical theory' known as the 'neo-gramscian approach' (Cox, 1995; Gill, 1993), after the Italian (post?) Marxist Antonio Gramsci. Gramsci's model of the political economy put much more emphasis on the politics of interacting and indeed organized socioeconomic coalitions, and the shifting alliances they formed around particular socioeconomic issues. These alliances and the success of dominant social forces, including capital, were contingent on the circumstances of the time and the open-ended interactions among coalitions of interest. Dominant coalitions constituted 'historic blocs' which could institutionalize their position in the apparatus of the state. Although it was by no means certain that capital would regularly dominate, and careful political strategies by other social forces might well challenge the hegemony of capital, nonetheless control of the means of production has historically remained closely correlated to the control of political resources.

There is of course no reason why these 'historic blocs' cannot project themselves beyond state borders through the policies of states on the one hand, and through the patterns of governance constituted by the transnational market on the other, with the one being interdependent with the other. This is precisely the model which Robert Cox developed in his volume, *Production, Power, and World Order* (Cox, 1987) and earlier writings (Cox, 1995). Cox's agenda, given his normative premises, however, was more concerned with the role of labour and other social movements challenging the transnational dominance of interests linked to the contemporary neo-liberal market order and multinational business. There is therefore little explicit attempt to conceptualize (although there is considerable discussion about) the place of business organizations in this regard.

Although Cox never focuses explicitly on business organizations, Cox's approach as a whole remains particularly fruitful for understanding the ways in which organized business and corresponding state institutions interact in an international milieu increasingly characterized by a transnational market economy. A number of studies in international political economy have done just that using explicitly Coxian assumptions (McDowell, 1994; Sinclair, 1994; Moran, 1991), seeking to explain the role of social forces in the symbiotic transformation of market structures and state policies.

Although international relations theory, through the field of IPE, has at least begun to integrate the role of organized business and corresponding firms into its conceptual models, there is still considerable work to be done. The principal task is to build models of how transnational economic structures, and the coalitions of organized market actors involved, are integrated into the policy processes of states at domestic and international levels of analysis, sometimes bringing (for example) protectionism in sectoral trade (Underhill, 1990, 1998), sometimes bringing greater liberalization (Milner, 1988). Unfortunately, most IPE accounts remain less than explicit on the precise role of organized configurations of business interests, but a point to emphasize is that as these coalitions of market interests become increasingly transnationalized, they begin to operate in the politics of several states simultaneously. While the organizational context of national states and national systems of interest intermediation remain distinct (which accounts for often contrasting outcomes), it is not surprising that the transnationalization of economic structures has correlated closely to changing state policies and often radical liberal-market reforms of domestic regulatory environments (Underhill, 1996).

Conclusion

The evolution of IPE away from state-centric sterility has served to bring the deliberately separated worlds of comparative political economy and international political economy closer together. The immediate catalyst has been the 'globalization' of domestic political economies, and the corresponding projection of domestic political processes into the domain once conceptualized as inhabited exclusively by unitary state actors maximizing their advantages in a setting characterized by anarchy. The agenda and the essential ingredients have been available for some time in the works of Strange or Cox, and in the work of comparative political economists such as Gourevitch or Hall (Gourevitch, 1978, 1986; Hall, 1986).

It is only, however, since the second half of the 1980s that empirical research has begun on a systematic basis to illustrate the crying need for synthesis at the theoretical level. For too long the politics of organized business was considered by IR specialists to be the preserve of the domestic level of analysis. The state form of political authority is clearly observable at domestic and international levels of analysis, but the politics of the state were conceptualized in fundamentally different ways depending on the discourse selected. All the while the state and the market were developing and transforming as interdependent patterns of political authority cutting across traditional discourses linked to abstract notions of separate levels of analysis.

Why should the politics of states somehow be fundamentally different because of the intervention of two abstract concepts: 'levels of analysis' and the separation of the economic and political domains? Empirically, domestic politics and international politics demonstrate considerable continuity, so there is no reason why the domestic and the international should not be conceptualized as on a continuum as well. Admittedly the institutional context does differ – the locus and nature of political authority and governance at the international level is much less certain, but this is not a difficult point to make. Likewise, if the political and economic domains are demonstrably an integrated ensemble, then why insist on their separation for conceptual purposes? Politics continues to be about the security of institutionalized socioeconomic arrangements across different layers of institutions, and who will get what out of them, including the arrangements established and coveted by organized business. An international relations theory which fails to conceptualize the role of non-state actors in general and of organized business in particular is not an international relations of the real world, and were it a boat it wouldn't float.

Note

1. To be accurate, it should be noted that the economic dimensions of the international system, and the interrelationship of these economic dimensions with the power structure and political dynamics of the system of states, had long been analyzed by radical approaches which emerged from the Marxist tradition. Of particular note was the dependency school and Modern World Systems theory (see below). I have not examined these approaches at any great length, not because they lack merit, but because they were regarded by mainstream IR theorists as on the margins of the discipline.

3
The Role of Organized Business in the Formation and Implementation of Regional Trade Agreements in North America

Henry J. Jacek

The impact of new and expanded trading regimes appears now to be substantial and evergrowing. Organized business, especially business associations that represent large firms in general or sectors with large firms, are the predominant players. Automobile production, banking, industrial chemical production and pharmaceutical manufacturing are the typical major proponents of these new or expanded trading regimes, whether at the regional or world level. Yet at the same time as the new trading institutions are put into place, these new regimes increase the power of business, especially large business. An important question is what is the impact on the societies of North America of this new global order and the increasing influence of business interest associations representing large business?

Unlike Europe, a rich panoply of formal North American-level business associations has not developed (Greenwood, 1997). Rather American business interest associations, with Canadian and Mexican members, are becoming the dominant North American business association players. A good example occurs in the North American steel industry. The dominant organization is clearly that of the American Iron and Steel Institute (AISI). On its web site, AISI makes clear that it views its geographical mandate as a North American one, it is concerned with promoting the world competitiveness of all North American steel companies.

Increasingly the Canadian–American Free Trade Agreement (CAFTA) and the North American Free Trade Agreement (NAFTA) impact on the

American, Canadian and Mexican governments and business in a number of ways. Although these agreements were the result of the combined influence of big business as conveyed through the Canadian Business Council on National Issues (BCNI), the American Business Roundtable (BRT) and the *Consejo Mexicano de Hombres de Negocios* (the Mexican Council of Businessmen), many individual firms and sectors now feel the uncomfortable hand of international coordination and regulation which constricts firm activities. No sector has felt this as strongly as the softwood lumber industry in the United States.

In a sense, this American industry overreached itself and set off the recent developments in North American regional trade agreements over the past decade. This industry along with some others constantly used 'US trade remedy law to harass Canadian exporters' (Doern and Tomlin, 1991: 43). This harassment forced the Canadian government into the Canadian–American Softwood Lumber Agreement Act of 1986, yet this pyrrhic victory hardened the resolve of Canadian business and the Canadian government to obtain a binational free trade agreement. The free trade agreements placed limits on the actions of the large American firms in the softwood lumber industry primarily through binational dispute settlement rulings which overturned American government actions that imposed border duties on imports of softwood lumber into the United States. The American firms, organized as the US Coalition for Fair Lumber Imports, argued that these binational panels violate in an unconstitutional way US sovereignty. The Coalition filed a lawsuit in the US Court of Appeal in Washington DC on 14 September 1994. It was later withdrawn.

The development of broadening and deepening regional trade agreements in North America with extensions into South America represents a clear opportunity for some businesses, a possible opportunity for others and a threat to traditionally protected firms. The NAFTA created the world's largest geographical free trade area with over 360 million people (Winham and Grant, 1995: 15), somewhat smaller than the European Union (EU). Big business has been the major source of pressure for trade liberalization. Large firms have a vested interest in international rationalization within their own firms and as well they have concerns about moving goods from one plant to another across borders. In North America the major voices are the BCNI and the BRT. They were enthusiastic while small and medium sized businesses and the organizations that represent them were confused and ambivalent (Jacek, 1994: 17, 28–9). Ideologically liberalized free trade is attractive to small firms; however, marketing limitations, less access to capital and low internal organizational trade capacity could easily lead to net market losses as large foreign firms enter previously protected markets without compensating net gains outside one's country for these smaller firms.

CAFTA and NAFTA have administrative sites spread over a vast geographic area. The major sites have been Washington DC, Mexico City and, in Canada, Ottawa as the site of political leadership and Toronto as the big business center. In addition, the North American Commission offices on the environment and labour were in still different locations. The 1980s was the key decade for both agreements. Although American and Canadian business cooperation on a joint free trade agreement goes back to the Great Depression and the passing by the US of the highly restrictive Smoot–Hawley Tariff Act of 1930, the free trade agenda began to really move when the BCNI made free trade its top agenda item. In the Mexican case, US–Mexico business cooperation began about the same time. However, the Canadian–US efforts paid off first.

Both Canada and Mexico gave strong consideration to the same 'third option', namely closer trade links with Europe. Both countries felt that the European countries and European business rebuffed their overtures, and by 1980 both felt their economic development and growth could realistically only be enhanced by closer economic integration with the US. The severe economic recession of the early 1980s hardened their resolve. In various ways public opinion in both countries was convinced that national protectionism was no longer viable and that free trade with the US was the only way to prevent economic stagnation and high unemployment.

Business interests have been active in designing and promoting the free trade agreements and supporting agreements on capital investment and safeguarding intellectual property rights across borders. At the same time, environmental and labour groups opposed to liberalized free trade have tried to entrench environmental safeguards and workers' rights into these agreements. However, it is clear the momentum lies with freer trade and the big business community in general. The institutions of the CAFTA and the NAFTA are very weak and consequently have not influenced or encouraged a major development in NAFTA-level business interest groups (BIAs). A good part of the problem is that government–business relationships are very different in each of the three countries. The US has always had a weak national state *vis-à-vis* BIAs and if anything this trend is even more pronounced under the weak Clinton presidency. The Liberal and Conservative governments of Canada view themselves as leaders of Team Canada, whose key players are the BCNI, the presidents of large Canadian firms and the provincial premiers.

Mexico provides a very different third case. Here we see the continuation of corporatist-like pacts among the federal president, the leading Mexican BIAs, the big labour unions and farmer organizations. The 'el pacto' is held together with the glue of patronage and corruption although the latter has become less important over the past ten years. The corporatist pact persists in Mexico even though in many other countries these are the relics of the 1970s and 1980s. Inflation still remains a serious problem. The limitation of workers' wages is as it was elsewhere, an important policy tool. Uncontrolled wage inflation always puts the peso at risk (Ley-Borras, 1997: 85–6).

In the USA agreements among business, labour and the federal government are unnecessary. The American labour movement has declined to a small fraction of employees and has little control over its members' wage demands. In any event, these demands are so weak they have confounded the inflation fears of economists about the US labour market. For 25 years the rule of thumb was that an unemployment rate under 6 per cent would set off an inflation of 5 per cent or more. For most of the Clinton presidency the unemployment rate has been below this, now even below 5 per cent, yet low stable inflation continues. In addition, US organized labour has little policy and political clout. It was unable to push through medical care reform in Clinton's first term and it could not prevent pro-business Republican majorities in both houses of Congress at the beginning of Clinton's second term.

In Canada, organized labour is much stronger from the national level down to the firm and plant levels. Politically, however, the union movement is closely aligned with the New Democratic Party (NDP), Canada's social democratic party which is not a major party at the federal level and in most provinces. Labour and the NDP are usually most powerful as the swing party in a minority government situation or when the NDP has a majority government in one of the Western provinces such as British Columbia, Manitoba or Saskatchewan. Since there has not been a minority government at the national level since 1979, organized labour has limited bargaining power there. Even with high national unemployment rates Canadian voters have supported five consecutive majority governments. Thus, the basic political dynamic is now played out among the federal cabinet, provincial premiers and the leaders of the BCNI and large transnational corporations.

Pulling the NAFTA countries together are various joint committees, many organized from within the Chamber of Commerce system. This system is probably the most complex aspect of business organization in North America. Not only are there chambers for domestic business, but organized chambers of foreign businesses are also important. Thus, the Canadian Chamber of Commerce in Mexico and the United States Chamber of Commerce in Mexico help tie Mexico, both economically and politically, to the other two NAFTA countries. Not only do these business committees affect current political relationships but they also have a longer history than most people realize. Work by the Committee on Canada–United States Relations, a joint American and Canadian chamber of commerce devoted to liberalized trade between Canada and the United States, began its efforts in 1933. US–Mexico business discussions go back to the administration of Mexican President López Portillo (1977–82). First of all, a US–Mexico Quadripartite Commission was established with the goal to link the business and government sectors more closely in both countries. The Commission was concerned mainly with development in tourism, food manufacturing, energy production and primary manufacturing (Gustavo del Castillo V., 1995: 38–9).

By early 1980, a US–Mexico Business Committee began to push for trade liberalization behind the scenes. The impetus came mainly from the US business community. By the end of June 1983, the Committee put forward a proposal for free trade to the United States Trade Representative (USTR). In March 1985, the USTR and the Mexican Secretary of Commerce signed an agreement to work towards a clarification of trade and investment rules applicable to both nations. By January 1987, a Mexican–US Binational Commission was working on a framework.[1] Only after all this background spade work was done did the BRT move openly to involve Mexican President Carlos Salinas de Gortari and its own membership in the mobilization of American public opinion in favor of a three-country free trade agreement (Jacek, 1994: 5–6).

NAFTA and employer–employee issues

So far, North America does not have integrated business interest associations (BIAs) covering Canada, Mexico and the United States. However, BIAs have had to concentrate their efforts on at least three broad issues, the broadening and deepening of the trade agreements themselves, employer and employee issues and environmental policies. The most contentious of these is the balance of power between employers and employees.

The business proponents of free trade agreements view these agreements as merely commercial agreements. Their view is that governments should not look at the components or input factors of the price such as labour costs or environmental damage. The notion of a level playing field across all domestic jurisdictions on these issues is clearly rejected.

The successful stance of business on this type of issue is nothing new. We can go all the way back to the difficulties of forming a viable economic and political union out of the thirteen original American states in the late eighteenth century. In particular, the conditions needed to complete any internal regional market are similar to what was needed for the thirteen American states 'to form a more perfect union' in order to facilitate business activity. The problem now in NAFTA and then in the American states centers on different regulatory regimes in the member units. The business solution is clearly a step towards deregulation as Wolfgang Streeck has noted for the European Union, but using the language 'mutual recognition as deregulation' (Streeck, 1989: 7–11). In the United States the language for the same concept involved the 'full faith and credit' clause of Section 10, Article I and the positive grant for regulation of all 'Commerce' to the common legislature, Section 8, Article I of the United States Constitution (Corwin, 1978: 46–86, 142–4, 246–55). At the same time we recognize that the world of business in late eighteenth century North America was a far simpler world than the one today. Regional subsidies were not recognized as a problem, environmental impacts were ignored and labour costs were not a subject of dispute. Yet the echoes of the 'full faith and credit' clause can be found in modern day Europe under the guise of 'mutual recognition'.

Yet concerns continually surface about what lies behind a traded commercial price. Are the inputs affected by hidden subsidies. In particular, are substandard working conditions and low wages part of fair and free trade? To business, labour payments and employment standards are input decisions which all trading partners must accept at face value. To business critics low wages and poor standards, resulting from the suppression of employee rights to engage in meaningful collective action are in fact a manifestation of 'social dumping' (Robinson, 1995: 475, 484) or an indirect government subsidy if based on government limitations of employee collection action (Adams and Singh, 1997: 161).

Out of this conflict came the *North American Agreement on Labour Cooperation Between the Government of Canada, the Government of the United Mexican States and the Government of the United States of America* (September, 1993), also known as the labour side agreement to NAFTA. This agreement was due to candidate Bill Clinton's commitment to organized labour in the 1992 presidential campaign. Although not thrilled with it, US BIAs viewed the side agreement as necessary to get the main NAFTA provisions through. The Canadian government was indifferent since its main concern was to be included in the main agreement. The organized business response in Mexico was more complicated. Over the past generation the model of employer/employee was a state-dominated corporatist one. Trade unions were incorporated into the ruling party and consequently the Mexican state. Trade union leaders and the political demands and political support of organized labour was clearly controlled by the state. Such a system is incompatible with neoliberal trade liberalization and its neoliberal assumptions about freedom of association.

In the late 1980s the Confederation of Employers of the Republic of Mexico (COMPARMEX) saw a need for a more liberal employer/ employee relationship as a way to improve productivity and to pave the way for North American free trade. This meant liberalizing the rules of the game by reducing state interference in internal union affairs. The Confederation of National Chambers of Commerce (CONCANAC) agreed but the more traditional manufacturing firms as represented by the Confederation of Chambers of Industry (CONCAMIN) preferred the old state corporatist system (Graciela Bensusán Areous, 1994: 58). However, all three BIAs continued to favour state control if not repression of employee strike action. In contrast, COPARMEX and CONCANAC advocated an evolution of the state corporatist system into a social corporatist system where the non-state social partners would have more autonomy, and where the economic goals are increasing firm efficiency and the stabilization of inflationary pressures (Alberto Aziz Nassif, 1994: 135). All of this was seen as a transition from a closed to an open economy.

American BIAs desired even greater changes in Mexican employer/employee relations. Their clear preference based on their success in the United States since 1956 was to reduce union density. From their perspective the maquiladoras program in Northern Mexico was the way to go (Kathryn Kopinak, 1993: 142). The American Chamber of Commerce's director of its specialized Mexican Maquila program noted with approval the low unionization rates in the maquiladoras compared to other Mexican cities (Robinson, 1994: 127). It is perhaps unrealistic for American BIAs to expect low unionization rates in traditional industrial areas compared to the rural greenfield sites of the maquiladoras.

Although initially viewed as weak by the American Federation of Labour/Congress of Industrial Organizations (AFL-CIO) and the Canadian Labour Congress (CLC), the labour side agreement is increasingly defended by organized labour. To the BIAs of Canada and the United States this agreement has become a dangerous precedent. It now looks more potent than expected to friend and foe alike (Herzenberg, 1996: 28).

Increasingly, North American political leaders are predisposed to insert labour accords as well as environmental and social charters into the core of possible regional trade agreements. This can be seen most clearly in a dramatic shift by the Canadian Liberal government which won a majority, albeit narrow, victory on 5 June 1997. Most of its losses were to a resurgent social democratic party, the New Democratic Party of Canada (NDP) that argued that the Liberals were not doing enough to reduce unemployment in Canada. Putting labour guarantees into new trade deals by the Liberals is seen as one way of meeting the criticism of social democrats. This position is opposed however by key business groups. The president of the BCNI has said his organization supports employee rights to free association, however it is opposed to making these side agreements as integral parts of regional trade deals (Eggertson, 1997: B1 and B4). On this issue we can expect more conflict in the future.

NAFTA and environmental concerns

In August 1993, another side-agreement to the NAFTA was agreed upon. This was the North American Agreement on Environmental Cooperation (NAAEC). As with the labour side-agreement, this was viewed as a temporary necessary evil by the North American business community. These two side-agreements were needed to gain the approval of the pro-labour, environmentalist Democrats in the White House and in the American Congress. This environmental accord was also compatible with the stated environmental goals of the new Canadian Liberal government of Jean Chrétien elected in October, 1993. Thus, publicly the Liberals were happy to sign it. Especially useful to a moderately nationalist Canadian government with sensitivity to the Quebec independence movement was that this new accord set up a new bureaucracy, a North American Commission on the Environment (NACE) in Montreal, Quebec's largest city now somewhat economically depressed (Howlett, 1997: 111).

The NACE contains three elements; the Council of Ministers, the permanent bureaucracy and a Joint Public Advisory Committee (JPAC). It is the latter group which allows a major entry for business influence on NAFTA environmental decisions. All three countries appoint an equal number of representatives expected to stabilize around 45 in total. In addition, each country appoints its own National and Governmental Advisory Committees to provide independent national advice. Business also has an opportunity to use environmental instruments against foreign competitors. NACE activity against the businesses of one country can be started by complaints of a business group in another country (Johnson and Beaulieu, 1996: 131–63).

Another place for conflicts among BIAs from different countries is in the area of environmental standards. On the one hand there can be downward pressure on environmental rules, the race to the bottom. On the other hand there are pressures for upward harmonization. The NAFTA text discourages both the relaxation of environmental standards and the creation of pollution havens. But more than that, the text calls for equivalence of national standards without relaxation. Implicitly, this means the highest national standard becomes the NAFTA standard. Business that conforms to the highest national standard now have a NAFTA trade advantage (Johnson and Beaulieu, 1996: 111–14).

One type of new business that has benefited from upward harmonization of environmental standards is the new environmental industry sector which in Canada is represented by the Canadian Environmental Industry Association (CEIA). This BIA advocates no relaxation of environmental standards. Indeed, its members' material interests are based on new higher regulatory strictness because these provide the technological innovation that gives these industries the edge over traditional firms (Toner and Conway, 1996: 138–44). As a result of the environmental side-agreement, the Canadian government developed an environmental industry strategy to benefit this BIA and its members. Among the policy components are a national environmental industry data-base, the collection of environmental industry statistics, training in environmental industries for trade promotion staff and environmental requirements for government procurement. All of this was especially significant because this policy was initiated at a time the Federal finance minister was cutting funding for business promotion (Westell, 1994: B4). This policy strategy builds upon the previously-created joint business–federal government Canadian Council for Human Resources in the Environment Industry (CCHREI).

The CEIA, founded in 1988, is a national federation of provincial environmental industry associations which in turn represent firms in the environmental industry. These companies are in the business of supplying technology, products and services. Canadian sales of business service exports is growing rapidly, and the fastest growing category of service exports are environmental services.

Despite the growth of environmental industries and their associations, the impact of the NAAEC is limited. The trade-offs between environmental protection and new economic costs to both industry profits and traditional jobs usually favor the status quo for economic reasons. As well, the bias in the organization of interests overwhelmingly resists change. A good example is air quality and its transborder character. At least half of the acid rain and greenhouse gases in Canada come from the United States. Especially damaging to Canada are the high-sulphur pollutants that are produced by American coal in American energy production, particularly in the American midwest.[2] American BIAs representing the coal producers, the steel industry, and the energy producers join with workers in these industries to thwart any positive improvements in North American air quality (Hoberg, 1997: 376).

The Business Roundtable (BRT), the chief organized voice of big business in the US, has argued that a serious assault on acid rain and greenhouse gases would cost over $30 billion and 500,000 American jobs. Thus, it opposes increasing environmental standards. The for-profit electric power generating industry is represented by the Edison Electric Institute. This BIA is opposed to increasing anti-sulphur dioxide emissions measures especially mandatory switching to lower sulphur coal.

The current battleground over the environment lies in regional and world international agreements. As we have noted above, BIAs take the position that environmental protection, as well as labour protection and human rights, are important values but they should not be integral parts of trade agreements or even as conditional side-agreements in the future. A second argument by BIAs is that international environmental agreements need to be tempered by national economic interest. Pressure is put on national officials not to agree to pacts that include mandatory measures and fixed timetables for compliance. Rather, flexibility and informal understandings are preferred. Energy BIAs constantly articulate this view in the face of increasing calls for the reduction of air pollutants, especially greenhouse gases such as carbon dioxide. In Canada, the Energy Council of Canada has taken the lead, but other BIAs convey the same message. These include the Canadian Association of Petroleum Producers, the Canadian Gas Association, the Canadian Electricity Association and the Canadian Energy Pipeline Association.

This whole issue will come to a head in Canada in the person of the new Trade Minister, Sergio Marchi, who recently left the environment ministry. Armed with a new majority mandate, albeit a reduced one, as a result of the Federal General Election of 2 June 1997, the Liberal government is now committed to including environmental, labour and social accords in all future trade agreements, a position in conflict with North American BIAs. The new trade minister, while in opposition between 1984 and 1993, opposed CAFTA and NAFTA. The door is now open to advance the cause of environmental improvements via North American trade agreement adjustments despite the objections of BIAs.

Business interests and binational dispute resolution

Beginning with the establishment of CAFTA, the United States and Canada decided to resolve their trade conflicts through a generalized dispute panels mechanism. This procedure was extended to NAFTA and later adopted by the World Trade Organization (WTO) (Davey, 1996: 1). Although legally the disputes are between two national governments, BIAs are often part of the political background of the trade dispute process.

The binational dispute resolution process itself has been part of conflicting expectations and differing evaluations. Some expected that the binational panels would seek to implement some concept of the public interest which might mean the general consumer interest or the common rules among the North American countries. Certainly many hoped for a near termination of trade conflicts. The latter expectation is now replaced by a more realistic view that trade conflicts are chronic and that the challenge is to manage these disputes. It is clear that the public interest has little to do with the dispute resolution mechanism. Consumer, labour and environmental aspects of disputes are ignored. Although ostensibly the disagreements are between national states, often governments are merely surrogates or agents of organized business interests. Also there are no clear common trading rules especially when it comes to government subsidies and corporate differential pricing policies. What the mechanism is designed to ensure is that each country applies fairly its own laws. The criticism from outsiders in the past was that domestic interest groups influenced unfairly the application of national rules and regulations so that domestic interests were given unjust but favorable treatment while foreign firms were not given the benefit of just implementation of the laws of the country to which they were sending their goods, services and capital.

Although BIAs are behind the disputes and heavily involved once the process gets going, at times they are even involved as panel judges themselves. So in one notable case in 1993 involving American restrictions on the importation of ultrahigh temperature (UHT) milk from Canada, a panel judge, out of five, from Canada was Frank Petrie, the president of the Canadian Exporters Association. Although the complex decision seemed to favor the US position, the panel's report pushed the two governments into a negotiated settlement two years later that allowed exports of UHT milk from Canada to resume (Davey, 1996: 57–62).

The initiation of binational disputes by BIAs and their participation as nominated panel judges are two important roles for them in the dispute resolution process. However, a third aspect is perhaps most important of all and especially so in the United States. This role is the provision of systematic information. Government decision-making bodies require accurate, systematic data that describes an economic situation as well as information that explains the consequences of the actions of economic actors as well as the potential impacts of a new state decision. State agencies find it costly to collect this information and analyze it competently. As well, there are compliance problems because some business firms distrust the state and are inclined to noncooperation. BIAs are in a much better position to collect economic data from their members. Thus, the BIA data is likely to be more accurate and complete and thus the basis for state decisions (Schmitter and Streeck, 1981: 229–30).

The weaker the state, the more reliant government agencies are on BIAs for the necessary information needed for state decisions. This is especially true for the United States. Traditionally the American national government has been weak by comparative standards. But the situation has become worse with the major downsizing of the civil service begun by Presidents Reagan and Bush. The US policy process is now almost totally dependent on domestic BIAs for the American perspective on trade disputes. What makes matters worse is that by American law, complex decisions have to be made quickly. Thorough investigations by American state agencies are now precluded. As a result these agencies rely on data provided by American BIAs to make state decisions (Moody-O'Grady, 1994: 124–6).

Although there were many forces in the 1980s that led to CAFTA and its distinctive settlement process, the long-term battle over softwood lumber imports was one of the most important. This American–Canadian 'Pine War' was used as a major, if not the most important justification, for adopting the CAFTA in Canada. The battle began in the midst of the deep 1980s North American recession when the US Coalition for Fair Lumber Imports was formed. The Coalition represents large, medium and small forest products companies in the US, but its leaders are the large firms such as the International Paper Company and Georgia-Pacific Corporation. In the slumping market of 1982, the Coalition argued that the Canadian business was unfairly subsidized by Canadian governments.

Initially Washington resisted the domestic pressure. But by 1986 the American government reversed itself and declared that Canadian provincial governments were unfairly subsidizing Canadian firms and by political threats forced the Canadian government to impose a 15 per cent export tax. With the CAFTA in place with its dispute settlement mechanism, the Canadian government in 1991 in the midst of the long Canadian 1990s recession boldly terminated its export tax. The US Coalition responded by lobbying the US government again for action. The result was that in 1992 the American authorities imposed a duty of 14.48 per cent on Canadian lumber imports. In 1994 a unanimous binational trade dispute panel overturned the US tax. As if often the case, the dispute panel found that US agencies were using questionable statistics whose origins were in briefs from US BIAs.

Before the panel, the US Coalition was confronted by data and analysis provided by the Canadian Forest Industries Council. As well in these battles other American BIAs have been mobilized. On the side of Canadian business is the US National Association of Home Builders. Their member firms depend on Canadian lumber, especially in upscale home construction since the Canadian product warps less than US material. The home builders have been joined by the National Lumber and Building Materials Dealers Association who have argued that Coalition efforts to harass Canadian exporters has contributed to higher inflation as a result of increased house prices ultimately based on higher lumber prices.

The second most important continuing dispute in CAFTA revolved around pigs and pigmeat so in addition to the long simmering pine war we now have a secondary swine conflict. Once again a Canadian

BIA, the Canadian Meat Council (CMC), an association of red meat food processors,[3] has been waging a long and difficult battle with American administrative tribunals since 1983 and before the enactment of the CAFTA. Without a binational mechanism with an arms length process from interest groups the CMC was at a clear disadvantage (Davey, 1996: 275–6). After the CAFTA, the Canadian Pork Council (CPC) joined the CMC in a battle to change the tenor of decisions by the American tribunals.

In a way, the American BIAs in the meat industry were even more bothersome than the lumber BIAs. Not only did the American groups such as the National Pork Producers Council (NPPC) get import tariffs placed on Canadian products for the unusual reason that American business may be injured in the future, but the American interest groups successfully lobbied US border officials in order to get them to apply the letter of American law to these imports. At border entry points, US inspectors were delaying the movement of Canadian goods and then applying very minor regulations that were not even applied to US pork. The result was a scaling back of Canadian exports and the reduction of production in Canadian meat packing plants.

For the most part through 1991 the CMC and CPC were painstakingly turning the tide of decisions in the US. Then in March of 1991, at the request of the NPPC, US trade representative Carla Hills demanded the formation of an extraordinary challenge committee. Once again the Americans lost the battle (Moody-O'Grady, 1994: 129–31).

The third area where BIAs have come into play is in the metal mining sector. The Nonferrous Metals Producers Committee in the United States attacked the idea of binational dispute resolution panels even before the CAFTA was approved in 1988 (Davey, 1996: 99). In the one case involving this sector, namely magnesium exports from Canada, once again the Canadian group won.

Since most of the decisions of this process have gone Canada's way, especially in the areas involving large amounts of goods such as lumber, food and mining, American BIAs have become increasingly hostile to the dispute settlement mechanism. Not only have Americans lost most substantive dispute decisions, they have also lost the two extraordinary challenges allowed by CAFTA. Now the intensity of the trade battle has moved up a notch to a higher level. A new BIA called the American Coalition for Competitive Trade, representing 21 constituent industry associations is going to the US courts with the express purpose to have the mechanism declared unconstitutional. In particular, the Coalition argues that the trade panels obstruct the rights of firms to use American courts for trade dispute purposes. In 1994 the lumber coalition filed the same type of petition to the US courts, but backed off when it was concluded that the case had little chance for success (Fagen, 1997: B7).

NAFTA and the converging attitude towards business

There is no doubt that large businesses in all three NAFTA countries pushed for regional trade integration. And again in general it appears as if business executives believe NAFTA has worked well. Perhaps the most tentative in their attitudes in the beginning was Mexican business. What did they want from NAFTA? From 1990 University of Michigan survey data, Mexican business indicated that it wanted a reprivatized banking system and more open government (Basáñez, 1995: 2–5). But business in all three countries may get more than they expected or want. They may be happy with what appears to be a basic trend, that is that North Americans are becoming more alike in their attitudes towards business. Fundamentally this involves American and Canadians moving closer to Mexicans while the latter becomes more like the other two publics.

A key issue being fought out in North America is the chronic issue of the relationship or balance of power between owners and managers on the one side and employees on the other.[4] How much autonomy should employees have? Traditionally, in the USA and Canada the public was clearly on the owners' side while in Mexico the most common view saw a balance of owners' and employees' powers. But this generalization ignores the recent trends. Americans and Canadians are moving to more of a balance and away from an owner-dominant position while Mexicans are slowly dropping their deep antipathy to business prerogatives (Inglehart, Nevitte and Basáñez, 1996: 107–15).

A second key issue for business is discipline in the workplace. Once again we find that US and Canadian mass opinion between 1981 and 1990 is moving in one direction while Mexican opinion is going in the opposite direction, yet all are converging. The first two countries show a public opinion, especially among younger workers, moving away from high deference to a work superior's instructions, while Mexican workers are becoming more docile. Over the 1980s, Americans and Canadians dropped 7 and 3 per cent in deference while Mexicans have increased 6 per cent (Inglehart, Nevitte and Basáñez, 1996: 115–18).

It seems reasonable to expect that NAFTA will accelerate this trend toward North American convergence on business values. This is an important generalization since many critics of the NAFTA negotiations thought the integration of Mexican political and economic culture with those of the USA and Canada was not possible. Unexpected was the pattern of convergence. Business leaders hoped and expected a change of Mexican values to those north of the Mexican border. What they didn't expect was that US and Canadian opinion would also change, and in the direction critical of traditional owner and management rights and prerogatives.

To what extent is NAFTA responsible for this attitudinal convergence? At first glance perhaps not at all since these trends became evident in the 1980s far before NAFTA. But on the Mexican side a pre-NAFTA attitude emerged early in the decade. In 1980 the US–Mexico Business Committee started working on a bilateral agreement by performing analyses needed to support it. In June 1981, the two presidents created the Joint Committee on Commerce and Trade, and in 1985 the US Trade Representative and the Mexican Secretary of Commerce signed an agreement to negotiate a protocol on trade between the two countries. From 1986 onwards, the Mexican government pushed the bilateral idea as the preferred solution to Mexico's economic underdevelopment.[5] At the same time, trade between Mexico and the USA in the last part of the decade doubled. Increased economic integration, and the prospects for more, conditioned the Mexican population to look North and emulate their rich neighbor and its perceived modal attitudes toward the rights of business owners and the proper role of the worker in the business enterprise.

The US and Canadian explanation seems to be different. The nature of these economies and their common severe economic downturns in the early 1980s and 1990s eroded American and Canadian loyalty to business prerogatives. Business was now seen as not delivering the economic goods. Unemployment rose and stayed higher than usual even after the purported recovery in the latter 1980s. It was the younger workers who suffered economic adversity the most and their anger toward business was clear. Their faith in American and Canadian business to create the conditions for prosperity weakened. The wealth and income inequality between older and younger workers has been increasing for over 25 years. Thus, these changing attitudes are independent of NAFTA.

Conclusion

This chapter has shown that business interest associations have been heavily involved in the encouragement, founding, shaping and implementation of regional trade agreements in North America. So far the institutional pulls of NAFTA are of much less importance than the push factors – the role of BIAs in shaping how NAFTA operates. To a large degree this is because there are no mechanisms to harmonize fiscal and monetary affairs, social policy or general labour mobility. With these crucial areas still completely in the hands of domestic governments, BIAs still look upon the nation-state as the primary target for lobbying. Even the political architecture of trade matters dampens any pull to organized business harmonization and integration that one might expect of NAFTA. In particular, the lack of common operational definitions for subsidies even prevents this trade agreement from being complete.

While the formation of a large number of true region-wide BIAs is still some time away in the future, the process has begun and cross-border alliances are underway either through overlapping memberships, the most common form, or through formal or informal horizontal relationships. The two side agreements on the environment and labour appended to NAFTA provide one type of focus while the dispute resolution mechanisms provide another. Just as we can expect a converging of business interest group activity we also see evidence of attitudinal convergence towards authority relations within business organizations.

As well, we are also beginning to see NAFTA strategies coordinated by BIAs to counter non-NAFTA competition. By being able to locate specialized plants in the most favorable locations in North America, North American firms are better able to meet outside competition. One of the best examples is the clothing and textile industry as coordinated by the American Textile Manufacturers Institute (AIMI). This strategy is explicitly aimed at containing, if not reducing Asian, and especially Chinese, imports into North America. A division of labour has been developed in which clothes are manufactured in Canada and Mexico by workers with lower wage and fringe benefit rates than American workers while the wearing apparel are manufactured out of US textiles (Lachica, 1997: B8).

In essence the debates about CAFTA and NAFTA are between business interest associations and government leaders on one side versus at least half of the public in the three countries. The latter are against changes being led by the new global order while the majority of BIAs and state officials believe liberalizing trade is a necessity. The mindset of the opposition is clear. These are people, employees, who fear losing the jobs they have and being reduced to part-time, nonstandard, contract positions and lower wages with few or no benefits. Their political defenders, such as Bill Ford, the Democratic chairman of the US House of Representatives' Education and Labour Committee during the NAFTA debate were adamantly opposed to NAFTA and the first proposed labour side-agreement. The latter was a commitment to a national reemployment scheme to improve employee skills and find them new jobs equivalent to the old jobs they would lose under NAFTA. The House Democrats blocked this initiative. They were opposed to retraining and new jobs; they wanted to fight to hold on to the jobs that now existed (Reich, 1997: 56, 123, 132, 255).

To date the most noticeable impact of CAFTA and NAFTA has not been the creation of new jobs, although the four years after the beginning of NAFTA have brought relative prosperity to North America. Rather, the major impact has been a political spillover. Most dramatically the decline of electoral corruption in Mexico has been startling even to NAFTA's strongest critics. NAFTA's dividends are primarily political, the extension of democracy, not economic benefits nor the creation of new jobs (Kantz, 1997: A16). Regional economic integration affects domestic political practices even though national BIAs who push these deals are slow to see their effects (O'Brien, 1995: 717–24). In general, they are less than happy with the moderate swing to the democratic left in Canada, Mexico and the United States.

In conclusion, at the present time, the future of North American BIA integration will not see any dramatic increase. Incremental moves here and there will occur but to have more dramatic change a deepening of NAFTA would be needed. There has been no movement to define subsidies, no attempt to forge a common legal framework for North American trade and no agreement to allow general labour mobility among the three countries. Given the deadlock between a pro-free trade president in the USA and a Congress reluctant to move any further on the trade front, we will probably not see any real deepening and widening of NAFTA until we see Clinton's successor, if then. And without the prospect of new trade initiatives, dramatic BIA integration is not likely. Then, what does all this add up to? First of all, we can say NAFTA is a trade bloc of very real importance. Yes to a certain extent the NAFTA agreement is partially a confirmation of what has been going on economically over the previous 15 years. But NAFTA brought with it unexpected political consequences. Converging attitudinal change for one but business was forced to accept environmental and labour standards they preferred to ignore. The BIAs such as the COM-PARMEX and the BRT had the power to execute the NAFTA but not enough power to prevent labour and environmental associations from adding on these new standards.

Finally, the NAFTA produced a US and Canadian media scrutiny of Mexican administration and political practices. The public's expectation was that Mexico would really follow through on its NAFTA commitments, ones the Mexican state expected to ignore with tacit American and Canadian acceptance. But the three governments could not do any of this.

Does the impact of BIAs on the development of North American trading rules aid us in evaluating current intellectual disputes in regional integration theory? I believe the answer is yes. Clearly our analysis by its very nature points out the weaknesses of neorealism interpretations. Hurrell (1995) argues that states are often playing catch-up to the extention of markets and interactions among organized business. In North America there is a growing interaction among the North American business community, convergent attitudinal change and more and more commercial interpenetration.

If economic and technocratic coordination across national boundaries is 'low politics', the higher politics of domestic institutional conflict and consensus-building sets the pace of regional political integration. BIAs can move governments but when there is political division within the hegemon as there is today between the Democratic President and the Republican Congress, progress in increasing formal political integration comes to a dead halt. Neorealism thus misses two important factors for change, the activity of powerful BIAs representing 'big capitalism' and domestic political dynamics especially in the hegemon.

Hurrell (1995: 349–50) argues that 'Neoliberal Institutionalization… [is] a highly plausible and generalizable theory for understanding the resurgence of regionalism.' What Hurrell describes fits North American experience if the word 'neoliberal' is dropped and 'organized' is substituted. In this way we can understand the interaction of state institutions with business, labour and environmental organizations. Together they all matter because of the information produced, the demand for transparency and monitoring (we can add the mass media here), the 'development of convergent expectations', and the overall thrust to regional cooperation. What this chapter demonstrates together with previous work on North America by the author and others is that Organized Institutionalization is perhaps the best explanation for the 'new regionalism'.

Notes

1. Information on these developments was provided to the author by Ian Robinson, then at the Institute for Labor and Industrial Relations at the University of Michigan, 23 August 1994.
2. In 1985, some 3.8 million tons of sulphur dioxide blew into Canada from the United States (Inglehart, Nevitte and Basáñez, 1996: 150).
3. For a systematic overview of the BIAs in the Canadian food processing industry, see Coleman and Jacek, 1983: 257–80.
4. For an especially bitter contemporary battle see Jacek, 1997: 308–10.
5. The author is indebted to Kathryn Ibata for this chronology.

4
Business Associations, Regional Integration and Systemic Shocks: The Case of the ABM in Mexico

Duncan R. Wood[1]

The North American Free Trade Agreement came into effect at the beginning of 1994. Less than a year later, the Mexican economy began a crisis that is only now being resolved. One of the causes of that crisis, and one of the sectors hardest hit, was the Mexican banking industry. The combination of new NAFTA rules on bank ownership, and the 1994/95 economic crisis in Mexico have combined to force changes in the banking sector that have dramatically altered the shape and business practices of the industry. This chapter will examine the response of the Mexican banking industry's business association, the Asociaciòn de Banqueros de México (ABM), to the challenges posed by the conjuction of the beginning of the NAFTA and the economic crisis. It argues that four effects must be considered. First, the new NAFTA ownership rules and the crisis have introduced new players into the Mexican banking sector and have in turn altered the internal make-up and priorities of the ABM. Secondly, the banking sector crisis has had a direct impact on the resources, both financial and human, available to the association. Third, the response of the Mexican government to the banking sector's problems can be seen to have placed certain restrictions on the autonomy of the association, at least in the short term. Lastly, the crisis has brought a new agenda to governmental banking authorities, an agenda which the ABM is helping to shape.

The chapter begins with a brief history of the ABM, a discussion of its structure, and its role in both industry and public decision-making. The discussion then turns to the changes brought about by the NAFTA and the economic crisis in the Mexican banking sector, and the consequent effects on the ABM. Finally, the chapter examines the role played by the ABM since the economic crisis and argues that its interests have been somewhat altered by the increasing level of foreign ownership, but more importantly that it has been able to secure a central role in helping to mould the future regulatory environment for Mexico's banks.

History and structure of the ABM

The Mexican Bankers' Association was founded in November 1928 with the express purpose of representing the general interests of the banking industry and to provide it with specialised technical services. The association has undergone many changes in its almost 70-year history, including alterations in its name, most recently from Asociaciòn Mexicana de Bancos (AMB) to Asociación de Banqueros de México (ABM). More substantially, the association has changed in response to structural change within the Mexican banking sector, and it is such change in recent years that form the focus of this chapter.

The ABM is organized along broad democratic lines – consulting with its members through both a General Assembly of associates and an Executive Committee, in which representatives from the administrative board of each member bank have a place. At the time of writing there were 52 associate banks, each having an equal voice in decision-making in the ABM, or at least in theory. In reality, the larger banks tend to have more influence, not least because banks pay membership dues according to their assets and loan portfolios, plus a fixed sum. Because the big banks pay more, they often claim a larger stake in the direction of the association, though this is publicly denied by them and the ABM (Jimenez, 1997). In addition to the General Assembly and Executive Committee, the ABM has seven assessment commissions in which each member bank is again represented. These commissions cover the functional areas of:

- Standards
- Operational efficiency
- Credit
- Savings
- Development banks
- Management
- New Banks

The ABM is headed by its president and has 5 vice-presidents. The president is the most highly visible spokesperson for the ABM, and the current holder of this position, Antonio del Valle, has been extremely active in voicing the association's opinion on government policy. In addition to the president and vice-presidents, the ABM has a general director who supervises subdirectors in three areas: technical, banking centres, and management and finance.

Objectives and services of the ABM

Broadly defined, the objectives of the ABM are to represent the banks and provide them with services. More specifically, the association has a mandate to:

1. Represent and defend the general interests of its associates in common efforts directed towards the public administration and private organizations.
2. Encourage the development of banking activities.
3. Conduct studies and research focused on the development and good-functioning of the banking and financial system in general, as well as those aimed at improving operating methods and practices.
4. Supervise the operation and good functioning of state banking centres.
5. Organize and promote courses and seminars that promote understanding and development of the banking system.
6. Work with similar foreign institutions and in international organizations to form relationships and facilitate exchanges. (Asociaciòn de Banqueros de México, 1995)

Up to the present time, the first of these functions has been the most important, for it concerns the relationship between the banking industry and the authorities that regulate it. In the future, it is to be expected that the fourth and sixth functions (supervision and foreign relations, respectively), will increase in importance as the principles of regulation and the level of financial integration in North America change. This matter will be discussed in more detail later in this chapter.

The association offers a comprehensive set of services to its associate members, including assessment, consultancy from the specialised commissions, information exchange through the ABM computing area, union services, information through memoranda, bulletins and journals, and training. Nontheless, the ABM is most important in providing an arena where banks can discuss common policy objectives, such as the current discussion over standardising cheques (Jimenez, 1997). These common policy objectives are then taken to discussions with the Treasury (Hacienda), the central bank (Banco de México) and the banking regulator (Comisiòn Nacional Bancaria y de Valores or CNBV). All three of these public bodies attend the bimonthly executive committee meetings of the ABM and there is a 'healthy, two-way dialogue' between the ABM and each of these authorities, 'not just at the senior level, but also at the intermediate level' (Jimenez, 1997).

It is this function of representing the interests of the Mexican banking sector in negotiations and discussions with public authorities that gives the ABM real importance in Mexican banking. It allows the ABM to be involved in the formation of policy, and in particular in the creation of banking regulatory and supervisory, as well as fiscal, monetary and exchange rate, policies. Since the economic crisis of 1994/95, such consultation has held increased significance, because of the many changes in both industry structure and banking regulation. Unfortunately for the purposes of this chapter, the relationship between the ABM and government bodies continues to go through a period of change and is difficult to assess. This change is due mainly to the privatization of the banking system since 1991 which dramatically changed the dynamic between public and private banking sectors.

NAFTA and foreign ownership

As part of the negotiations for the North American Free Trade Agreement (NAFTA), Canada, the United States and Mexico agreed upon new foreign ownership rules for their banks. During the negotiations, the Mexican banking industry put forward its policy preferences to the Mexican government negotiating team through the Asociaciòn Mexicana de Bancos (AMB). This communication was of little consequence, save for technical advice, because the AMB position differed little from that of the government. This was, of course, because the banking industry at the time remained nationalized, and therefore the industry's association was de facto state-controlled. Its interests were, in any case, more political than business-oriented, and public rather than private.[2] However, the NAFTA negotiations did succeed in revolutionizing the area of foreign ownership of banks in the three NAFTA countries. In Mexico's case, the policy change was a dramatic one. When the privatization of the Mexican banking system began in 1991, the Mexican government opened up the system to bids from foreign financial institutions, as well as Mexican.

The government set July 1995 as a deadline for approving applications for banking licenses in Mexico and a number of US and Canadian banks were successful.[3] Few, however, have so far taken up the opportunity (or challenge as many see it) of participating directly in the Mexican banking system. We can explain the reluctance of many North American banks to involve themselves in Mexican banking by reference to the economic crisis that hit the system in 1994 and 1995. Paradoxically, we can also explain the willingness of those banks that have decided to 'take the plunge' into Mexico by reference to the same crisis: they have done so in large part because the devaluation of the peso made Mexican banks a very good bargain for US and Canadian banks operating in dollars. Before talking of this involvement, it is therefore important to explain the crisis.

The Mexican banking crisis, 1994–97

Beginning with the peso crisis of 1994/95, the Mexican economy has undergone, and continues to undergo, a period of structural adjustment that has been extremely costly in economic and social, as well as, it appears, political terms. Little need be said about the economic crisis itself in this chapter – it has received excellent journalistic coverage to date and is already the topic of many a scholarly dissertation in progress. What is less well known, however, is the banking crisis that both preceded the onset of the broader economic crisis in Mexico, and which has prevented a more speedy recovery. Thus far it has been the topic of discussion in financial circles in Mexico, and in some of the more rarefied and esoteric circles of finance in the USA and Canada, but has not received substantial academic attention.

The first thing to say about the Mexican banking crisis of the 1990s is that it was not caused by the peso crisis of 1994/95. The devaluation and ensuing economic crisis merely brought to the surface and exacerbated the already existing problems afflicting the country's banking system. To quote a representative of the central bank, 'Mexico's banking problems preceded the economic crisis and began with the privatization of the banking system' (Schwartz, 1997). The privatization and liberalization of the Mexican banking system was an abrupt and poorly managed transition that involved the sale of the nationalized banks at vastly inflated prices, prices which did not reflect the underlying value of their assets, nor the looming problems in their loan portfolios (Heath, 1997). The privatization of 18 commercial banks during 13 months in 1991 and 1992 returned the banking sector to private hands after the nationalization of the system in 1982. The privatization process raised essential income for the state – more than $10 billion which was used to pay off part of the public debt.[4] In addition to the privatization of the banks, regulations preventing universal banking were removed and non-bank banks and thrifts were authorized.

New banks were licensed in 1993 and new financial products were authorized. The securities market was deregulated and foreign bank participation was made legal under the provisions of the NAFTA. It is difficult to exaggerate the scale of the changes that deregulation brought to the Mexican banking system in the early 1990s – or, indeed, the new risks to which the system was exposed. Competitive pressures were brought to bear on Mexican banks from all quarters – from new national market participants, new non-bank banks, and new foreign competitors. In addition, Mexican banks were placed in a position where they had to learn quickly, not only how to survive in this new competitive atmosphere, but also how to master new financial products and techniques of risk management.

Supervisors, too, felt the effects of the liberalization process. They found themselves facing new forms of financial activity, higher levels of industry competition, and outdated forms of supervision technique. Indeed, this appears to be a factor common to banking crises in emerging markets. *The Economist*, in a recent survey of banking in emerging markets, pointed to financial liberalization as a short-term threat to banking stability. Though liberalization is generally held to be healthy in the long term for a banking system, it brings certain problems with it:

> The trouble is that liberalization exposes banks to new risks which, without proper precautions, can make a crisis more likely... The switch from a cosy, state-directed system to one driven by competition also requires commercial bankers to develop a new way of thinking. Banks that have grown fat on a captive market must learn how to analyze credit risks, which takes time and training. (*The Economist*, 12 April 97: 11).

This last quote shows the interconnectedness between financial change and knowledge. Within the industry itself change brings new challenges that can only be met with improved expertise. But the challenge extends to banking authorities. The 'proper precautions' of which the article talks can only come from the authorities charged with regulating and supervising the system. These authorities in Mexico have been insufficiently endowed with such knowledge and expertise. The reform process that has removed regulations and privatized the banks has been in progress since 1988; however, this liberalization was not 'matched with improved supervision' (de Luna, 1996) until after the peso devaluation, and even now improvements have a long way to go.

The current crisis was preceded not just by liberalization but also by a massive expansion in the amount of credit in the system. Between 1988 and 1992, 'the real annual growth of bank financing to the private sector ... reached a remarkable average of 30.9 per cent, about 10 times the rate of economic growth in the period' (*LatinFinance*, September 1997: 32). The growth in bank financing was particularly rapid after privatization. The opening up of the banking system brought a rush to buy into the banking system; 'so fierce was the bidding that some buyers shelled out over three times the bank's book value in the expectation of many years of rosy returns' (*The Economist*, 12 April 1997: 19). Though they had paid inflated prices for the banks, the new owners soon discovered 'that they were short of capital and that conventional banking was less lucrative than they'd imagined it to be – unless they could find a way to expand assets quickly' (Tangeman, 1995: 119).

The massive expansion of loans was not matched by an improvement in methods of risk assessment: credit-rating agencies were only authorized in 1995. Most Mexican banks increased the size of their assets, without taking note of the decreasing level of asset quality.[5] These 'halcyon' days, of course, foretold problems that were soon to afflict the system. At the same time as demand began to drop off in 1993/94 as a result of an economic slowdown and a rise in interest rates, the banks also experienced a rise in non-performing loans and corporate bankruptcies, making their position untenable. Even before the peso crisis, Mexican banks' past due loans had reached 8.3 per cent of gross loans (*The Economist*, 7 January 1997). The crisis of 1994/95 brought all of these problems to a head in a very short time and heaped a considerable set of new problems on the banking system. Interest rates were forced upwards by the government, reaching the incredible level of 110 per cent in March of 1995. Increasing numbers of bad loans hit the system, and dollar-denominated liabilities increased in value, due to the peso devaluation, at the same time as bank asset quality was deteriorating. Banks experienced a severe drop in their capitalization levels to the point where their capital/asset ratios no longer provided them with sufficient coverage in the event of wide-spread default (*LatinFinance*, September 1996: 34).

The continuing problems of the Mexican banking system and foreign involvement

What problems remain in the Mexican banking system? Two main problem areas can be identified: low levels of capital and banking expertise. The first of these problems is one that affects only the industry directly. However, indirectly it limits the number of new loans issued by the banking system, and complicates the work of supervisors and regulators seeking to ensure the safety and soundness of that system. The second problem, as noted above, affects both industry and authorities alike.

The first problem is one that will have to be solved before the Mexican banking system, and hence the Mexican economy, can regain a stable and healthy balance. Without higher levels of capitalization, banks will not be able to safely extend credit to the economy, credit which is desperately needed to provide a boost to growth. This is a problem that has been partially solved by the government's rescue schemes, which have been key in stabilizing Mexican banks' capital levels during the ongoing economic crisis and which will be discussed in more detail in a later section of this chapter. However, another of the government's initiatives, that of opening up the Mexican banking system to foreign competition, has also been crucial. Foreign bank involvement in the Mexican system currently stands at around 27 per cent of the market – a substantial advance on the beginning of the decade. In terms of voting shares, foreign banks now hold an astounding 53.1 per cent of the total (Salgado, 1997). When asked what benefits foreign bank participation brings to the Mexican system, the head of the CNBV, Eduardo Fernandez Garcia, replied that 'the immediate effect is the fact that they are bringing capital to Mexican institutions' (*LatinFinance*, September 1996: 33). However, Mexican regulators had hoped that the level of foreign bank participation would be much higher than this (de Luna, 1996). Mexico is still experiencing a credit crunch – in 1996 the economy grew by 5.1 per cent but 'bank loans to the private sector shrank at nearly twice that rate' (*The Economist*, 12 April 1997: 25). There is widespread agreement that the quickest way to increase Mexican bank capital levels would be to secure increased foreign bank participation, and both the CNBV and the ABM argue that foreign involvement will be useful in the restructuring of the banking system (CNBV, 1996: 44) and in increasing competition (del Cuesto, 1997).

The provision of capital, however central as it is to the immediate recovery of the Mexican banking system and economy, will not solve the longer-term problems afflicting the system. These concern the lack of expertise, on the part of both banks and banking authorities, in the area of modern financial practices. Mexican banks have begun to adapt. But they have had such a long way to come to catch up with their counterparts in advanced national financial systems that an area of what can accurately be called 'significant ignorance' still exists. Banks lack the technical know-how to enable them to develop effective strategic plans, to adequately measure risk, and to be able to safely adopt new financial products. As the president of the Mexican banking association recently put it, the 'banks of Mexico must bridge the technological gap setting them apart from their industrialized-nation counterparts' (del Valle, 1997). This, of course, is the same problem that contributed to the banking crisis in the first place. In describing the roots of the crisis, CNBV president Eduardo Fernandez Garcia argued that in 'some cases, the moral ethics of administrators were clearly not what they should have been... In others, I would say there was a problem of a lack of knowledge of the banking business' (Tangeman, 1995: 119).

Much of the blame for this problem can be laid at the door of the nationalization process of 1982. During the ten years of state control, a generation of bankers and their expertise was lost to the Mexican banking system. When the banking system was liberalized, and bank lending expanded at the beginning of the decade, 'banking institutions had not by that time completed the establishment of adequate internal controls as well as proper criteria and procedures for lending' (de Luna, 1996). To recover that knowledge and expertise is a challenge that will require foreign participation. The experience of the Filipino banking system that began in 1994 is testament to this. Since encouraging foreign bank participation, the Filipino system has benefited from a much-needed injection of expertise; it is widely held that foreign banks 'bring know-how – from streamlined loan approvals to the latest branch automation systems' (*The Economist*, 12 April 1997: 33). Such changes in Mexico will bring improved customer service and greater safety and soundness.

But what has been the extent of foreign involvement in the Mexican banking system since the crisis? Two Canadian banking institutions have taken an active role in Mexican banking since the onset of the economic crisis. In late February of 1996, two of Canada's largest financial institutions, Bank of Montreal and Bank of Nova Scotia, each became part owners of Mexican banks. Bank of Nova Scotia has invested in one of the nation's largest banks, Inverlat by taking on a 16 per cent share of the bank, with the option of purchasing a further 39 per cent of the bank in March of 2001. The initial investment on the part of Scotiabank was US$50 million, plus US$125 million in eight-year bonds which can be swapped for the optional 39 per cent later. Bank of Montreal similarly took on a 16 per cent share in Bancomer, the nation's second largest (and now largest) bank at a cost of between US$424 million and US$477 million.

Interestingly enough, Canadian banks did not appear on the lists of foreign financial institutions granted licenses during the liberalization of the Mexican banking system. Most permits went to US financial institutions, but they have waited until recently to become seriously involved in the Mexican system, when GE Capital Bank bought a Mexican bank, Banco Alianza, and Citibank expanded its Mexican operations with its take-over of Confia in August of 1997.[6] This relative reluctance on the part of US banks can be explained by two factors. First, US banks are adopting a 'wait-and-see' approach to involvement in Mexican finance, waiting to see how the system reforms itself before investing heavily therein. Secondly, US banks are deriving significant profits from lending to Latin America through international financial markets, and as long as these profits are forthcoming, they see little point in risking a long-term fixed investment in Mexico's banking marketplace.[7] The other nation whose banks are becoming increasingly active in Mexico is, of course, Spain. Three Mexican financial institutions are now owned or part-owned by Spanish banks, one to the level of 75 per cent, showing the importance of cultural and linguistic factors in industry mergers and alliances.[8]

The relative weakness of US bank participation in the Mexican system is lamentable for its consequences in terms of capital. However, the strength of Canadian involvement stems from the advantages in terms of both capital and expertise that Canadian banks have brought to the system. According to one Canadian regulatory official, it is 'Canadian, not US, banks that have retail banking expertise' (Fecser, 1996). Indeed, Canadian banks' strength lies in the provision of financial services, not merely loans. This is the direction in which Mexico's banks are heading and to which Canadian financial institutions can make the greatest contribution to future profitability and system stability. According to the same official, 'Expertise is the main thing that Canadian banks have to offer' the Mexican system. Due to the stability and high level of competition of the Canadian financial system, as well as pressure from Canadian regulatory and supervisory authorities, Canadian banks have developed their internal controls to a high level which can be of great benefit to the Mexican banks in which they have invested.

The direct cause of Canadian banks' decisions to invest in Mexico can be traced to the veritable bargain they received due to the devaluation of the peso (Randle, 1996). Indirectly it was the stability, as well as the saturation, of the Canadian market, that has enabled Canadian banks to develop international strategies in recent years. Due to the saturation of the Canadian banking marketplace, the Canadian banks which have taken the plunge into Mexico have made the decision to invest for the long term. Scotiabank has developed a strategy in recent years of keeping equity holdings in banks in other countries, so this is not a new development for them. As for Bank of Montreal, it appears that the institution has developed a North American strategy, which now embraces all three national North American banking markets: Bank of Montreal in Canada, Harris Bankcorp in the USA, and now Bancomer in Mexico (Dowbiggin, 1996). The goal of Bank of Montreal 'is to seamlessly provide product' across the NAFTA marketplace (Dowbiggin, 1996). Because of the need to seek profits and high returns outside of Canada, both these institutions seem to have made a long-term commitment to a presence in the Mexican banking system, a factor that can only be beneficial to the long-term health of that system.

What impact has this had on the ABM? Well, increased foreign presence in the Mexican banking system has meant a reordering of the association's priorities. The new foreign owners are pushing issues related to their start-up concerns in the ABM's executive committee. It is to be expected that this will not last for long; as these new participants become established, 'their interests will converge with those of established banks' (Jimenez, 1997). This is more or less what happened in the early part of this decade when the banking system was again privatized.

New foreign owners have brought with them new technology to the Mexican banking system and this has been viewed very favourably by the ABM. What is less clear is whether it is the new members of the ABM that have been responsible for the calls by the ABM for less governmental and more private regulation of the banking system, focusing on internal management standards and risk assessment. There is certainly an echo here of the concerns of banks in the United States and Canada and it must be noted that banks from these two countries now operating in Mexico or holding shares in Mexican banks can provide the technologies and techniques necessary to allow for greater self-regulation.

Despite the increased foreign presence, the ABM has not actively sought to attract more foreign capital. Neither is it trying to deter higher levels of foreign investment, but it must be remembered that the ABM represents the interests of its associate banks operating in Mexico, and when new banks enter the marketplace, they take business away from those already established here. Thus it would be wrong to see the ABM as an organization working to further internationalize Mexican banking.

State involvement in the Mexican banking system

What have been the results of this banking crisis? In short, the banking system experienced a massive contraction in the value of its assets, a rise in the value of its liabilities, and a sharp drop in the level of capital in the system. New lending virtually dried up for 1995 and 1996. The government was forced to intervene in the banking system to rescue a number of institutions through a series of schemes designed to recapitalize the banks and render them capable of re-entering the market. In effect, the state found itself compelled to renationalize many of the banks which it sold only 5 years previously. Six of the 18 banks that were privatized have been taken over by the government; in addition, a large proportion of banks loans have been sold by the banks to the Fondo Bancario de Protección al Ahorro (FOBAPROA), and the Programa de Capitalización Temporal (PROCAPTE)[9] has played a key role in recapitalizing Mexican banks.

These schemes have proved remarkably successful. In two years they have succeeded, in conjunction with foreign investment, in stabilizing the Mexican banking system to the point where it is now beginning to issue new loans. However the cost of the banking system's rescue has been enormous. The recapitalization program alone has cost the Mexican government 100 billion pesos. The head of the banking commission estimated in September of 1996 that the rescue programs together 'should cost about 8 per cent of 1996 gross domestic product' (*LatinFinance*, September 1996: 32). A more recent estimate claims that the banking crisis 'will eventually take a total of 12 per cent of the country's GDP, or $30 billion, to clean up' (*The Economist*, 12 April

1997: 18). Of more direct importance to the current chapter, the state has taken control, or guaranteed, a huge portion of the banking system's financial assets. Under FOBAPROA and PROCAPTE alone the government now controls over 111 billion pesos worth of assets. This has meant that the privatization effort of the early 1990s has, in effect, been stalled. It would be surprising if this has not had an impact on the level of autonomy exercised by the ABM.

Of greater direct importance, though, to the ABM has been the cost of these programs for the banks themselves. Though most of the initial funds for FOBAPROA were provided by the government, the banks have been required to contribute 'major sums' each month and 'the weight of their cumulative contribution in the total is rising fast' (del Valle, 1997). In addition, the government contribution came in the form of long-term financing from the banks themselves rather than cash, and this financing was granted at a discount. By the time FOBAPROA finishes, banks 'will share a loss liability ranging between 25 per cent and 30 per cent' (del Valle, 1997).

The association played an important role in the period directly following the onset of the banking crisis. First it provided a forum where the banking industry could develop common policies that could then be taken to discussion with public authorities. Secondly, it has been intimately involved with the authorities, in particular the central bank and the CNBV, in drawing up the government's solutions, both short- and long-term, to the crisis. In these discussions, many of which occupied 'long nights' according to one source (Jimenez, 1997), it was not always a question of what should be done,but rather how the measures should be implemented. Throughout the main goal was to secure minimal pain for both government and the banks.

The ABM and changing regulation in Mexico

The crisis in Mexico had an direct impact on the ABM. First, the association has lost a great deal of money because it receives its funding from the banking sector relative to the assets and loan portfolios. The contraction of the banking system that was witnessed in 1995 and 1996 thus hit the ABM directly. The association has halved its personnel and has implemented an austerity program. Secondly, the effective nationalization of banking assets that has taken place under FOBAPROA and PROCAPTE, as mentioned above, has diminished the impact of the privatization of the country's banks in the early years of this decade, and has necessitated closer cooperation rather than confrontation between the ABM and the government. Third, the ABM, though halving its staff numbers, has shifted its priorities towards hiring fewer, but more highly trained, more technical personnel. This new hiring strategy dovetails nicely with the association's demands for more self-regulation – the ABM will in the future be better placed to provide technical assistance and training for the new challenges in Mexican banking.

What response has been made by Mexican banking authorities? Mention has already been made of the dramatic changes that were imposed on the Mexican regulatory system in the early 1990s. What is vital to note here, though, is that changes and improvements in supervision did not coincide with the liberalization of the Mexican banking system. As one banking commission put it, 'the rapid growth of banking loan portfolios was not accompanied by [stronger] prudential regulations and supervision, that could discourage new privatized entities from taking excessive risks' (de Luna, 1996: 1). The challenge for Mexican regulatory authorities since the crisis, and for the future, has been to improve prudential regulation in the form of 'higher provision requirements, new capitalization standards which incorporate market risks, new accounting and disclosure principles highly consistent with international standards' and to improve banks' internal controls (de Luna, 1996: 2). Supervision, too, requires drastic improvement. Significant steps have already been taken, such as changing the focus of surveillance 'from one oriented to auditing to one oriented to the monitoring of those risks' (de Luna, 1996: 3). However, the CNBV still has a long way to go: it must develop techniques to ensure consolidated supervision and needs to train its supervisory officers in modern methods of supervision.

It is here that the role of the ABM has been vital. They have been engaged in an ongoing consultative process with the CNBV. The views of banks have been central to the reforms being pushed by the CNBV, an outline of which is given below:

- *First objective*:   ensure the stability and solvency of the financial system;
- *Second objective*:   protect the interests of savers and the investing public;
- *Third objective*:   promote the constant improvement of the moral and technical quality of Mexican financial institutions' administration, as well as their systems of internal control;
- *Fourth objective*:   encourage the efficient and safe development of the financial system, so that it responds to the needs of saving and

of the financing of diverse sectors of the economy, and so that it promotes economic growth and development; and
- *Fifth objective*:   strengthen the institutional development of the CNBV. (CNBV, 1996: 7)

These five points amount to nothing less than a revolution in the way the Mexican financial system is regulated and supervised, most importantly with regard to the latter. According to observers of the Mexican banking system, the problem in the past has not been lack of regulations. Rather, the underlying weakness of Mexican banking authorities has been their outdated and inadequate methods of supervision (Dowbiggin, 1996). Rules are all well and good, but they are worth little in the way of ensuring systemic safety and soundness if their application is not tightly supervised.

The supervision of the Mexican financial system is currently being shaped according to a plan involving *Manejo de fondos* (fund management), *Adecuaciòn de capital* (capital adequacy), *Calidad de activos* (asset quality), *Rentabilidad* (profitability) and *Organizaciòn* (organization). This is an advanced and sophisticated plan that will require high levels of supervisory expertise from those charged with its implementation.

One area that threatens to be a destabilizing force in the Mexican banking system in the next few years if adequate safeguards and methods of supervision are not adopted is the issue of self-regulation. One of the goals of supervisory change named in the CNBV's strategic plan is the need to improve self-regulation (autoregulaciòn) in order to 'delegate, under specific conditions, certain functions of supervision' to the financial sector itself (CNBV, 1996: 23). Whilst such an objective is far from revolutionary in advanced financial systems, in Mexico's it poses a high level of risk. This was explicitly recognized by one of the CNBV's own officers, who stated that the choice between official and self-regulation

> depends on the level of development of a financial system. Whilst a developed system can provide its own regulation, an underdeveloped system needs guidance from regulators and supervisors. The Mexican banking system is not well equipped enough to self-regulate at this time. (de Luna, 1996)

To make a system of self-regulation work efficiently, without compromising systemic safety and soundness, a considerable injection of expertise at both industry and authority level is going to be required. Corporate governance and management standards are a 'top priority' for the CNBV. If Mexican authorities are not successful in bringing Mexican banks up to speed in this regard, the area of significant ignorance that exists in the industry, combined with that in regulatory and supervisory circles, threatens a future Mexican banking crisis.

The ABM has been key in pushing this new approach. Despite fears among some analysts that Mexican banks are not ready for self-regulation, the association has made it very clear that it supports giving greater responsibility to the private sector for its own stability and soundness. The ABM has argued that its own training schemes and technical assistance and the injection of foreign expertise that has already taken place will be able to secure the transition from the former system of regulation to one based on self-regulation and public supervision. One area where this argument is particularly strong is in the area of derivatives trading and it has clearly not gone unanswered in the banking commission. At time of writing the CNBV was drafting new rules that, though strict, focused on internal risk management in the banks themselves. The CNBV has decided to concentrate the new rules on developing risk management departments in each bank, with Chinese walls, high levels of information disclosure, and an emphasis on self-regulation. A similarly market-oriented response that focuses on information disclosure has been the adoption of Generally Accepted Accounting Procedures (GAAP), in which the ABM was similarly involved. Though it is unlikely that the commission has taken these measures solely in response to pressure by the ABM, and likely reflects both other pressures and a general change in regulatory philosophy on the part of the commission, it would be wrong to underestimate the influence of the association.

One last, specific example of ABM involvement in the drawing up of new regulations is the reform of FOBAPROA. The association has been active in arguing for a reduction in coverage under the program, so that investors and depositors alike can choose banks according to their soundness. Though the program was essential in shoring up confidence in the banking system immediately following the crisis, the ABM initiated discussions with the CNBV aimed at reducing the extent of the program now that relative stability has returned to Mexico's banks. As the vice-president of the association argued in 1997, FOBAPROA is having the undesirable effect of restricting competition:

Providing virtually universal protection to all kinds of deposits no matter its size, be it a minor depositor, a mid-range depositor, or the treasury of a massive and complex corporation, fails to offer an adequate framework for competition. For competition to work, both depositors and sophisticated investors must be able to choose the soundest institutions, with trustworthy information to this respect provided for the general public to know their actual financial position, and be able to demand premiums for weaker institutions over the returns offered by their stronger counterparts. (del Cuesto, 1997)

The government's response to this line of argument from the ABM has been to announce that FOBAPROA coverage will gradually decrease, beginning in 1998, with a new focus on low-income investors. This, of course, will be a great relief to many of the ABM's more stable members. As one source put it, whilst the government's 'programs have been successful, they have been very expensive for the banks' (Jimenez, 1997).

Conclusion

This chapter has attempted to demonstrate that the structural change in the Mexican banking system brought on by the conjunction of two events, the signing of the NAFTA and the country's severe economic crisis in 1994 and 1995, has had a significant impact upon the business association representing Mexico's banks. Four elements have been identified in this chapter:

- First the NAFTA allowed for increased foreign participation in the banking system, and that possibility has been realized because of the effects of the 1994/95 crisis. New foreign participants have introduced new concerns to the banking association, but have also given the association new technical resources on which it can call, and new regulatory priorities.
- Second, the crisis hit the association hard, reducing its budget and personnel and forcing it to reevaluate its priorities.
- Third, the governmental response to the banking system's crisis imposed severe costs on Mexican banks and also saw the effective renationalization of a large portion of bank assets (in addition to six of the banks themselves).

- Fourth, the crisis has brought about a new regulatory and supervisory agenda on the part of the nation's banking authorities, and the ABM is playing a central role in the shaping of new approaches.

What more general conclusions can we draw from this case study? Primarily, the experience of the ABM shows that deep structural change in one sector of the economy, such as that following from the NAFTA and the economic crisis, not only brings costs for the business associaiton representing that sector, but also new opportunities. The injection of new and different members into the ABM, and the reform of Mexico's regulatory and supervisory agenda that has followed the crisis, has helped to define a new role for the association. What remains to be seen is if similar new roles have been made available to banking associations in other Latin American countries that have undergone liberalization and crisis in their banking systems in recent years.

Notes

1. Special thanks are due to my research assistant, Gabriela Valero, for her help in the background and translation work on this chapter.
2. Private finance was represented in the drawing up of Mexican policy on NAFTA by the Asociacion Mexicana de Intermediarios Bursatiles (AMIB).
3. Part of this was due to the fact that banks were required to meet capital requirements of only US$5 million.
4. At the 1992 exchange rate, this was approximately 33.7 billion pesos.
5. The exceptions were the two largest banks, Banamex and Bancomer, which both diversified and acted more cautiously in their loan expansions. Serfin, the third largest bank, was not so well-advised or fortunate.
6. In addition to these banks, BankBoston, which is already involved in the new Afores system, is rumoured to be interested in buying the Mexican bank Ixe.
7. I am indebted to Matthew Shepherd for this explanation.
8. Banco de Santander of Spain now owns 75 per cent of shares in Banco Mexicano.
9. Bank Savings Protection Fund and Temporary Capitalization Program, respectively.

5
Organized Business and the European Union

Justin Greenwood

Business is more intensively organized at the European Union (EU) level than at any other transnational level in the globe. Whilst the European Economic Community (EEC) was created by politicians against a backdrop of disinterest from business, 'Euro enthusiasm' is more marked today amongst business interests. There are now over 600 formal European level business associations (European Commission, 1996; Landmarks Publications, 1997), a variety of informal business public affairs clubs and alliances, and approximately 250 firms with representative offices in Brussels.

As well as responding to the competencies of the European Union, business interests have been a significant influence in developing the course of European integration. Indeed, the 'relaunching of Europe', culminating in the Single European Act (SEA) of 1986, arose in part from the demands of a group of business leaders from Europe's largest companies, concerned about losing out in global competition to Japan, America and the newly industrializing countries of Southeast Asia. For the businesses they represented, a European single market was, at the bottom line, a strategy for survival. In a manner predicted by Ernst Haas's early neofunctionalist account of European integration (Haas, 1958), business interests thus sought and encouraged the progressive transfer of competencies from the national to the European level. Today, Cowles has estimated that some 60 per cent of all legislation directed at industry in Europe has a 'made in Brussels' stamp on it (Cowles, 1995a). Policy outputs in the governance of some business sectors cannot be accounted for without acknowledging the extent of input from private interests.

The European level impacts upon business in a number of ways. These include: regulation, concerned with restriction and governance of activities, usually on public interest grounds; promotion, such as action designed to develop industrial application of key technologies or to support export campaigns; integration, such as measures to ensure free and fair competition between producers throughout the single market, and delegated authority for product standardization; funding, such as the structural funds for regional policy, support under the EU research framework programmes, and sums awarded to business groups for project and consultancy work on behalf of the European Commission; and enablement, where responses are made to pressing problems with support measures, such as measures designed to promote a cleaner environment which do not fall into the category of 'regulation'. These categories are not mutually exclusive, nor are they precise. Regulation and integration activities have clearly been interlinked in initiatives designed to achieve the single market. Public procurement legislation, for instance, insist that large public works and supplies contracts are advertised for tender throughout the EU to ensure market competition, rather than permitting protected and cozy national and local 'champion' agreements with favored suppliers which tend to inflate costs and make industry uncompetitive (Cecchini, 1988).

The entire single market project represents an opportunity and a threat for business; an opportunity in the sense of having access to over 370 million potential customers under conditions of similar market supply; and a threat in that one's traditional, and perhaps at one time protected, customer base is open to competition from other suppliers. The logic of these forces is that large, mobile firms well able to compete outside their national markets would find the single market a glorious opportunity, whereas many smaller firms which had benefited from national rules, sometimes protectionist in nature, might struggle. In part for these reasons, the run up to the single market therefore saw a wave of mergers, acquisitions and strategic alliances as firms sought to maximise from the opportunities presented by the single market (Jacquemin and Wright, 1994). These conglomerations had a vested interest in a transnational, rather than a series of national, set of rules governing market exchange. Besides the opportunities presented by, and need for, one single market, there was the chance to tear up the national rules and help create a whole new set, sometimes based around liberalisation. Indeed, the most competitive firms have been the loudest voices for liberalisation, whereas struggling rivals prefer more regulated systems; such a pattern is evident in the case of airlines, where British Airways is a strong supporter for liberalisation while many of their rivals oppose it (Young, 1995).

Business interests have certainly been present in Brussels since the start of the EEC. But for large firms, in particular, interest in 'project Europe' can be traced to the 1970s, when the Commission established programmes directed at multinationals, and the European Court of Justice made a number of key rulings concerning competition policy (Cowles, 1995b). These, together with the severe economic recessions which characterized western economies following the 'oil shock', convinced firms to seek transnational solutions, and in turn these interests exerted significant influences upon the perceptions of member states that national protectionism would inevitably lead to the loss of ability of European firms to compete in international markets. These elite of 'super firms' were multinationals which operated across national boundaries, and which did not depend for their survival upon the support of a single host government to protect their national market. Rather, by virtue of their size, the interests of these firms was more to open up markets to transnational competition. Evidence such as that provided by the Cecchini report on the costs of 'non Europe' (Cecchini, 1988) also provided essential rational information to help build a climate of support among national governments for the deconstruction of national protectionism, and the reregulation of rules of market exchange at the European level to ensure free competition.

Indeed, market exchange arises within a framework of rules, and market building has brought with it not just deregulation of national rules, but also reregulation at the European level. Business interests have been active in the process of designing these rules, encouraging the progressive transfer of competencies to the EU level, sometimes manipulated by a Commission anxious to transfer power from the member states to its own transnational power base. Certainly, the early 1980's represented a considerable sea change for the role of business in the European Community, not least because of the mutually supportive relationships developed between business and the Commission dating from the period of Etienne Davignon as DG III (Industry) Commissioner (1981–85).

The European institutions have exerted significant influences upon the development of business interest political action at the European level. In order to encourage interests to organize on a Europe wide basis, the Commission, in its early days, operated a policy of dialogue only with European level (Euro) groups. Although this proved unworkable, the Commission still favors dialogue with encompassing Euro groups as a means of encouraging loyalty transfers, and of simplifying its dialogue with outside interests, which in turn has ensured the maintenance and stability of these structures as more direct forms of interest representation has evolved. In addition, the Commission hands out places on its advisory groups to Euro groups first, which provides a considerable membership incentive. Taken as a whole, the Commission has become dependent upon specialist input from outside interests. The European Commission is so small that there might be just one official with responsibility for the affairs of an entire business domain. It has therefore become dependent upon input from specialist outside interests, sometimes to the extent that European business interest groups write Commission reports. Indeed, a report from the Commission in the early 1990s recorded in its opening paragraph that

> The Commission has always been an institution open to outside input. The Commission believes this process to be fundamental to the development of its policies. This dialogue has proved valuable to both the Commission and to interested outside parties. Commission officials acknowledge the need for such outside input and welcome it. (Commission, 1992: 3)

'Outside interests' certainly have the capacity to make such an input. If the Commission's own estimates are to believed, excluding translators, there are as many individuals working in the Brussels interest representation environment as there are working for the Commission. Groups such as CEFIC (European Chemical Industry Council), for instance, draw on the resources of 4000 experts from amongst their membership constituency, as well as an in-house secretariat of 80 based in Brussels, to represent the interests of the European chemical industry at the European level (Grant, 1995). Multinational firms, in particular, are undoubtedly valuable political actors to the European institutions. They bring with them to European politics experiences of operating in a wide variety of regulatory regimes around the globe. They provide the Commission with the means to develop key structures in European public affairs, from leading edge new technologies as a basis for future wealth creation, to technical standard setting. Without their involvement, a European single market would not be possible.

The organization of business interests at the European level

Business interests have been present in Brussels since the start of the EEC. Indeed, around three-quarters of all business Euro groups in existence today had established themselves prior to the start of the single market project (Aspinwall and Greenwood, 1997). The large, cross sectoral business groups are among the best known of all interest groups working in Brussels. These include: UNICE (Union of Industrial and Employers Confederations of Europe), comprising national federations; ERT (European Round Table of Industrialists) and AMCHAM-EU (The EU Committee of the American Chamber of Commerce), both representing primarily large firms, and probably the most influential of all Euro groups; EUROCHAMBRES (Association of European Chambers of Commerce and Industry), representing Chambers of Commerce; and, amongst those dedicated to representing small firm interests, UEAPME (European Association of Craft, Small and Medium-sized Enterprises) which recently incorporated EUROPMI (European Committee for Small and Medium-sized Enterprises).

UNICE and EUROCHAMBRES were formed in 1958 in direct response to the 1957 Treaty of Rome, and are both confederations of national associations. ERT and AMCHAM-EU, on the other hand, were formed in the 1980s as direct member associations, partly because, as is explained below, confederated structures were seen as insufficiently dynamic to represent the strength of business interests in an era when the European Community needed to develop a strategic response to the growing internationalization of markets and politics. ERT and AMCHAM-EU, whilst different animals, are modern transnational interest groups geared to the needs and demands of European politics approaching the twenty-first century. The great strength of UNICE and EUROCHAMBRES is, however, that they are encompassing organizations representing much of the constituency of business interests, whereas the ERT (and to a lesser extent AMCHAM-EU) is more an exclusive club representing interests drawn from rich firms.

UNICE

UNICE was designed to represent the interests of industry as a whole. It is a confederation of 32 national federations of 'peak' business and employers associations from 22 European (that is, not simply EU) countries, of which the majority are in turn comprised from sectoral associations. It therefore represents members which themselves have a wide of interests to represent. It has a staff of 30, whose work is supported by an Executive Committee consisting of the director generals of member federations (Stern, 1994).

In order to arrive at 'an opinion', UNICE has to seek to reflect the broad constituency of its members interests and positions, which are in turn very often the result of compromises made at the national level. To help it arrive at common positions, UNICE uses its network of permanent committee structures, which in turn heightens the tendency for compromise. Thus, the organization is well recognised for providing generalized, 'lowest common denominator' positions which are not always very helpful in providing the institutions with a clear signal to act upon. Indeed, Commission officials generally have to read between the lines of UNICE position papers in order to establish the differences and basis for compromises between members. However, the organization does provide a means to institutionalize a range of interests in European public affairs. The most obvious illustration of this concerns the role of UNICE as a 'macroeconomic' (first level) social partner, together with the trade union organization ETUC (European Trade Union Confederation) and public sector employers CEEP (European Centre of Public Enterprises), where these parties are empowered (through an annex to the 1992 Treaty on European Union, substantially written by the macroeconomic social partners) to progress European integration in labour market fields by mutual agreement. The first of these initiatives to be agreed by all three parties and carried forward into EU policy was the Parental Leave Accord, enabling leave for up to three months for a parent in the first eight years of the life of a child, emerged in June 1996.

The social dialogue illustrates how far UNICE's role has changed in recent years after its refusal through much of the 1980s to engage in meaningful dialogue with ETUC. Significant sections of business have been generally more interested in non-decision-making in employment-related issues at the European level, and in ensuring that the wider business community was not drawn into dialogue with ETUC. A number of UNICE's members have therefore sought to prevent the organization from developing the capacities to enter such a dialogue, and there is a suggestion that UNICE may historically have been deliberately under resourced for this reason (Ebbinghaus and Visser, 1994). Nevertheless, UNICE's own position has shifted with the tide of European politics following the development of the social market. The legal powers this confers upon the social partners has considerably strengthened their role in European public affairs. UNICE now has a limited mandate from its members to bargain with ETUC, whereas previously it had none. UNICE, whose own role as the voice of business during the 1980s came under threat from the establishment of ERT and AMCHAM-EU, has to some extent, therefore, developed an interest in the social dialogue mechanism.

Without doubt, UNICE continues to act as a brake on the rapid expansion of social Europe. But what is important is that it has an institutionalized role through the social dialogue mechanism. It is now to some extent enmeshed within a structure from which it cannot escape. Tangible results have now emerged from the social dialogue, and there is no turning back to the days when business refused to do anything other than talk to ETUC without commitment. To a limited extent, something similar applies in the case of UNICE's membership constituency. Thus, some 20 per cent of multinational firms have already negotiated voluntarily with trade unions in advance of EU requirements for a 'works council' to provide information to, and consultation with, workers, an initiative originating from the Social Dialogue and now a requirement for firms with more than 1000 employees (*Financial Times*, 23 September 1996: 3). Whilst caution should be exercised about the use of the 'corporatist' label at the EU, not least because of the absence of state like authority, the dialogue does resemble a limited form of private interest government, where interests have delegated authority for agenda setting and implementation (Falkner, 1995). In a manner resembling Haas's concept of 'spillover', the Commission, interested in developing the pace of integration, has now signalled its intention to introduce the measure for all firms with more than 50 employees. Once European business has become familiar with the culture of information to, and consultation with, its workers, extending the concept may not be too problematic.

By participating in European public affairs since 1958, throughout the full range of formal structures of European policy-making, UNICE has to some extent 'gone native'. It cannot help but to have been influenced by its own historic participation in all the structures of the European Community. To some extent, the institutionalization of UNICE has also been a deliberate strategy by the European institutions with these outcomes in mind, and, as such, supports the emphasis in neofunctionalist accounts of the role of these institutions in developing European integration.

UNICE has also sought to address the difficulties it faces as a result of its confederate design by establishing a more direct relationship with multinational firms, most notably through the creation in 1990 of an Advisory and Support Group, and by ensuring that committee chairs come from large firms. Although this cannot be said to have transformed the organization, Grant (1990) notes something of a revival in UNICE's fortunes. Amongst the factors the responsible for his, the stimulus of other, cross sectoral organizations with a direct membership structure, such as AMCHAM-EU, and ERT, cannot be discounted. Indeed, in part, the presence of ERT can be attributed to the frustration felt by multinational firms at the lack of effectiveness of UNICE and its inherently cumbersome nature, during the early 1980s, when an effective voice for big business interests was urgently required.

EUROCHAMBRES

EUROCHAMBRES, like UNICE, is a confederation of federations, bringing together 32 national associations from EU, EFTA and other countries, which between them represent 800 local chambers of commerce, and, through them, some 14 million enterprises, of which approximately 95 per cent are SMEs. Some of the national associations of chambers of commerce have their own offices in Brussels, or structures for members and policy officials to meet up.

EUROCHAMBRES has intervened effectively in European public affairs on selective issues, such as the downgrading a Commission proposal for a directive requiring all firms to have vocational training programmes and to report on them on a bi-annual basis, to the status of a non binding recommendation. Its institutionalized role in public affairs includes an agreement with the Commission to provide European Information Centres (EICs), whose activities are substantially aimed at business users, within the premises of Chambers of Commerce; currently, these account for some 35 per cent of all EICs (Eurochambres, 1996). Like UNICE, its importance in the future seems to be guaranteed by its 'social partner' status, although it is a 'second level' organization in the social dialogue, whereas UNICE has 'first level' status.

European Round Table

The European Round Table is altogether a quite different type of organization to either UNICE or EUROCHAMBRES. Formed in 1983, it is a 'rich club', with membership by invitation only, of (in February 1996) 45 chief executive officers (CEOs) of some of the largest European firms spanning key sectors of the European economy, and which are multinational in character and thoroughly global in outlook. The firms managed by ERT members have combined sales exceeding 550 billion a year, and which employ in excess of three million workers worldwide (ERT, 1996). Its views, therefore, command considerable respect in European public affairs, while the high-profile nature of the individuals concerned make it a highly powerful voice. Original members included such household names as John Harvey Jones (ICI), Wisse Dekker

(Philips), Umberto Agnelli (Fiat), and Pehr Gyllenhammar (Volvo), while present members include the CEOs of firms such as Nestlé, British Petroleum, Fiat, Bosch, Petrofina, Olivetti, Hoffmann-La Roche, ICI, Shell, Lyonnaise des Eaux-Dumez, Airbus Industrie, Bayer, Daimler Benz, Renault, Carlsberg, Unilever, Philips and Pirelli (European Round Table, 1996).

Whereas UNICE is more of a 'workhorse', involved in the everyday business of European public affairs and in responding to Commission initiatives, ERT is more of a strategic player, geared more towards seeking to create the longer term European agenda in the interests of its members, and, it would argue, for Europe as a whole. Indeed, Stern (1994: 144) has described it more as a 'elite think tank' (sic) than a traditional interest group functioning at the operational level of political influence. Thus, it has been widely credited with providing the impetus and blueprint for the single market project, whereby the largest firms in Europe sought a European response to wealth creation through the creation of one single market for business to exploit, in recognition of the need to provide European firms with a strategy for survival and growth in the next century in response to the development of trade blocks in Japan, the USA, and the newly emerging economies of south east Asia (Stern, 1994; Cowles, 1995b). However, its role has not been restricted to one of ideas generation. As Cowles comments,

> When member states wavered in implementing the single market programme, the ERT lobbied European heads of state and government directly with a simple message: support the single market programme or European industry will move its investments out of Europe. (Cowles, 1995b: 226–7)

Following its work on the single market, the ERT report on 'Beating the Crisis' was launched by the then President of the Commission, Jacques Delors, not least because it demonstrated support for Delors own White Paper on Growth, Competitiveness and Employment. Similarly, Commissioners sometimes seek out ERT members to help them present a report or issue at a press launch. The ERT also recommendations to EU Summit Meetings, and meets every six months with the Presidency of the Council of Ministers. Unsurprisingly, it also became engaged in the 'high politics' of the 1996 Intergovernmental Conference, and in particular European Monetary Union. Indeed, the ERT has provided the lead in European public affairs on a range of high politics' issues. It is well suited to working on issues of strategic importance to wealth creation in the European Union, and its highly authoritative reports invariably make a major contribution to agenda setting the areas of concern. Thus, it has been active in, inter alia, fields such as the development of Trans-European Networks (TENs) (an initiative it has been widely credited with prompting), and information technology, where strategic concerns of European infrastructure are involved as a basis for economic development, and in 1994 created a dedicated think tank, the European Centre for Infrastructure Studies, based in Rotterdam.

As an organization with a relatively small number of members, the ERT does not suffer from the cumbersome problems of democratic overload which confront UNICE. UNICE is essentially a confederation of national associations of business, whereas ERT is a membership organization of a select number of CEOs of some of Europe's largest companies. In style, therefore, the ERT is well suited to exerting influence through the most effective methods of interpersonal contacts with key figures in the European institutions, and through the status of their firms and CEOs in member states. When members leave their firms, or firms are taken over, so individuals lose their place on the ERT. Similarly, individuals who are not active in the organization can be removed (Cowles, 1995b). This means that the ERT is regularly reorganized and restructured, as frequently as every three to six months, creating a dynamic organization where membership is highly prized (Stern, 1994).

There can be little doubt that the ERT has been one of the most influential of all European interest groups. Cowles comments:

> President Delors himself publicly states that the industrialists were critical to the success of the single market programme. Perhaps the most important contribution of the ERT, however, has been its promotion of what one Commission official terms a 'new culture' within the Community regarding Europe and the global economy ... the ERT also influences the member states ... Michael Heseltine, head of the Department of Trade and Industry (DTI) in the UK, for example, returned a draft copy of the DTI's paper on competitiveness to the authors and asked that they incorporate the ideas of the ERT report, *Beating the Crisis*. (1995b: 235)

In many respects, the ERT has provided to other Euro groups a role model of success. UNICE, for instance, has established its own think tank in an effort to shape the European agenda after witnessing the success of ERT in this role, and a number of federated structures have sought to establish a more direct relationship with the CEOs of the firms in membership of national associations.

EU Committee of the American Chamber of Commerce

Like the ERT, AMCHAM-EU, created to represent the interests of European firms with American parentage, is one of the most effective, and admired of all Euro groups. However, while the ERT focuses on strategic issues, AMCHAM-EU tends to focus more on specific legislation. Although the present structure was established in 1985, with a membership constituency of 40 companies, AmCham has had a Belgian office since 1948 and a European level interest representation mechanism since the foundation of the EEC. The organization has grown rapidly in recent years to around 150 companies, including almost all of the largest American firms. This reflects the growing realization among American firms of the impact, or potential impact, of the EU upon its interests. AMCHAM-EU has a full-time staff of 17.

AMCHAM-EU is less of an exclusive 'rich firm club' than is the ERT because it speaks for the European Council of American Chambers of Commerce, an association of 14 American Chambers in Europe which together represent in excess of 18 000 firms (Jacek, 1995), and whose structures predate the formation of AMCHAM-EU. These firms are responsible for an estimated economic investment of $200 billion and 10 million employees in Europe, and it therefore has a powerful voice in European public affairs (Stern, 1994). These firms can sometimes also exert considerable influences upon member state governments. Indeed, there are examples of American trade associations intervening decisively (although sometimes clumsily, as is described later) in European public affairs. Thus, Jacek provides an example of how the Motion Picture Association of America was a significant influence on the decisions of the governments of Denmark, the Netherlands, and Germany to vote against a directive requiring half of all television time to be occupied by shows made in Europe (Jacek, 1995).

American firms can also exert influence where they are incorporated as full members into European sectoral trade associations. However, the exclusion of American firms from some domestic trade associations has meant that they have either operated as troublesome 'free agents' in pursuing their interests on the European stage, working against collective agreements reached in European trade associations, or found an alternative voice within AMCHAM-EU. Indeed, exclusion from sectoral trade associations in Europe has if anything strengthened the collective identify of American firms in Europe, and in consequence the ability of AMCHAM-EU to organize its members to act collectively. The exclusion of American firms from trade associations in Europe, on the whole, has not helped the interests of European firms. American owned firms may be more of a threat to the interests of European industry outside of European trade associations than inside, and consequently there is now a tendency to include them, rather than the common practice of exclusion in the 1970s and 1980s. However, Jacek still detects a hostility in the attitude of some European business associations towards American business in Europe, most notably, and significantly, from the ERT (Jacek, 1995).

AMCHAM-EU has also sought to provide a European interest perspective on issues which affect American firms, and, where possible, to use European figureheads in its campaigns, and to staff its offices with officials from a European background. Similarly, it has sought, with mixed success, to socialize American firms to adopt stances which better fit the continental European model of social democratic, rather than US style free market, capitalism. On the whole, however, American firms have been the staunchest opponents of Commission measures for industrial democracy, and it is this lack of cultural affinity to European traditions which Jacek identifies as the biggest hurdle to American business influence in European public affairs (Jacek, 1995). Nevertheless, on the whole AMCHAM-EU is regarded within the Commission as a supportive ally in favor of European integration. Without such a strategy on the part of AMCHAM-EU, it would be easy for the interests of American firms to be excluded from European public affairs.

AMCHAM-EU is particularly noted for the high quality and thorough nature of its publications and reports, which have become sought after handbooks and 'guides to the European Union' amongst European firms, and which are often used by EU officials as the basis for drafting legislation (Jacek, 1995). But above all, the key to its effectiveness is its ability to reach meaningful collective positions quickly, facilitated by its role as a direct membership driven organization. It has proved itself reform minded to maintain capacities for speed and adaptability to changing circumstances (Jacek, 1995), including the recent creation of a structure for high-level executives to meet, the European American Industrial Council, an idea partly inspired by the role model of ERT (Cowles, 1994). One high ranking Commission official has commented that 'AMCHAM is fast and it establishes good positions – as a result its contributions are always well received by the

Commission, even though it represents US rather than European companies' interests' (quoted in Stern, 1994: 144). This capacity is one of the major factors responsible for its effectiveness.

Despite such advantages, AMCHAM-EU does not have the institutionalized ability to exert influence in fields such as social policy, which UNICE does by virtue of its social partner status. This is an area where UNICE can, and does, broker and lead coalitions consisting of itself, ERT and AMCHAM-EU, such as when these actors needed them to act in concert to block Commission proposals on consultation of workers. Indeed, where these cross-sectoral associations work together they can constitute an almost irresistible force in European public affairs, and there is some degree of loose coordination between them.

Other cross-sectoral groups

Formal cross-sectoral groups are also present in issue based arenas, such as the Paris based Association for Monetary Union in Europe (AMUE). The association was created in 1987 by high-profile European industrialists who agreed on the objectives of establishing monetary stability and a single currency for the success of the single market. Current board members include names such as Etienne Davignon (president) and Giovanni Agnelli (vice-president). Over 250 companies and 30 banks, employing between them more than six million workers, are members of the association, including some of Europe's largest firms. Because of a high degree of membership overlap, the group works closely with the ERT, and a number of sectoral associations on an ad hoc basis. In addition to large firms, however, a number of national employers confederations (France, Greece, Ireland, Italy, Spain) are also members, providing a further means of coordination between federated and large firm member business structures. As a group operating in the 'high politics' field, where it is one of a number of actors (including, of course, member states) – and therefore lacks the opportunity for monopolistic access to (and influence of) public affairs characteristic in some 'low politics' fields – the Association operates mainly at the level of ideas generation. The association has produced a number of important studies and publications, including those completed for the Commission and the Parliament.

Small and medium sized enterprises

Although UNICE and EUROCHAMBRES seek to incorporate the interests of SMEs, there are a plethora of European-level interest groups dedicated to the representation of SMEs. The most encompassing of these include UEAPME (European Association of Craft, Small and Medium-sized Enterprises) and EUROPMI (European Committee for Small and Medium-sized Independent Companies), scheduled for merger at the end of 1998, resulting in the award of 'second level' social partner status. However, both the Council and the Commission are extremely concerned at the fragmentation of interest representation in the domain, and the Commission has recently (1996) responded by working with some of the key actors to fund the creation of an 'SME Forum', linking the range of associations in the field. At least in terms of rhetoric, SMEs are pushing at an open door with the Commission. Following the Delors White Paper on Growth, Competitiveness and Employment, where SMEs were identified as a major sector to target support at, the Commission adopted a major action programme for them, and specifically identified the importance of interaction with SME interest associations as a means to achieve the objectives of the programme.

Sectoral organization of business interests

Business sector (or, where sectoral definition is difficult such as in tourism, 'domain') trade associations account for the overwhelming majority of Euro groups. Many of these actors have become indispensable to public policy-making and implementation in Europe because of the types of resources they bring to these arenas, becoming institutionally involved with European public policy-making and implementation. Brussels is very much an 'insider's town', where operating effectively depends upon a dense network of interpersonal and inter-organizational links. It is very difficult for 'outsiders' to arrive, 'win the day' through persuasion, and go home again.

There is now a wealth of sectoral case studies identifying patterns of interest representation, investigating concepts of collective action, and examining the contribution of business interests to the integration process (see, for instance, the collection of case studies on information technology, pharmaceuticals, consumer electronics and broadcasting, aerospace, bioindustry, cement, banking, retailing, tourism, water, textiles, automobiles, shipping, firms and cross-sectoral associations, in Greenwood, 1995a; and those on Philips, Airbus Industrie, fruit companies, Euro Disney, airlines, couriers, gas, automobiles and information technology, in Pedler and van Schendelen, 1994). In some policy fields, both the outputs and outcomes of European public affairs cannot be understood without reference to the behaviour, presence and stances of sectoral trade associations. The members of some business sector associations have more resources at their disposal than do some member states, and they are bound therefore to be significant political players. They are often incorporated fully within European policy-making structures right from the outset, sometimes by setting the agenda, sometimes in implementation at the European and national levels, and sometimes in influencing the draft which emerges from the Commission. As Claveloux comments,

> The frequent contact between the Commission and sectoral interest groups means the outside association is allowed onto the inside track, so it knows what proposals are in the pipeline and which Commission official is drafting them. These single sector associations, particularly the European federations, are often asked to give line by line analysis of texts before they even become draft legislative proposals. (Claveloux, 1993: 20)

Some are so deeply ingrained within the structures of the European institutions that it is difficult to draw a distinction between 'public' and 'private'. Many have formal consultative status, and some form a lasting and ingrained policy community type of policy network with the relevant parts of the public institutions, which acts as a governance mechanism for the sector concerned. Some of the Commission services have become entirely dependent upon the information, expertise and other resources which these actors bring to European public affairs. DG XIII, for instance, contains many staff on secondment from the European consumer electronics firms, and the development of strategically important technologies would simply not be possible without the work of major firms such as Philips (Cawson, 1992; 1995).

Another example of ingrained interest intermediation is provided by the example of the European Federation of Pharmaceutical Industry Associations (EFPIA), where the association's involvement in the governance of selling standards in medicines at the European level through self regulation bears all the hallmarks of neo corporatism. Here, as an alternative to a Commission proposal to regulate, EFPIA proposed a scheme it had developed through the International Federation of Pharmaceutical Manufacturers Associations (IFPMA), and through experiences at the national level, in responding to regulatory threats at the international and national, levels. The Commission accepted EFPIA's proposals, and in doing so enabled the pharmaceutical industry to retain control of its key strategy to produce profits through its dominant position in providing medical practitioners with product information, particularly through its highly effective network of medical representatives (Greenwood, 1988). Thus, the industry's responses at the European level were conditioned by its experiences of political action at other territorial levels. EFPIA also persuaded the Commission to take the governments of Belgium and Italy to court over pricing arrangements to which the industries in those countries had once been a party to, indicating the extent to which the industry has been able to achieve more at the European level than once seemed possible at the national level. It turned a regulatory threat of a restricting directive on medicine prices into a directive requiring member states to produce transparent criteria for pricing decisions, and to provide detailed justification where price rises were refused.

Similarly, EFPIA provided the blueprint for the extension of the patent period for medicines in Europe, when the Commission had initially been reluctant to do so. It also gave encouragement to the idea of the creation of a European Medicines Agency to ensure recognition of medicinal products throughout member states, and to ensure a faster process of pre-market product evaluation by regulatory authorities. In doing so, EFPIA helped form a climate of ideas which persuaded member states to seek a transnational solution to the registration of medicinal problems, in that it was able to illustrate the losses which accrued from the need to seek repeat authorizations for products in every member state. Together with other business associations, EFPIA also prevented insertion of a 'fourth hurdle' criteria of 'social acceptability' in the registration of medicinal products. Through its position as one of Europe's major wealth creators, and its potential for wealth creation in the next century, the pharmaceutical industry has becoming the driving influence behind public policy outputs in the pharmaceutical sector. Indeed, the industry continues to improve its performance, set against a general loss of competitiveness and declining performance of European industry as a whole (Greenwood, 1995b). Nevertheless, on a note of caution it is well worth recording how powerful business interests such as EFPIA, and the large firm interest group Senior Advisory Group Biotechnology (SAGB) (since merged with another group to form Europabio), have discovered to their cost that public interest groups have increasingly shown their ability to use the European Parliament (EP) as a means of asserting themselves by politicizing issues.

As the cases in Greenwood, Grote and Ronit (1992), Pedler and van Schendelen (1994) and Greenwood (1995a) indicate, EFPIA is by no means an untypical case, although it is arguably perhaps the most influential of all sectoral interest groups in sectoral European public affairs. Whilst EFPIA is a clear example of EU-level sectoral corporatism, Streeck and Schmitter (1991) had a different variant in mind when they famously proclaimed the absence of corporatism at the European level, and indeed that the European level would be disruptive to national level corporatist relationships. Their focus was upon macro-corporatism, involving peak exchange over high-politics issues between business, labour and a bureaucracy with state-like properties, whereas they had little to say about meso (sectoral) corporatism. However, some accounts (Hix, 1994; Lewin, 1994; Hayward, 1995) have over-generalized Streeck and Schmitter's arguments to suggest that corporatist arrangements *per se* are not present in the EU, or that it is somehow a type of 'pluralist' type environment. Apart from the deductive fallacy of 'if it's not corporatist, it must be pluralist' implicit in these, Schmitter has, in a subsequent paper, explicitly identified the presence of 'islands [that is, sectoral] of corporatism at the European level, and has acknowledged in a study of Austria with Franz Traxler, that the European level need not be disruptive to national level corporatisms (Traxler and Schmitter, 1994).

Large firms as single and coalition actors in European public affairs

Large firms provide the 'powerhouse' for both cross-sectoral and sectoral European-level business associations, providing resources, experience in political action, and status for collective structures. Firms with their own dedicated Brussels office can have as many as eight public affairs specialists based there (Stern, 1994). Many large firms selectively share out responsibilities within groups for taking collective issues forward. Collective structures can offer the opportunity for large firms to achieve the cloak of identity; in the case of Philips, the EACEM has in previous incarnations been little more than a 'front' organization for its interests (Cawson, 1992). Group participation is also a means of accessing the institutional structures of the EU, in that Commission preferences for collective actors means that committee places are handed out through groups first.

Increasingly, structures less formal than federated and direct membership Euro groups have emerged in recent years, primarily based around large firms. These range on a spectrum from visible groups with a loose organization, through to privately organized occasional dining clubs. Some are issue-based, others are built around sectors, while others are cross-sectoral. Some are open membership structures, sometimes initiated by the European institutions, while others are more exclusive clusters of a select number of firms. Some are developing into more recognizable and formal Euro groups, whereas others are transient, or are likely to remain, by design, as informal meeting points. These more informal types of groups have become somewhat fashionable in recent years as the interests within them find such structures valuable; as Cram has suggested, cooperation in one type of structure can lead to collaboration elsewhere (Cram, 1995). But, equally, such structures can lead to the foundation of similar fora by outsiders who witness their effectiveness, or who seek to find ways of responding to their exclusion. In turn, this illustrates how the presence of collective structures, and participation within them, can influence the behaviour of private interest actors themselves.

At the more visible end of the spectrum are an increasing number of 'round tables', such as those which have sprung up in information technology, and banking. Some 'round tables' have become formal groups, while others are either a semi permanent structure of dialogue between firms. Other visible structures include issue alliances. In the information technology domain, two of these emerged in response to proposals which eventually became the 1991 Directive on the legal protection of computer software, representing competing positions on the desirability of allowing the retranslation of computer software. In turn, these organizations began to spawn further issue alliances, with slightly different configurations of interests. These collective structures emerged partly because of the inability of sector-wide groups to accommodate the competing interests (Pijnenburg, 1996). An example of another type of issue structure from the IT sector illustrates Cram's point about how participation in the structures of the European institutions can yield cooperation. Thus, collaboration within the CEN/CENELEC framework facilitated the creation of the European Workshop for Open Systems (EWOS) in 1987 as a means of drafting standards (Greenwood and Cram, 1996).

Other visible groups have emerged along cross-sectoral, multi-issue lines. Thus, the 'European Business Agenda' (formerly the 'Business in Europe') group, a Brussels-based group comprising a handful of large British firms, sought to influence the behaviour of the British government towards Europe and the 1996 Intergovernmental Conference by, amongst other activities, the production of papers for internal and external use. Following the IGC, the group disbanded. These papers were sent to UK Commissioners, UKREP, and to British interest groups with a Brussels presence. The organization was formed in 1994 from a dinner meeting amongst a circle of friends who were the European directors of their respective companies, including British Aerospace, British Gas, Guinness, ICL, Marks & Spencer, National Westminster Bank and Rolls Royce. The group had no formal secretariat, was kept deliberately small and informal, and operates primarily through inter-personal exchanges between a group of friends based in Brussels. Such features meant that group members could exchange 'gossip' freely about developments in Brussels without problems of accountability, and work very quickly together as issues demanded. It was, however, not a splinter group in any sense, and its presence was made quite open within UK Brussels circles. Collective tasks were divided between members, and information exchanged at monthly meetings held in the premises of a Brussels public affairs consultancy. Because of the nature of the group and its focus upon 'high-politics' areas, it was not a 'lobbying' organization, but operated more at the level of ideas and information (Greenwood and Stancich, 1997).

There are now a plethora of these kinds of structures encompassing a variety of interest domains. Some are caucuses of firms seeking to provide a particular direction to the activities of a particular interest group. They can provide important 'think tank' capacities, ideas leadership, as well as providing a 'short and unclogged' (Pijnenburg, 1996: 27) information channel and socialization network for members. Their exclusive and informal nature, together with their roles as networking structures, mean that decision making and collective action problems either do not arise or are relatively small in comparison to those of some formal groups. They provide flexible structures for firms to respond to the unpredictability of the European business environment, whether they act as issue networks, information and socialization networks, idea forums, or quick response mechanisms. They can enhance identity and interest cohesion, and carry few risks of a loss of autonomy that might arise from compromising positions through Euro groups (Cram, 1995; Pijnenburg, 1996). As significant actors themselves, large firms have the ability, and sometimes need, to act as a 'small club', or alone, in seeking to influence public affairs. These structures can quite comfortably sit alongside formal group structures.

For some large firms, therefore, the formal Euro group is just one of a variety of means of fulfilling its needs. The ERT, in particular, provided large firms not previously involved in direct membership structures with direct experience and involvement in political action at the European level, and a role model for them in inter-firm collaboration (Cowles, 1995a). Many large firms now have to maintain multiple membership of different groups to satisfy the range of product interests they might possess. This is indicative of the relative ease of associability at the European level. In the first instance, a collective action 'problem' may have been 'solved' by the time a Euro business group is formed, in that constituent members are those which are already politically active. A collective European-level structure may thus be one of a number of avenues of political voice for a large firm, alongside national and other more direct forms of EU representation (Gray and Lowery, 1995). From the Olsonian perspective of fixed preferences (Olson, 1965), working though the list of selective incentives produced by Euro groups indicates that, for most interests, the costs of non-membership of Euro groups is too high. Thus, whilst few Euro groups provide material, economic forms of incentives in the form of discounts or access to services on cut price terms, most produce essential outputs which few serious business players could afford to be without. Formal and informal information needs in a relatively uncertain environment, networking, the need to influence collective strategies, and the Commission preference for collective actors, amongst other factors, make participation essential, even if only from an 'insurance' perspective, particularly when set against costs which may be hidden or negligible.

Some two-thirds of Euro groups are federations of national organizations, where there may be a culture of associability deriving from the organization's needs to service its members, from the role of these groups in forming Euro federations, and from the social and career networks and aspirations of officials, while for the firms of national associations there seem to be few reasons to prevent their national associations from membership (Aspinwall and Greenwood, 1997). In the case of direct firm membership associations, the need to exercise voice in reconstructing a new market may also make European-level associability, as one of the routes of influence, indispensable. From the perspective of socialized preferences, the reasons for EU-level associability seem even clearer. Firstly, the preferences of interests may have been socialized through collaboration in national or international level groups, or through working together in market operations in a variety of regional contexts. For the multinational pharmaceutical industry, for instance, issues tend to be very similar throughout a variety of regulatory contexts (a proven wealth creator, set against concerns of medicine prices, and standards of safety and selling), and experiences developed through participation in national and global associations appear to have been reproduced at the European level. Elsewhere, some direct firm membership associations are exclusive 'rich firm clubs', and simply contextualize market cooperation, or provide an incentive to associate through their elite nature and without the need to compromise with smaller players. Secondly, the experience of participating in EU structures may produce a 'going native' effect, or assist in developing collaboration with other actors at the EU level (Aspinwall and Greenwood, 1997). Cooperation may thus be iterative (Cram, 1995). The entrepreneurial role of the European Commission, in particular, in funding the start up of Euro groups, in delegating public functions to them, and in providing an institutionalized context for them to participate, may thus ease collective action in a manner foreseen by Haas's neofunctionalist integration theory, where a manipulative role for the Commission in the process of actors shifting their loyalties to the European level was posited.

Whilst no one would today claim that 'spillover' works in a unidirectional way towards further integration – indeed, such a claim was never made in the original neofunctionalist accounts of European integration – the role of business interests such as EFPIA in the integration process has reawakened interest in mechanisms of political spillover. As Underhill (Chapter 2) argues, mainstream international relations accounts continue to see states as the main actors in integration, and fail to conceptualize the important role performed by private interests. In 'high-politics' arenas, business interests are just one amongst a multitude of players, although they do contribute towards a climate of ideas. But in 'low-politics' arenas, business interests can and do operate as players with monopolistic access to exclusive policy communities which progress the course of European integration.

Even in high-politics fields, big business interests, such as the ERT, have made a distinctive contribution, both at the European level itself, and in socializing the preference of state actors for transnational solutions, and amongst the participants of groups. Indeed, some of the actors in the integration process, such as is the case with UNICE and the Social Dialogue, find themselves enmeshed in a process with its own momentum, and their positions and those of their members have tangibly shifted as a result. In turn, their own actions contribute to the course of European integration, and their own organizational prosperity comes to depend upon further integration. In 'low-politics' fields, the dependence of the Commission upon the resources business interests bring to European governance, the absence of member-state involvement until later stages of the European policy process when agendas have been set, or in conditions of uncertainty where member-state input is not clear-cut, and the role of business interests in socializing member-state preferences, partnerships between business interests and the European Commission are often responsible for developing the course of European integration.

6
Asia-Pacific Business Activity and Regional Institution-Building

Nicole Gallant and Richard Stubbs[1]

Compared to Europe and North America, economic integration in the Asia-Pacific region, which is proceeding apace, is developing in its own very distinctive way. Indeed, this chapter will argue that, unlike in Europe and North America where governments have played a key role in forging regional frameworks which have served to shape regional business activity, in the Asia-Pacific region it has been the activities of the business community which have to a great extent forced governments to consider ways of regularizing regional relations. Certainly, the actions of the business community have driven Asia-Pacific regional economic integration. As Vinod Aggarwal (1994: 54) has noted, 'at this point, the interactions we see in the region, be they investment choices, trade patterns or capital flows, are not being significantly affected by a regionally-based regime'.

There is, of course, an irony in this development. Within the countries of the region the state played a major role in managing the rapid economic development that preceded the 1997 crisis. Strong states, bolstered by the need to centralize authority in the face of the Cold War threat posed by Asian communism, developed ties to the business community which allowed them to direct capital; favour particular sectors, industries and even companies; and encourage export-led growth.[2] This 'embedded autonomy', as Peter Evans (1992: 163–6) labels it, was enhanced by the fact that the states and the economies of these countries were given a major boost by the significant levels of aid injected into the region by the USA during the Cold War and especially in fighting the Korean War and the Vietnam War (Stubbs, 1994: 366–71). The general prosperity in the region, outside the theaters of

99

war, created an environment in which governments could facilitate economic growth and businesses thrived. Yet, while the governments led the way in expanding the domestic economies, businesses have led the way in developing the regional economy. The non-governmental and inter-governmental institutions that have been formed to help integrate the regional economy have, so far, lagged far behind what has been happening in the rapidly evolving private sector.

Regional economic growth

Economic links across the region have been developed by both Japanese firms and overseas Chinese family businesses. In the post-Second World War period it was initially the Japanese who had the biggest impact. In the 1950s the American government officials encouraged Japanese businesses to develop contacts in other parts of the Asia-Pacific region. Helped by US economic grants and technical assistance to various countries which were tied to purchases of Japanese goods and services as well as by Japanese reparations, Japanese companies gradually expanded their regional trading relations. In the late 1960s South Korea and Taiwan, both of which had been colonized by Japan during the first half of the century, became increasingly tied to the Japanese economy. For example, declining Japanese heavy industries were transferred to both Korea and Taiwan along with the needed financing and technology. During the 1970s, with the full removal of restrictions on the export of capital, there were increasing flows of Japanese foreign direct investment (FDI) into all parts of the region. This in turn led to increased trade among the Asia-Pacific countries.

The major catalyst to increased intra-regional economic activity came in the mid-1980s. In September 1985 the G-5 finance ministers (France, Germany, Japan, the United Kingdom and the United States) agreed to work towards raising the value of the yen and the lowering of the value of the dollar in an attempt to reverse Japan's growing trade surplus with the USA. The Plaza Accord, as the agreement was known, led to a doubling of the value of the yen. This, combined with the structural changes that were taking place in the Japanese economy, forced an increasing number of Japanese export-manufacturing companies to relocate outside Japan. At first these companies looked to South Korea and Taiwan; however, as their currencies also began to appreciate in value so the countries of the ASEAN (Association of Southeast Asian Nations) region (Brunei, Indonesia, Malaysia, the Philippines,

Singapore and Thailand) became alternative destinations. As a consequence, Japanese FDI in the ASEAN region rose from $855 million in 1986 to $4.7 billion in 1989. By 1994 the accumulated total of Japanese FDI in the ASEAN countries was $48.8 billion (*ASEAN–Japan Statistical Pocketbook*, 1991 and 1996 issues).

The attempt by Japanese companies to seek out low-cost production platforms in East and Southeast Asia forced their competitors, many of whom are overseas Chinese businesses, to do likewise. As a result in 1994 Taiwanese businesses constituted the largest group of foreign investors in Malaysia; Hong Kong businesses were the largest investors in China and Indonesia; and Singaporeans were the largest group to invest in Vietnam (*Far Eastern Economic Review*, 12 October 1995: 54–60). This increase in FDI produced a rapid increase in trade within the region. For example, ASEAN trade with Japan jumped from $28 billion in 1986 to $126 billion in 1995 (*ASEAN–Japan Statistical Pocketbook*, 1996: 27). And, importantly, in 1993 both the ASEAN states as a group and China exported more to the Asia's Newly Industrializing Countries (Hong Kong, South Korea, Singapore and Taiwan) than to Japan or the United States.

The rapid integration of the Asia-Pacific economy was reinforced by the emergence of country-specific as well as region-wide production networks (Stubbs, 1995). This development was a particular feature of the most recent wave of Japanese FDI with Japanese companies developing subcontracting links to local and Japanese businesses as well as to Asian NIC, ASEAN, US and European affiliates. Similarly, although networks established by overseas Chinese businesses are usually more tenuous and fluid than those set up by the Japanese, they are nonetheless crucial to their business success. Moreover, increasingly Japanese and overseas Chinese firms are to be found in the same regional networks. For example, some overseas Chinese companies have teamed up with one of Japan's large general trading companies to set up production sites in China (*Far Eastern Economic Review*, 1 February 1996: 47).

Overall, then, economic development and cooperation proceeded at a rapid pace during the last two decades that preceded the 1997 crisis. Yet none of the escalating business activity that produced this increasing regional prosperity was shaped by the regional economic institutions that have emerged. Indeed, in large part those outside the business world, especially government officials have been scrambling to try to catch up to the rapid pace of economic integration that has swept over the region.

Regional institution-building

Efforts to organize regional economic cooperation in the Asia-Pacific have been underway for over 25 years. Academics, officials and business leaders in Japan and Australia have been particularly active in pushing for the institutionalisation of regional economic relations. Over the years these efforts attracted the attention of an ever-widening circle of like-minded individuals from around the Pacific Rim. Their activities eventually culminated in the establishment of the inter-governmental Asia Pacific Economic Cooperation (APEC) forum in 1989.

PAFTAD, PBEC and PECC

The idea of a series of Pacific Trade and Development (PAFTAD) conferences was first proposed by Kiyoshi Kojima, a Japanese economist, in the mid-1960s and was in response to perceived European protectionist sentiment. Membership was initially confined to economists from Japan, Australia, New Zealand, Canada and the United States and has since been extended to include economists from Southeast Asia, Latin America, Russia and Greater China. The first of the annual PAFTAD conferences took place in January 1968 to discuss the viability of a Pacific free trade area involving the industrialized nations. The PAFTAD approach to regional economic issues, then, proved to be primarily policy-oriented, largely academic and geared to the interests of the more developed countries of the region. As a result, the regional response to the PAFTAD initiative, especially from the business community, was lukewarm, at best (Woods, 1993: 43).

The Pacific Basin Economic Council (PBEC) was established in the late 1960s on the initiative of business leaders from Japan and Australia as well as from New Zealand, Canada and the United States. These members were joined in 1984 by South Korea and Chinese Taipei. Mexico and Chile joined in 1989, followed by Hong Kong and Peru in 1990 and Malaysia in 1991. In 1992, Fiji and the Philippines became members. Other regular participants include Indonesia, the Philippines, Singapore, the South Pacific Islands and Thailand. As of 1994, PBEC had an estimated 1000 fee-paying corporations and business executives (Woods, 1991: 315). Until most recently, PBEC was the only organization in the Asia-Pacific region organized specifically to address the needs and interests of the private sector. It was intended to function as a forum where business people from different countries could share their policy concerns both as members of the same region and as members of the business community. However, just as PAFTAD was seen as reflecting the interests of the more developed countries so PBEC was seen as 'a rich man's club' which generally had little relevance to most in the region's business community (Woods, 1993: 88).

Building on the efforts of PAFTAD and PBEC and recognizing the rapid economic changes that were beginning to overtake the region, the Pacific Economic Cooperation Conference (PECC, later Council) held its first conference in Canberra in 1980. PECC conferences were, and still are, held every 18 to 24 months with task forces set up to operate on a continuous basis. The tripartite country delegations which bring together business leaders, government officials acting in their private capacities, and academics have driven the PECC process. By the mid-1990s, PECC had 22 full members making it the largest regional organization in the Asia-Pacific region. The organization sees its role as 'encouraging regional consultation, coordinating information, trying to solve economic problems and reduce friction, promoting Pacific interests in global discussion and promoting public awareness of the increasing interdependence of the Pacific economies'. (AUSPECC, quoted in Higgott, 1994: 87). PECC views business as the principle stakeholder in the organization and the primary generator of change in the Asia-Pacific region. As a consequence, Mark Borthwick (1994: 165), Chairman of the PECC Coordinating Group, notes 'the private sector needs to find better ways to communicate its experience and knowledge to policy makers'. The participation of business in the PECC process is, therefore, perceived as vital in achieving the three main goals of trade liberalization, trade and investment facilitation and development cooperation. However, a number of businessmen have been unhappy with the PECC process and have asked for tangible results. For example, they want to know how PECC can help them consummate business deals (Simandjuntak, 1994: 362). PECC, then, has come in for the same kind of criticism from the business community that has been leveled at PAFTAD and PBEC.

APEC

These attempts at non-governmental institution-building, as well as the rapidly growing interdependence of the Asia-Pacific economies, led to a call by Prime Minister Bob Hawke of Australia for a meeting of Foreign Affairs and Trade Ministers from around the Asia-Pacific region to discuss regional trade and economic issues. Tensions which had been created by a number of global developments, including the emergence of regional trading arrangements in Europe and North America and the possible failure of the Uruguay Round of GATT negotiations, meant that the proposal was received relatively favourably by regional governments. Hence, despite the trepidation of some participants from ASEAN, the first APEC meeting was held in Canberra in November 1989. It was attended by representatives from 12 economies: Australia, Canada, Japan, New Zealand, South Korea, the United States and the six ASEAN countries (Brunei, Indonesia, Malaysia, the Philippines, Singapore and Thailand). From the Canberra meeting emerged a consensus on the principles of economic cooperation in the Asia-Pacific. Notable among them were the objectives of maintaining regional growth and development, the insistence that their efforts be directed towards strengthening the open multilateral trading system and not encouraging the formation of a trading bloc, and that APEC should focus on the advancement of common economic interests rather than political or security issues.[3]

Since 1989 APEC has developed at what many would consider a remarkable pace. Ministers have met annually and membership has expanded. In 1991 China, Taiwan and Hong Kong were admitted using a formula which stated that membership was granted to economies rather than countries. Also admitted in the 1990s were Mexico, Chile, Peru, Russia and Vietnam. In 1993 a small Secretariat (which is comprised of twelve staff) was set up in Singapore to act as a support and coordinating mechanism and to disburse funds for APEC activities. The first APEC leaders summit was hosted by President Clinton in Seattle in November 1993 and leaders and ministers have attended each of the annual meetings since then. Most importantly, in Bogor, Indonesia, in November 1994, the APEC leaders committed their countries to achieving free and open trade and investment by the year 2010 for developing countries and 2020 for the others. At the Osaka summit in Japan in November 1995 the leaders agreed to their 'Action Agenda' which sets out a framework for achieving free and open trade and investment. More detailed proposals, or individual action plans, were considered at meetings at the summit in the Philippines in 1996 and reviewed and updated at the Vancouver Kuala Lumpur summits in 1997 and 1998.

At the same time as these defining initiatives were being taken additional work was being done by ministers and officials in committees, working groups and *ad hoc* groups. In order for APEC to try to create results-oriented, practical programmes that would produce tangible benefits, it was decided at the first meeting in 1989 that working groups needed to be established. A number of broad areas were identified as the basis for the development of projects and plans for action: economic studies, trade liberalisation, investment, technology transfer and human resource development, and sectoral cooperation.[4] At the second Ministerial Meeting in Singapore in 1990, seven working groups were established for the following areas; trade and investment data; trade promotion; expansion of investment and technological transfer; human resource development; energy cooperation; marine resource conservation; and telecommunications. Since then, additional working groups have been formed. They address issues such as fisheries, transportation and tourism. Within the working groups, sub-committees and networks have been set up. For example, the working group on Human Resource Development has established a number of networks in attempts to coordinate information. Key projects have been identified for most of the working groups, and every year the APEC Ministers stress that efforts must be made to further involve the private sector in the working group projects.

From the beginning the ministers were especially intent on involving the private sector in these working groups. In the words of the ministers, 'engagement with the business/private sector, particularly through Working Group Activities, ensures APEC's efforts are relevant to real world challenges and opportunities'.[5] In Seattle in 1993, the APEC Economic Ministers asked regional business leaders to establish a Pacific Business Forum (PBF) to 'identify issues APEC should address to facilitate regional trade and investment and encourage the further development of business networks throughout the region' (Report of the Pacific Business Forum, 1994: i). The PBF was composed entirely of people from the Asia-Pacific business community; they were in effect the private sector counterparts to APEC's political leaders and officials. Each member economy appointed two people from the private sector, one representing the interests of large business and the other representing small to medium enterprises (SMEs), to provide suggestions regarding the actions APEC should take in its attempts to liberalize trade and investment.

The PBF met three times in 1994 and presented their report to the Ministerial Meeting in Bogor, Indonesia in November of that same year. Based on the core principle of open regionalism and with the goal of preserving and promoting the region's dynamic rate of economic growth and improving everyone's standard of living, the members of the PBF agreed that four factors need to be considered in order to make APEC more relevant to the private sector. First, there needs to be further trade and investment liberalization and deregulation. Second, there is a need to develop business and human resources support mechanisms such as infrastructure, technology transfer, information exchange, structural adjustment programmes, education and training programmes and support for small and medium enterprises. Third, there is a need to facilitate existing and future business. Finally, the private sector recognizes the need for a partnership between government and business (Report of the Pacific Business Forum, 1994: i).

The PBF report also clearly states that in order for APEC to become more relevant to the private sector, it must be active in

> making substantive and practical progress towards a predictable trade and investment environment in the Asia-Pacific region ... business will not, and cannot, wait for governments. Business will go where bureaucracy is minimal and procedures straightforward and transparent. (Report of the Pacific Business Forum, 1994: ii)

APEC, the PBF argued, must achieve applicable and practical results if it is to become more than just another forum for dialogue. The 1995 PBF Report provides APEC leaders with 15 specific measures to generate concrete and pragmatic results, thus providing the business community with tangible evidence of APEC's ability to deliver. Making APEC more relevant to business requires APEC working groups to encourage the participation of the private sector in the formation of relevant policies. In part as a response to this pressure the APEC leaders at the Osaka meeting in November 1995 agreed to combine the PBF and the *ad hoc* Eminent Persons Group (EPG), which had produced the 'Vision' for the Asia Pacific region, to form the permanent APEC Business Advisory Council (ABAC). This, it was hoped, would provide an even better channel for private sector input into the APEC process. Overall, it is obvious that business wants results.

Yet, so far, APEC has had little or no impact on business activity in the Asia-Pacific region. As one commentator has noted, 'businesses, of course, are impatient with the posturing of leaders and want APEC's promises to start appearing on the bottom line. (Hulme, 1996: 34). A Hong Kong businessman has noted in the *Far Eastern Economic Review* that he took an informal poll among his friends around the region and 'could not find anyone who could come up with a single APEC initiative that has made goods cheaper for Asian consumers, opened markets or spurred investment and development' (Simon, 1995: 35). And *The Economist* in an article, entitled 'No Action, No Agenda', which assessed the work of the leaders at the November 1995 Osaka summit noted that the meeting 'avoided real action, and "agenda" is a flatter-ing word to describe the vague programme that the delegates agreed upon'.[6]

The key question, then, is 'whether or not APEC can translate suc-cessfully its many activities into a work program that has significant meaning for the real economies and daily lives of people in the region' (Morrison, 1994: 81). APEC must start to produce concrete results. There are some indications that APEC is attempting to accomplish just that. At the Bogor summit in November 1994, the ministers adopted the investment principles proposed by the Pacific Business Forum. While these principles are non-binding, as a Singaporean delegate stated at the summit, 'it's the most concrete signal to the business community that APEC members want to encourage investment in the region' (*The Straits Times*, 13 November 1994: 1). However, in the Eminent Persons Group's Report for 1995, an assessment of APEC's progress on the investment issue concluded that the non-binding Investment Principles represent a useful first step, but they need to be strengthened and they need to be incorporated into national policies. A review of the deliberations of the various committees and *ad hoc* and working groups shows that concrete actions which could help busi-nesses in such areas as investment, customs procedures, dispute media-tion and business visas are being developed and some could be in place in the very near future. Certainly, APEC could play a facilitating role in a number of areas. But the APEC skeptics will continue to be in the majority until some of this potential is actually realized in more than the most minimal of ways. Clearly, at present APEC has no impact whatsoever on business activity in the region.

Sub-regional institutions

While APEC has come to dominate economic discussion in the wider Asia-Pacific region other, subregional institutions have emerged in the last few years. The one which has the potential to challenge APEC is the East Asian Economic Caucus (EAEC). The idea of an East Asian Economic Grouping was first put forward in December 1990 by the Malaysian Prime Minister, Datuk Seri Dr Mahathir Mohamad.[7] Later, in response to concerns that it sounded too much like a proposal for a trading bloc, Mahathir began to talk of it as a Caucus which would consult on regional economic issues. Mahathir's proposed membership of the EAEC would bring together the ASEAN states, Taiwan, Hong Kong, South Korea, Japan, China and eventually the countries of Indochina. Like

APEC, the EAEC emerged from fears over the collapse of GATT, and the rise of NAFTA and the EU. In addition, proponents of the EAEC also state that they fear the United States will use APEC to dominate the entire region. Importantly, the EAEC would be an Asian-only group which would seek to advance the interests of the East Asian economies. Indeed, for this reason the United States opposed the formation of such a grouping. Moreover Japan, which was seen by the Malaysians as the obvious leader of the group, has been reluctant to make any commitment which might possibly upset the United States. Other regional governments were also somewhat ambivalent. However, the Malaysian government continued to push the idea, and with considerable diplomatic skill the Singaporeans were able, in 1993, to arrange for the EAEC to be formally established as a caucus within APEC.

The EAEC represents an alternative vision of the Asia-Pacific region to the one which is embodied in APEC (Higgott and Stubbs, 1995). The narrower region defined by the EAEC tends to underscore the fact that its members have much more in common in terms of historical experience, political systems and culture than do the more geographically dispersed members of APEC. Moreover, the EAEC tends to be increasingly integrated through the formation of production networks. However, like APEC the EAEC has had no influence whatsoever on the region's economic activity. It is still very much at the embryonic stage of its evolution as an institution.

The one organization in the Asia-Pacific region which has become entrenched in the life of the region is ASEAN. It was established in 1967 with its primary purpose being to 'accelerate the economic growth, social progress and cultural development of the region through joint endeavors in the spirit of equality and partnership in order to strengthen the foundation for a prosperous and peaceful community of Southeast Asian nations' (Colbert, 1986: 196). However, while economic cooperation was ostensibly a feature of the Association, during the 1970s and 1980s it was the political dimension of regional cooperation which was most important. The Vietnam War and the threat of the spread of communism were the major factors which helped to unite the members and led to the creation of an effective regional institution. Progress on the economic front was largely symbolic. For example, the Declaration of ASEAN Concord signed at the Bali summit of 1976 identified a number of areas of economic cooperation[8] and the 1977 ASEAN Preferential Trading Arrangement (PTA) cleared the way for the gradual decrease in trade barriers and tariffs. Yet, progress was very slow. Attempts at economic cooperation through schemes such as the ASEAN Industrial Projects and the ASEAN Industrial Joint Venture Agreement proved to be of very little value. Moreover, despite the fact that by the end of the 1980s nearly 16 000 products were listed under the PTA, they constituted less than 1 per cent of total intra-ASEAN trade (Ravenhill, 1995: 853).

However, with the end of the Cold War and the reversal of the role of Vietnam from sworn enemy to possible ally, ASEAN needed to find a project which would once again give its members a sense that the Association was moving forward. As a consequence at the fourth summit in Singapore in January 1992 the ASEAN leaders signed a framework agreement known as the ASEAN Free Trade Agreement (AFTA) which was intended to further regional economic cooperation. The goal of AFTA, through the Common Effective Preferential Tariff (CEPT) scheme, is to reduce intra-regional tariff barriers on all manu- factured goods and processed agricultural products to 5 per cent or less over a 15-year period. This framework was initially to be implemented on 1 January 1993, but negotiations took longer than anticipated and the whole process appeared to be in danger of disintegrating. In late 1993 the scheme was relaunched with a streamlined CEPT and a new starting date of 1 January 1994. Renewed impetus was imparted to the process in 1994 when the period over which the target reductions in tariffs were to be reached was changed to 10 years and again in 1998 when the target date for full implementation of AFTA became 2002.

Before the advent of AFTA, ASEAN's attempts directly to bolster regional economic development and cooperation had been limited at best. As Ravenhill (1995) has noted, 'While ASEAN's success in defus- ing regional conflicts provided the political prerequisites for the rapid growth of the economies of the region, the direct contribution to this growth made by regional economic arrangements was negligible.' ASEAN's lack of success in the past in orchestrating economic coopera- tion and development suggests that the CEPT–AFTA scheme may still run into political roadblocks. The most common criticism voiced by the private sector is that the ministerial decisions made to speed up the process of economic cooperation are grounded in political compromise and not in economic reality. On top of this Hadi Soesastro, the Executive Director of Indonesia's Centre for Strategic and International Studies, has chided the bureaucrats noting that they are responsible for some of the problems that have plagued AFTA. 'They haven't done their homework. It was not sufficient for them to have made the decision to launch AFTA. They should have made a lot of technical preparations before that' (*The Straits Times*, 6 October 1993: 36).

Yet AFTA clearly has the potential to have an impact on business activity in Southeast Asia.[9] This will certainly be the case if AFTA manages to build on the 'growth triangles' that are being set up around Southeast Asia. The model is the growth triangle that links Singapore to the Malaysian state of Johore and the Indonesian province of Riau. The three governments have agreed to facilitate investment and trade within the triangle and Singapore businesses in particular have responded by locating in the relatively low-cost Johore and Riau. Indeed, there is significant private sector support for growth triangles and for the wider AFTA in all member countries. The ASEAN Chambers of Commerce and Industry (ACCI) has promoted economic liberalization and developed a good working relationship with a number of ASEAN's committees. However, rather like APEC, ASEAN still has to prove itself to the regional business community.

Overall, then, the institutionalization of Asia-Pacific economic cooperation has generally lagged far behind the regional economic integration that has been promoted by the activities of regional businesses. It is, of course, possible that the economic crisis of 1997–8 which shook the region will force governments to implement some form of comprehensive regional economic 'regime' based on ASEAN or APEC and that it will serve to shape the way in which companies do business. The tariff-reduction goals that the two organizations have established would suggest this might occur. However, past practices, entrenched and institutionalized as they are in the state–business policy networks of the various countries, were up to 1997 very successful and it may be politically difficult to abandon them altogether and move towards the essentially voluntary, liberalization goals that leaders have set for the region. Certainly, a NAFTA or EU form of economic arrangement for the Asia-Pacific region is highly unlikely. In all probability business will continue to lead government in terms of regional economic cooperation.

Notes

1. Nicole Gallant would like to thank the Canada–ASEAN Centre for a travel grant which allowed her to undertake research on APEC in Singapore, and Richard Stubbs would like to thank the Social Science and Humanities Research Council of Canada for a grant which allowed him to undertake research in Asia. Thanks go to Larry Woods for his helpful comments on aspects of this paper.
2. See for example, Chalmers Johnson (1982) *MITI and the Japanese Miracle: The Growth of Industrial Policy, 1945–1975,* Stanford: Stanford University Press; Alice Amsden (1989) *Asia's Next Giant: South Korea and Late Industrialization,*

New York: Oxford University Press; Robert Wade (1990) *Governing the Market: Economic Theory and the Role of Government in East Asian Industrialization,* Princeton: Princeton University Press.

3. Asia-Pacific Economic Cooperation Ministerial Meeting Canberra, 6–7 November 1989. Joint Statement. Article 16. in *Selected APEC Documents: 1989–1994.* Singapore: APEC Secretariat. February 1995: 40.

4. Joint Statement, APEC Ministerial Meeting. Canberra. 6–7 November 1989.

5. Ministerial Meeting, Joint Statement, Seattle 17–19 November 1993, section 39. See also the Ministerial Meeting, Joint Statement, Singapore, 1990.

6. 'No Action, No Agenda', *The Economist,* 25 November 1995. See also the response to this assessment in Fred Bergsten, 'The Case for APEC: An Asian Push for World-Wide Free Trade', *The Economist,* 6 January 1996.

7. 30. On the origins on the EAEC see Linda Low (1991) 'The East Asian Economic Grouping', *Pacific Review,* vol. 4: 4.

8. 'Declaration of ASEAN Concord. A Common Bond Existing Among the Member States of the Association of Southeast Asian Nations, Denpasar, Bali, 24 February 1976'; Hans Christoph Rieger (1991) *ASEAN Economic Cooperation Handbook,* Singapore: ISEAS, pp. 105–8.

9. 37. For a positive view of AFTA see Lee Tsao Yuan (1994) 'The ASEAN Free Trade Area: The Search for a Common Prosperity', *Asian-Pacific Economic Literature,* vol. 8 (May 1994), pp. 1–7.

7

A Differential Organized Business Response to the New Regional Trading Regime in the Southern Cone: The Experience of Argentina and Brazil's Car Industries

Martha Diaz de Landa and María Carola Sajem

On 26 March 1991, Argentina, Brazil, Uruguay and Paraguay signed the Treaty of Asunciòn establishing MERCOSUR. This integration project is quite different from previous regional arrangements,[1] particularly concerning its tight schedule to achieve a common market, its ambitious goals, the firm willingness of governments to implement an irreversible structure, and the private sector participation in the design of the project.[2]

While it is true that the political decision of member states constituted the primary stimulation for the integration process, it is also true that without the support of the private sector this new agreement could never have materialized. One of the most important transformations has been the granting of autonomy to enterprises to make international agreements without government intervention. Cooperation between firms of different countries is an increasingly frequently-used strategy to adapt to the new regional context.

The result of this growing cooperation has been a large increase in trade among MERCOSUR members, almost doubling in some two-year periods (Hurrell, 1995: 259). While a great deal of trade is firm-led, the whole process is reinforced by the formation of new business interest associations with a MERCOSUR perspective. These BIAs in turn push for further regional integration setting up a dynamic to push further the new regionalism in the Southern Cone.

This chapter attempts to illustrate this trend by outlining the response of Argentina and Brazil's car sector business organizations to the challenges and opportunities arising from the implementation of MERCOSUR. This sector has shown a great dynamism in the integration process and, as a result, has reached high levels of trade and intra-industry integration compared with other sectors. The first part of this chapter explores essential features of industry structures and industrial policy approaches of both countries in order to analyze the political and economic factors that led to the improved business environment. The chapter then turns to the responses of organized business to such a framework, taking into account both sector characteristics and the firm size. The conclusions are intended to highlight the main trends observed in Argentinean and Brazilian organized business behaviour relating to the impact of market and political changes.

The political and economic context of organized business behaviour

In the process of integration, specific sectors often demonstrate a far greater intensity of exchanges and deepness of integration than other sectors in Latin America as elsewhere (Vera and Bizzozero, 1993: 77; Schmitter and Lanzalaco, 1989: 207–9). In both Brazil and Argentina, manufacturing has generated the biggest rise in expectations, and consequently the most political demands. It is not surprising, then that manufacturing constitutes the most active field of real investment, technological innovation, productivity and new employment. Thus, the coordination of industrial policies in MERCOSUR is the core concern of government, associations and firms.

Industry in MERCOSUR's main partners shows a remarkable asymmetry.[3] This concerns not only particular features of production structures of both countries, but also the approach of government officials toward industrial restructuring. In this context, the Treaty of Asuncion lead to the shaping of a Sector Complementation Agreement (SCA) to encourage a rational specialization within industrial sectors on the basis of each country's comparative advantages and cooperation to compete in third markets more efficiently. However, private enterprises have not used the SCA to reform the industrial system, rather, it has been used to ward off the impact of market integration. Therefore, a brief review of the main aspects of industrial policies of both sides of the frontier is useful.

Argentina and Brazil's industrial restructuring: two different approaches

In the early 1990s, Brazil's industrial policy dramatically changed from a planning system integrated by sectors and administered by government through sectoral chambers, and providing support for sectors in structural crisis such as automobiles. This was an attempt to create conditions conducive to moving enterprises from a purely defensive policy, appropriate for the first stages of an industrial restructuring process, to an offensive policy, focused on productive capability, growth and technological innovation. That aim was realized in the development of horizontal programs for the generation of improvements in such fields as technological innovation, management and staff training (Todesca, 1996: 40–3). To reach the above-mentioned objective, specific instruments such as the Industrial Technology Development Program (PDTI), created in 1988 and consolidated in 1993, and the Quality and Productivity Program (PBQP) of 1990, were created. The latter includes sectoral subprograms aimed at overcoming obstacles to the development and modernization of several industrial complexes. Brazil's intention was to use the sectoral chambers as agents in the application of the PBQP. Their function was saved and enhanced through a new policy coordination instrument called the Sectoral Policy Executive Group. As a result these sectoral chambers have acquired an important role as administrators of the sectoral programs that are orientated to quality and productivity improvement.

Brazil's new industrial policy has fostered exports to the world market by managing the rate of exchange and granting businesses some financial incentives. Further assistance comes in the form of the Brazilian Regional Promotion Policy, which exempts certain provinces from the payment of specific taxes, especially the Tax on Goods and Services (ICMS). Such industrial promotion programs at a regional and provincial level, combining credit support with tax exemptions, are consistently used in Brazil. Moreover, one of the most remarkable traits of the Brazilian taxation system is the independence given to provincial states to handle their own taxes, with the purpose of encouraging the development of regional industry promotion programs.

At the same time that Brazil was changing its industrial policy, parallel events were taking place in Argentina. To a large extent, the developments in both countries were due to rapprochement between the two and a desire to consolidate civilian rule (Hurrell, 1995: 254–63). The Argentinian government implemented an extraordinary commercial opening in 1991 as part of a much larger program called the 'Plan de Convertibilidad Economica'. The consolidation of a dynamic export sector is one of the pillars of the Argentinean Economic Plan. Nevertheless, the restrictions resulting from macroeconomic stability limited, from the start, the possibilities for elevating the real rate of exchange. As such, different instruments of trading policy (such as tariff increases, statistics tax and exports duties restitution) together with tax reductions and deregulation of certain markets were applied. Despite this, it is not possible to speak here of a global design of industrial policy. The country has neither examined nor defined the productive fields in which it possesses or could develop competitive advantages so as to reassign resources and specialize. Instead, Argentina has adopted a strategy of Selective Sectors Regimes in order to support industrial productivity.[4] This strategy comprises the Capital Goods Policy,[5] the Special Car System,[6] some protective measures for certain industries, such as paper and textiles, and the gradation of tariffs and duties restitution in accordance with the elaboration degree.

As for industrial help for SMEs such as research and development incentives and staff training, government initiatives are rare. Indeed, SMEs constitute the weaker link of the country's industrial fabric, often acting as suppliers to big companies, and lacking current or future defined development plans. The government has restructured the energy system in order to reduce industrial production costs, redefining the SMEs as big consumers of energy. This allows them to benefit from the payment of a special lower tariff, hitherto awarded only to big enterprises. Such redefinition was the result of strong lobbying from a coalition of the BIAs representing the SMEs. The rights of the latter are used by large firms to justify their own demands; in other words, the fostering of SMEs is a mobilizing argument used by large companies to encourage decision-makers' approval of mutually beneficial policies. In general, the greatest profits are taken by the large firms but, at the same time, the quiet voice of SMEs gets louder in their interaction with the state for the purpose of getting help to engage in the exposed market.

A scarcity of both energy and equity prevents SMEs from affording the necessary investments in product completion and packaging modifications. Despite this, the joint actions of the SEBRAE-Sao Paulo and Northeast of Brazil Bureau in Buenos Aires and Fundacion Export-ar are working to ameliorate the situation. SEBRAE-Sao Paulo and Northeast of Brazil Bureau in Buenos Aires, between January and November 1995, mobilized 225 Argentinean SME which, in turn, contacted about 2200 Brazilian counterparts at business meetings and fairs. This was intended to help SMEs to adjust their business expansion projects. In that way, business of about US$1337 million was generated. Fundacion Exportar, a recently-created agency, depends on the Argentina Foreign Affairs Council. During the last two years it has initiated a broad range of activities to help medium-sized firms to thrive in the transformed market. However, the results of such action is not sufficient to satisfy the demands of business. It is important to note that initially SMEs attended trade fairs and meetings purely with the aim of selling their products or services. Now, they are actively seeking to participate in joint ventures; their purpose is to transform comparative advantages into competitive ones. This is a qualitative leap for small and medium entrepreneurs compared to their previous MERCOSUR approach.

Economic and political influence on Argentinian and Brazilian organized business behaviour: the case of automobiles

It is frequently possible to observe significant contradictions between the speech and behaviour of officials among MERCOSUR's main partners. On one side, governments are always showing a great interest in the integration process success but, on the other, they often take decisions that do not fit at all with such declared integration objectives. These political contradictions form the basis of the arguments proffered by Argentina and Brazil. Evidently, the structural asymmetries of both countries play an important role in the difficulties faced in their industry harmonization policies, but other significant elements have to be considered in order to understand the behaviour of organized business.

One of the most vigorous and active sectors in the integration process is, at the same time, one of the most troublesome for MERCOSUR's completion. The car industry is well-organized in both Argentina and Brazil, with a great deal of influence over their respective government's decisions. Argentina's lack of macro-industrial policy design has led to the car industry taking sectoral measures with the aim of fostering technology-intensive industry development. Although this is positive for the country's economic development, these measures threaten the decision-making autonomy of public officials. Firms that work in technology-led sectors wield an economic power due to the politically desired characteristics of those industries. In Brazil, powerful industries use their influence on governmental decisions to seek protection from sectoral balance of trade deficits. To this end, they appeal for the application of sectorally-protective measures by the government even if such measures contradict integration aims.

As an example from mid-1995 shows, the Brazilian government introduced the Medida Provisoria-MP 2410 (provisional measure) whose main point was to place import restrictions on cars, including from MERCOSUR's members.[7] On one hand, the country's balance of trade deficit is an important factor in understanding Brazil's behaviour. But on the other hand, efforts to encourage multinational corporations in the car industry to invest in the region, and the desire for having them set up in Brazil instead of in Argentina played an important part too. The General Motors of Brazil corporate affairs vice-president, who is also vice-president of the powerful Automobiles Producers Brazilian Association (ANFAVEA), acknowledged that Brazil's Automobile sector BIAs had significant influence upon President Cardoso's decision to establish special rules for the sector.

Furthermore, and as has already been stated, regional and provincial industry promotion policies through fiscal subsidies and tax exemptions are very common in Brazil. This fact, combined with the jealously defended autonomy of Brazilian provincial states over taxation policies which is particularly prone to subsidizing production and exports, has a major influence on the location of production and investment by large firms.[8]

One of the most recent commercial disputes between Argentina and Brazil is rooted less in economics than in politics. By the middle of December 1996, the President of Brazil had signed a decree creating a special system of rules encouraging companies to invest in the north, northeast and center-west of the country.[9] One of the main problems faced by the Brazilian government in its pursuit of economic reform is the explosive atmosphere in the northeast, one of the most densely populated and poorest regions of the country, which urgently requires assistance to achieve its economic development. The atmosphere of civil unrest in the northeast, combined with President Cardoso's desire to win a consecutive re-election when his term of office ends in 1999, despite a constitutional prohibition, undoubtedly played a major role in the president's decision to encourage investment in the region.

Furthermore, it is in the northeast that Cardoso has his allied governors and deputies who support his political ambitions and who were expected to give their favourable vote to eliminate from the Constitution the rule that prohibits Cardoso's re-election.[10]

Fiscal incentives, combined with cheaper labour than that available in Argentina has resulted in a high level of establishment of new businesses in the region. Asia Motors Corporation announced 500 million US$ investment for its plant in Bahia (northeast of Brazil) a week after the signing of the December 1996 decree. The decree is also intended to influence negotiations with Hyundai, Asia Motors (South Korean) and Skoda (Czech–German). The shift of major firms to the region has been at the expense of the remaining three MERCOSUR partners, particularly Argentina.

On the Argentinean side, the largest business associations seek to guide the government decision-makers in order to overcome the lack of definition in the design of a productive structure. One such organization is the Argentinean Group. It comprises 10 peak-level Argentine enterprises (whose combined turnover is US$11 500 million per year) which have recently invested in Brazil. A good example of the influence exerted by these powerful industrialists over the Argentinean Government is this latter group's attitude toward Cardoso's decree on investment in northeast Brazil. Although Argentina's President Menem is sympathetic to Cardoso's political needs, the real explanation of the cautious Argentinean official's posture towards a measure that clearly infringes MERCOSUR commitments is the pressure from powerful car industry organizations as well as the other industrial sectors. The car industry organizations particularly sought a prompt and favourable solution to the unfixed car quota system for terminals without subsidiaries on the other side of the frontier,[11] such as Sevel, Ciadea – though Renault has started to build a plant in the Brazilian state of Parana – and Toyota.[12] Cardoso's decree could be, in such circumstances, a useful card for the Argentinean government to bargain with and then reach a good deal. Meanwhile, Argentina's government officials speculated on the (unlikely) possibility of Cardoso reversing his decree due to heavy lobbying from the southern governments and car sector businesses that, in the new context, see themselves deprived of their advantages.

But Argentina's car industry is much more than a restrained sector of organized business. The Motor Car Factories Association of Argentina (ADEFA), representative of this sector, has attempted to defend its members against the possible damage arising from Cardoso's decree, but so far has lobbied without success. ADEFA's president accuses Brazil of attracting investment by permitting favoured business organizations to incur lower costs over the long term. ADEFA therefore requested that goods produced in the plants covered under the new system of rules be considered 'outside zone', as if its goods were produced outside of MERCOSUR, and therefore excluded from tariff advantages that the recently implemented regional trading regime entails. Another proposed solution was that Brazil's government compensate Argentina's car industry for damages. However, such compensations lead Brazil, which has already contravened the WTO guidelines, to a confrontation with the WTO. Nevertheless, Presidents Menem and Cardoso decided to negotiate compensations. The activities of business interest associations alone cannot explain the way business firms are adapting to MERCOSUR commitments and rules, but they may shed light on some current and future general integration patterns.

Argentina's and Brazil's car industry BIA response to MERCOSUR

Economic liberalization and regional integration processes raise challenges and obstacles for business firms which must be overcome in order for them to profit from the opportunities brought about by the new situation. The effects of those challenges and obstacles depend on the features of individual businesses. This analysis will consider their sector characteristics, firm size including very large transnational corporations, big domestic companies and medium and small firms. These factors help account for differences between Brazilian and Argentinian BIA responses to regional integration.

First of all, it is useful to introduce a brief comparative review of the organized business behaviour evolution in Argentina and Brazil from the Iguazu Declaration of 1985 to the present. During the last half of the eighties, the establishment of subsidiaries of Argentinean companies in Brazil, often in partnership with local firms, was common. The factors encouraging these investment flows are, among others, the international experience acquired by many export companies in the early eighties, the size of the Brazilian market, and the favourable reception in Brazil given by consumers to Argentinean products. In addition, Brazil's tariff restrictions on imports hindered the Argentinean companies' exports to their neighbour's market, and thus, encouraged them to directly invest on Brazil's territory.

Between 1990 and the end of 1994, the trend began to reverse and Argentina's investments in Brazil diminished while Brazilian capital started to enter Argentina. The investment pace in that sense sped up in 1993 and 1994. Joint ventures, mergers and the absorption of Argentinean firms by Brazilian counterparts was the most widespread manner of investment.

Since the second half of 1995, a new trend in business integration began. In 1991 only 5 per cent of Argentine investments were influenced by MERCOSUR, in 1994 this figure had changed to 21 per cent, and in 1995 45 per cent (*El Economista*, 24 November 1995: 14). Out of 258[13] joint ventures completed by Argentinian and Brazilian companies up to the first half of 1995, 45 per cent have had some kind of productive impact by means of either setting up new plants or purchasing enterprises. About 40 projects had a solely commercial impact and were carried out mainly through trade agreements. The remaining undertakings (106) belong to the service sector as either operational or cooperation agreements or the opening of subsidiaries. These latter activities are supported by the Treaty for the Establishment of Argentine Brazilian Bi-national Enterprises, an important instrument in ensuring that the coming Common Market is not merely a Customs Union. The agreement allows for the new enterprises to receive the same treatment as the guest country's enterprises.

As for the type of business firms, it is argued that MERCOSUR was created as a large firm project. We have seen the same argument made by Cowles (1995) for the European Union, Doern and Tomlin (1991) for the Canadian–American Free Trade Agreement and Jacek (1994) for NAFTA. The participation of SME BIAs in MERCOSUR was rendered problematic due to domestic recession, difficulties in participating in the enlarged regional market, and lack of adaptation to the globalized economy. As such, their reaction towards the new trading regime was slow to develop and uncertain in its direction, once again a characteristic of medium and small BIAs elsewhere.

For transnational firms, the new integration attempt has turned out to be a magnet to many of them who see the free market as a good chance for making a higher profit with lower costs. Indeed, MERCOSUR affords an opportunity for a division of labour which allows the firms to recoup their sunk costs (Bielschovsky and Stumpo, 1995: 10). The current integration scheme in the Southern Cone implies the completion in the future of a great common market which the transnational could easily supply. In fact, they generally possess subsidiaries in both main country markets, where they are already in leading market positions. The majority of those enterprises are taking measures to rationalize and complement their activities in both countries. The companies with subsidiaries in only one of the markets are seeking cooperation agreements on production and trade with other companies in the same situation (Kosacoff and Bezchinsky, 1994: 148).

Briefly, the general trend in the behaviour patterns of the transnationals could be summarized as follows. Early on, they responded to MERCOSUR by means of reacting and adapting to the established facilities in order to 'wait and see'. So, they were not indifferent to the changes taking place in that region but in general they displayed caution. In the second stage, when the process seemed to be developing on a solid and irreversible basis, they decided to move more confidently into MERCOSUR territory. Most of these corporations, already known in this region as importers, invested in local companies that had a strong presence in domestic markets, so as to take over control, or to at least obtain a strong minority interest. From this position they are now becoming local producers in the new free market.

Car sector organized business activities within the framework of MERCOSUR

The automobile sector is an illustrative case of intra-industry regional integration dynamism. Here the trade flows have a noticeable influence on intra-MERCOSUR exchanges, namely on Argentina and Brazil's balances of trade and on each country's global balance of trade (Nofal, 1996: 18). Argentina, which now mainly produces spare parts (gear boxes and motors), used to produce older models at an extraordinarily high price. However, the sector is still undergoing a process of rapid change and investment[14] as a result of industrial integration within MERCOSUR, a fact that determines this industry's position in the globalization process. According to Fundacion Invertir of Argentina, which has kept a record of initiatives in every industrial sector since 1994, 242 projects have taken place. Investments have reached US$18.089 million, 22 per cent of which corresponds to the car and auto parts industry (Sosa, 15–21 December 1996: 24).

Brazil has comparative advantages in commercial vehicles, and possesses one of the world's largest bus markets. Since 1994, the country also ranks eighth as a world car producer, having overtaken Italy. In MERCOSUR, this sector comprises the major part of foreign investment and regional exchanges (see Tables 7.1 and 7.2), as well as the biggest number of business initiatives.[15]

Projects establishing new factories count on manufacturing about three million vehicles per year; Brazil attracts most of this capital inflow. As for business initiatives, the car sector absorbs more than a quarter of the total cases with 60 per cent of these initiatives having a productive impact. Productive Complementation Agreements between

Table 7.1   Assembly plants in Argentina: investments in the 1990s (US$millions)

Ciadea	500
Chrysler	165
Fiat	642
Ford	1000
General Motors	1100
Iveco	125
Mercedes Benz	100
Scania	60
Sevel (Peugeot)	500
Toyota	150
Volkwagen	280
Total	4600

Source: Gazeta Mercantil Latinoamericana, 15–21 December 1996, pp. 21–I.

Table 7.2   Argentina and Brazil car sector bilateral trade evolution (in units of vehicles)

Year	Exports (from Argentina to Brazil)	Imports (from Brazil to Argentina)	Balance
1990	0	350	−350
1991	3 900	17 000	−13 100
1992	13 200	64 500	−51 300
1993	23 700	39 500	−15 800
1994	35 200	31 000	+4 200
1995	32 600	20 300	+12 300
1996*	36 800	15 600	+21 200

*First Semester.
Source: Gazeta Mercantil Latinoamericana, 15–21 December 1996, p. 9–I.

spare parts and terminal firms of both countries are the prevailing norm. Half of them take place between branches of MNCs operating both in Argentina and in Brazil. In addition to this, Brazil's investment in Argentina has targeted the transportation industry, especially motor cars.[16] One of the growing tendencies in business behaviour is the production of different models in each country with the aim of augmenting the economies of scale for cars and spare parts. Another very widespread tactic is the simultaneous launching of new models at their headquarters and their branches[17] abroad.

Finally, it is important to point out the apparent contradiction between, on one side, the high number of initiatives registered in the sector and, on the other, the conflicts related to the trade's particular organization administered by domestic and common mechanisms within the MERCOSUR regime. The predominance of MNCs with branches in both countries (particularly in the terminals segment) and the strong lobbying aimed at reconverting both countries' car industries, all inside the framework of trade liberalization, are elements that help explain the notable dynamism of the agreements,[18] the growth of BIAs and strategies of cooperation which have taken place since the inception of MERCOSUR.

Concluding thoughts

MERCOSUR, and particularly Argentina–Brazil integration, was seen from the beginning as a tool to reconvert and modernize those industrial sectors that had lost competitiveness, as well as a means to foster new technology intensive sectors. Thus, the challenge is as important for enterprises as it is for governments. Business people, through their BIAs, are playing a central role in the success of this new attempt at integration in Latin America. In fact, the entrepreneurial sector is charged not only with the development of productive resources, and to make the common market become an every-day reality; they also have to coordinate the new processes of competitiveness development and introduce these processes to their countries in the new global trading network.

One of the most significant influences on the behaviour of organized business is the different way Argentina and Brazil approach their respective industrial policies. While the encouragement of productive activities is barely perceptible in Argentina, it is very common in Brazil, not only at national level but also at provincial and subnational stages. This exacerbates the already existing asymmetries between the two main partners of MERCOSUR. Indeed, most of the commercial disputes originate from such asymmetries. As Argentina lacks a clearly defined industrial policy, the problem of asymmetry is never fully resolved. From this point of view the words of the President of the Argentinian Industrial Union (UIA), the peak association which represents the whole country's industry, are perhaps the most accurate explanation of the real causes of those problems. He recently stated that so long as there exists a country (Brazil) aiming to strengthen its production and another (Argentina) releasing everything to market forces, such asymmetries would keep deepening and producing intra-regional controversy.

However, such disputes are not always devoid of political interests. The political challenge of local enterprises in both countries seems to be as great as the commercial one. This is due to the necessity for negotiating with their respective governments for more advantageous concurrence conditions. In that sense, Brazilian business organizations are better positioned, for they always bargain as a bloc within their respective chambers. In both countries enterprises are damaged as a result of infringement of MERCOSUR principles. This has the effect of preventing enterprises that have organized their productive activities across borders from achieving projected results, which weakens the credibility of the integration process for those actors. Nevertheless, their trust in the process is very important. If businesses give up on investment plans on both sides of the frontier, the political will to make MERCOSUR work will also decline.

MNCs seem to perceive the integration project as an easy way to conquer new markets. In fact, from Brazil and Argentina, where high quality raw material is easily accessible at low prices, MNCs can launch themselves to the whole Latin American market at very low cost to themselves. Moreover, the lack of customs tariffs permits them to enter otherwise distant or difficult markets at very competitive costs (and also makes it more difficult for local enterprises to compete). For the moment, MNCs have become involved in Brazil, Chile and Argentina, but if association agreements multiply and the customs union weakens further, big corporations will take the greatest MERCOSUR gains. In such a framework, Brazilian and Argentinian firms find it difficult to profit from the rich possibilities engendered by the enlarged market, with the exception of some large national firms. It remains, however, that Brazil's biggest enterprises are, in general, better prepared to adapt and participate more readily in the new markets than their peers in Argentina.

Argentinean SMEs face the greatest difficulties of all groups, as they are not actively participating in the integration project – even despite the risk of perishing. The problem is not only the lack of information and financial support for SMEs, but also their weaker ability to compete with Brazilian SMEs. However, SMEs should be playing a very important role in any Free Trade Area constitution, not least because they are a major labour employer in comparison with large enterprises, and are better positioned to distribute the benefits of increased trade among the population. Given their scarce resources and small size, however, they are less able to conduct the necessary research into neighboring markets.

One of the ways in which SMEs have sought to overcome this starting disadvantage is through forming associations by sectors. In forming such associations they seek to strengthen their export capabilities by diminishing marketing costs and increasing bargaining capabilities. Nevertheless, such strategies are not yet widespread. Another way to surmount the obstacles they find in new regional markets is the formation of a front constitution together with the stronger firms, to lobby on the government's decisions so as to obtain positive responses to their vital demands. The sector to which an enterprise belongs also has an important bearing on the enterprise's behaviour – sometimes as important as the size of the business. As was explained earlier in this chapter, Argentina's system of rules for the car industry is benefiting multinational and Brazilian companies that invest in Argentina and bring their own suppliers to that country. It is fair to say that they are creating employment too; Fiat, for example, utilizes spare parts manufactured by Argentinian enterprises.

Last, but not least, the legal framework is essential in the first stages of integration, motivating states to help local enterprises to adjust and specialize. A good relationship between the public and private sectors, supporting the development of regional associations between enterprises, assists the foundation of a fair and firm integration process in any region, but particularly in the developing Southern Cone Region.

Notes

1. It is fair to say that MERCOSUR is just the most recent stage of the South American integration process: the two immediately previous experiences were the Latin American Free Trade Area (LAFTA) and, its successor, the Latin American Integration Association (LAIA), created in 1980 by the Treaty of Montevideo.
2. MERCOSUR is an intergovernmental organization based on cooperation, with an international legal status conferred by the Protocol of Oura Preto of December 1994. The Functional objective of the Treaty of Asuncion is the setting up by December 1994 of a Common Market, to allow the free circulation of goods, services and productive factors; the establishment of a Common External Tariff (TEC) and a Common Trading Policy towards third states; coordination of macroeconomic and sectoral policies on every area and harmonization of laws wherever pertinent to strengthen the integration process.
3. Brazil tends to have greater competitive advantage in mass production, with cheaper labour and greater investment. The Argentinean quality is

generally better, as is the labour force. Taxes are generally higher in Argentina than in Brazil; Brazil tends to have more up to date technology and equipment, though both countries have relatively little in terms of research and development.

4. Argentina protected its most sensitive sectors by putting a large number of products on the exception lists (221 compared to Brazil's identification of just 29 products to be exempted from the common market), justifying it in terms of the necessity to permit the short-term avoidance of the intra-national trading regime effects, and by making those industries conform to a regional scale.

5. Former Economic Minister, Domingo Cavallo, lowered tariffs almost to zero on capital goods imports from the world market, replacing trade protection on these goods with a subsidy to the local producer. This measure damaged the metal machinery sector – an important sector due to its potential role in technological progress.

6. In 1991, Argentina implemented a Car System of Rules that had to last till 1999, mainly a matching of imports with exports. Such a policy encourages the assembly plants to register a balance of trade: otherwise, the firm had to pay a 2 per cent tariff on each non-matched dollar.

7. Briefly, it established an in-aid system of rules favouring raw materials, spare parts and capital goods imports coming from outside the FTA, with preferential duties provided that those benefits were similarly counterbalanced. The MP 2410 redefined the whole Car Industry context of MERCO-SUR dramatically curtailing Argentina's FTA advantages.

8. GM's decision to establish new factories in Rio Grande Do Sul was especially inspired by the Enterprise Operation Fund Program (Fundopen), part of a state restructuring program.

9. This measure consists of a 50 per cent tariff rebate and other tax exemptions to make production costs substantially diminish. Cardoso's decree endows the same tariff rebate (a tariff of 35 per cent on car imports) in spare parts to the factories established in this region before 31 March 1998. The whole car sector is granted tax rebates on equipment and inputs purchasing until 1999 and been promised some benefits extension till 2010, ie., 10 years after the deadline set for an Argentina–Brazil common system of rules.

10. Early in 1997, the Brazilian Constitution Amendment was approved.

11. Early in 1996, it was agreed that Argentinean plant would be free to export 85 000 cars to Brazil without duty until the year 2000, and without having to compensate Brazil with the same amount of Brazilian imported units. That is to say, Argentina was exempted from Provisional Measure 2410. But those companies based in Argentina without a branch in Brazil would be ruled by another system. Under the pressure of business in this, Argentinean officials requested permission to export free of duties, up to the equivalent of 60 per cent of the Brazilian market, which implies 2 million vehicles per year, and offered in exchange the same treatment for the Brazilian car industry up to the equivalent of 40 per cent of the local market, i.e., 400 000 units per year.

12. Brazilian enterprises in the same situation are Volvo, Hyundia and Honda.

13. This information is drawn from data compiled by the Argentine's Embassy in Brazil where all the Argentine–Brazilian Joint Ventures carried out between 1986 and August 1995 were counted.

14. To mention but a few examples, *Toyota* will start to produce Hilux pick-ups and *Mercedes Benz* built a plant to manufacture utilitarian cars, both in Buenos Aires. *Ciadea,* which fabricated models of *Renault,* invested in the launching of a new model; *Ford, Volkswagen* and *Sevel* also injected great investments in the sector; *Chrysler* will open a new plant in Cordoba this year; and *Iveco,* of the *Fiat Group,* will make investments to start production of a new model.

15. Regarding investments, the following examples illustrate this assertion. One of them is the establishment of General Motors (GM) in Argentina (two factories, one in Cordoba and another in Rosario) through its Brazilian subsidiary, aiming to sell a third of overall production in the Argentinean market and export the remaining to Brazil. Exports also permit the import of GM's cars from Brazil to be sold in Argentina without paying any customs duties due to the Argentina car system of rules. Its strategy is a 'functional partitioning system of production' that allows new plants to exchange spare parts and cars between them. To strengthen it, GM established two other factories in Rio Grande Do Sul and contemplates the building of one more in Porto Alegre with US$600 million of capital disbursement. Another example is Mercedes Benz, whose gear boxes are manufactured in Argentina, while the Brazilian subsidiary supplies motors, axles and cabin parts to the Argentinean counterpart. The Mercedes Benz assembly plant has two units in Brazil and one in Argentina, all of them directly subordinated to the headquarters in Germany. They concentrate on trucks and buses production in Brazil while the Argentinean branch focuses on spare parts production.

16. Among the pioneers in the integration between Argentinean and Brazilian factories, Scania, the leader in Brazil's heavy vehicles market, is a good example. Manufactures in both countries are constantly exchanging the components in which they specialized.

17. An instance of that trend is the high complementation process developed by General Motors headquarters with its Brazilian Branch.

18. Deutz of Argentina and Agrale de Calzas do Sul (Brazil) signed an agreement of parts and wholes so as to assemble trucks and tractors in Argentina. Allied Signal signed a trade agreement with the Argentinean group Armetal for selling the Bendix products of the former firm in Argentina. The company Iochpe Maxion, situated in Brazil, associated to Armetal constituting Estampados Argentinos. Cofap, the Brazil's greatest spare parts factory acquired 50 per cent of the stock packet of the Argentinean Indufren. Afterwards, the Brazilian enterprise Freios Bega built its branch jointly with those companies (*El Economista*, 24 November 1995: 14).

8
Business Interest Groups and the State in the USSR and Russia: Change of Models

Sergei Peregudov

Among the dramatic changes in today's Russia, one of the most important is the process of the building up of new relationships between organized business and the State. This process began some years ago and despite the very short period of change, it already has its own history. But before coming to this, we need to look first at the prehistory of those changes, which continues to influence organized business–state relations to a great extent.

Organized interests and the State in the post-Stalinist USSR

State-interest group relations in the USSR before perestroika can be characterized as bureaucratic corporatist. In contrast to some Western sovietologists who also defined those relations as corporatist and virtually considered the Soviet Union as a corporatist state (Kelley, 1980), the understanding of Soviet corporatism used in this chapter is narrower. Whilst agreeing with the corporatists' (together with the pluralists) (Solomon, 1983, Ball and Millard, 1986) identification of real interest groups in the USSR as economic ministries and, especially, various 'complexes' (the military–industrial, agrarian–industrial, metal–engineering ones and so on) the 'bureaucratic corporatism' used in this chapter differs in that it does not put corporatism in the same category as pluralism and totalitarianism. This is because both latter terms refer to the nature of the political system and political regime as a whole. Soviet 'socialist' corporatism, it is argued here, was not a political regime on its own account, rather, a 'subsystem', a model of relations between organized interests and the state. As for the regime itself, it remained totalitarian, although not to the same degree as that which existed in Stalin's time, and whose main features were formalized by Brzezinski and Friedrich in 1956.

One of the main arguments of the pluralists was that in the post-1960 Soviet Union, a plurality of interests existed and was developing. While accepting this, it must be borne in mind that this pluralism must be placed within a corporate concept. 'Low-level' pluralism exists within virtually every corporatist mode. The best proof of this is the pluralism of business and other interest groups which existed within the corporatist model of fascism (Pitigalini, 1934). But the plurality of interests was subordinated politically and institutionally to the state corporatist system. The Soviet corporatist system was 'based' on a plurality of interest groups, but this pluralism was very limited, and not only by its nature, but by the fact that within each interest group a strict hierarchy was maintained and the number of groups was limited. Each had a monopoly of representation for a certain sphere of activity, usually according to a branch of industry or economy. And because all of them belonged to the state, it was a 'state corporatism' of a special, Soviet kind. The state not only directed the activity of interest groups, it also 'possessed' them.

Since the intermediation was within the state, it can be called 'bureaucratic'. But this term has wider meaning; it also describes the bureaucratic character of relations and behaviour within that subsystem. The subjects of the intermediation were not the 'usual', 'normal' interests of groups, their participants and members, but mainly bureaucratically-oriented interests. First among the latter were the careers and careerist aspirations of the leaders of groups, which materialized in many ways. For example, in efforts to squeeze out or 'knock out' as much in the way of resources (financial, technical, and so on) as possible without any relation to the genuine needs of production; and in various tricks to minimize their obligations and obtain such plans which would enable them to show the best results. According to the rules of the game, bureaucratically determined agreements were reached and fulfilled. Such behaviour was most obviously demonstrated by the use of 'apparatus' ties and connections, the administrative hierarchy, by the selected supply of information and the ways 'achievements' were reported.

The interests of the State as a whole (in real, not 'decorative' achievements) were represented by a central power structure – the central committee of the Communist Party and its Politburo, the Council of

Ministers, the state planning authority (Gosplan). But the more the system underwent bureaucratic degeneration, the deeper they were involved in bureaucratic games and came under the influence of sectional interests. Nevertheless the role of the centre as an integral and powerful body was not reduced to the role of a broker between competing interests as the pluralists argued. It ceased to act as a dictator suppressing and 'silencing' interests, but it did not become a powerless mediator. The downgrading of the role of ideology did not result in the abdication of the priorities, dictated by it in domestic, foreign and defence policies. The preservation of the vanguard role of the party, the emphasis on the development of heavy and especially military industry, the encouragement of 'socialist' regimes and communist parties everywhere retained the same significance as in previous decades.

It was therefore natural that the military–industrial complex and its particular units became pressure group number one, interested first of all in the further militarization of the economy. Its growing influence encouraged the military and expansionist ambitions of the top leadership and further stimulated the growing imbalance of the economy in favor of military and heavy industry production. But it would be wrong to evaluate the results of the growing influence of interest-groups in the USSR only negatively. By weakening and modifying the administrative-command system the bureaucratic corporatism stimulated more flexible and businesslike relationships between various levels of decision making and increased the capacity of the regime to react more quickly to changes in the sphere of production and in the society in general. It stimulated a more active involvement of low-level units of economy and industry in the process of consultation and accommodation both in vertical and horizontal ways. It is this development, leading to the creation of the so-called 'bureaucratic market', which according to V. Naishul (1982), had become a basis for a more genuine market, which began to emerge during perestroika and after it. Nevertheless, it remains true that this widening participation in the decision-making process in the economy only involved bureaucratic-administrative elements and did not change the hierarchical character of economic relations.

The collapse of the old regime and the emergence of the new business interest groups

After the failure of some more or less serious attempts to 'improve' the old economic system and to make it more efficient, Gorbachev and his associates initiated a number of unprecedented measures which started off the process of dramatic changes in the Soviet society. One of them was the adoption in 1987 of the 'Enterprise Act'. According to the Act, enterprises were able to exercise more autonomy over prices and wages and were given more possibilities to influence the planning process. Even more important was the right given to working collectives to elect enterprise management, and to participate in the management (through their councils) and in the distribution of incomes.

By widening the prerogatives of enterprises, the Act struck a heavy blow to the whole hierarchical system of administrative relations and, first of all, to the hierarchy inside interest groups themselves. The former system of orders and instructions was weakened not only by narrowing the sphere and range of ministerial regulation, but also and mainly because the management of enterprises was pulled out of the 'cartridge clip' of the party and state leadership.

The disintegration of interests which followed led to the development of more direct relations between big enterprises and the central state authorities. As the former minister in the Russian government Sergei Glazjev writes, 'top state authorities became the object of direct lobbying by the enterprises, leaving aside the central economic ministries' (Glazjev, 1993: 233). The key word in this quotation is 'lobbying' because it means a change in the very principle of interest group–centre relations. Not only the number of these increased, but the former, corporatist relationship, based on mutual obligations, began to erode. In its place came another, pluralist relationship (and the world 'lobbyism' means exactly that). The ministries themselves were rapidly becoming lobbyists too, acting in many cases as 'tools' of their subordinates. Formally, that subordination remained (as did the whole system of planning and other bureaucratic corporatist structures), but in fact it virtually stopped functioning in the old way.

Almost at the same time a second assault on the old bureaucratic-corporatist system began. Some months after the Enterprise Act, a 'Cooperative Act' was adopted by the Supreme Soviet (both of them were enacted from the beginning of 1988). As with the Enterprise Act, it was intended to renovate the socialist system, not to destroy it. The idea behind the Act was to realise the 'cooperative plan' sketched by Lenin just before his death and 'spoiled' by Stalin's 'Kolkhoz system'. But in reality that Act legalized small business and private property, though still on a minor scale. The act allowed the new cooperatives to hire labour and in this way to function as small business enterprises. Even more important was the permission granted to industrial enterprises to create cooperatives, and they used this permission to the full. About 80 per cent of all cooperatives were created in this way. The consequence of this was the start-off of the process of privatisation and private ownership. The managers and especially the directors of enterprises began to acquire state property and to function not only as managers but as property owners as well. Of course, this increased their autonomy even further. The liberalisation of foreign economic relations and the liquidation of the state monopoly in the field stimulated this process too.

Political reform, initiated by the XIX Party Conference in 1988, and especially the General Election of 1989 and the new Soviet Parliament, created most favourable political conditions for the further liberalisation of the economy and for the disruption of the old economic order. The position of interest groups was strengthened still further when political reform legalized strikes. A wave of strikes in 1989 was directed against the government and in many cases they were supported or virtually organized by management and sometimes even by ministries. Joint pressure of management and personnel against the government brought the latter almost to its knees.

A further factor greatly influencing government-interests relations was the creation by Ryzhkov's government in the late 1980s of huge state concerns (and, later, holdings companies), such as Gasprom, Agrokhim, Rosugol, and many others, based on the former ministries and their departments dealing with particular branches of industry. In addition to this some large industrial enterprises, such as the giant lorry-producing KAMAZ, the AUTOVAZ and others were transformed into joint-stock companies. Despite the fact that all of them remained, at that time, in state-ownership (the control of which was delegated to their management), the degree of their autonomy increased substantially. This development, which was considered by its initiators as a route to the 'planned market economy' (Abalkin, 1991: 77), accelerated the disintegration of previous economic relations.

The failure of the August 1991 coup which was intended, among other things, to bring 'order' to the economy, put an end to the perestroika period of reforms in the Soviet Union. The unnatural symbiosis of the old bureaucratic corporatist and the new, anarchical-pluralist systems had led to the paralysis of the economic machinery, and it was the task of the new authorities to find the way out.

From an 'anti-lobby' to a 'super-lobby' government

Two main tasks stood before the new Russia leadership in the area of interest group–state relationships. First, the complete destruction of the old bureaucratic-corporatist system and, second, the creation in its place of a model which would correspond to new, market priorities of economic development.

In accordance with its the neo-liberal approach, Gaidar's government (1992) aimed to 'minimize' industry–government relations, if not completely eliminate them. For about three or four months it refused to make any contacts with business interest groups and enterprises and became known as the 'first anti-lobby government'. But very soon reality intruded and compelled the government to change its approach. Money was printed and given out to industry, inflation became a permanent and distressing phenomenon. At the same time some new people, 'generals of industry', representing a different, directors' view, took important positions in the government (Prime-minister Chernomyrdin was among them). As one of the new ministers, G. Khizha, said at the time: 'The people who are in the government [that is, Gaidar and his associates] and the people working in industry spoke different languages' (*Nezavisimaja Gazeta*, 23 July 1992).

The new people in the government behaved mainly as some sort of 'insider' lobby, reinforcing the efforts of the 'outside' one. The predominant subject of lobbying was again money (in the form of credits, subsidies, as well as various concessions in taxes, duties and so on). As a result, Gaidar's government within six months was transformed from an 'anti-lobbyist' into a 'super-lobbyist' one.

Not only the 'reform' government was turned 'into a body, representing real interests' (to quote a well-known businesswoman and politician I. Khakamada) (Krasheninnikov, 1993: 121); the representative institutions embarked, firmly, on the same path. The whole system of functional representation lost even formal signs of order and rationality. By the beginning of 1992 the reorganization (or more precisely, the liquidation) of the old system of management of the economy had been carried out, and the state and semi-state concerns, holding companies and associations of various types replaced the old system of ministerial administrative management. Only enterprises of the military industrial complex (MIC), railway transport and some others of that kind remained under administrative supervision. But even they, especially in the MIC, were allowed much more autonomy than they had ever had.

Nevertheless, the old command system did not want to die peacefully and, as a special inquiry by a group of experts of the Institute of Economics discovered, the departments of the Ministry of Industry began to curb the newly acquired autonomy of the businesses, trying to dictate the ways of profit distribution, formation of wage funds and so on (Boeva, Dolgopolova and Shirokin, 1992: 17–18). It was quite natural that in doing so they met vigorous resistance. Even those directors and managers who were hostile to Gaidar's reforms understood, in their hearts rather than in their minds, that the most secure guarantee against a return to the past was not just their will to resist but their new social positions and status as property-owners. As it was proved by various sources, the striving for independence and real economic power was one of the strongest impulses behind their campaign for property ownership (Gordon and Keopov, 1993). Management's only rivals were the workers' collectives, who had some real opportunities to become owners of 'their' factories, enterprises and so on. But there have been a lot of formal and informal ways of 'disenfranchizing' workers. It is worth noting that, despite their alliance with the workers' collectives in their pressure on the state, the directors and their organizations were from the very beginning decisively opposed to the worker-ownership projects, and only a small minority of them agreed, voluntarily, to manage such enterprises. By the middle of 1993, or even earlier, the trend of property-acquisition by directors and top management teams had become irreversible, and their position as property owners was secured.

Business interest groups and the state in present-day Russia

As a result of dramatic changes in the economic system and in property relations a principally new kind of business interest group emerged. Parallel to the process of their formation a more complicated system of their relations with the state began to develop. The general disposition of those groups is reflected quite adequately in the sphere of business organizations which began to emerge from the end of the 1980s and the beginning of the 1990s. It is worth mentioning, perhaps, that before that time no such organizations existed in the Soviet Union. The sole 'business organization' was the Chamber of Commerce of the USSR. But in reality it was a state-administered organization for promoting the interests of the USSR in foreign economic relations.

As of 1995, there were more than a hundred business organizations in Russia, but only few of them are strong enough to influence the decision-making process. The oldest among them is the Russian Union of Industrialists and Entrepreneurs (RUIE), which has among its members the bulk of big Russian industrial enterprises and sectoral business associations. It was organized (as the 'Scientific-Industrial Union') in 1989 and for some years acted as the only representative of the top management of big state enterprises. Because of this it was called a 'directors lobby' (or even 'red' directors lobby). After the beginning of large-scale privatization it attempted to assimilate some powerful privatized industrial units and banks, and a number of them are now among its members. Nevertheless, even today it is rightly considered as mainly a voice for the directors of state-owned and semi-state companies. The climax of its political influence was in the second half of 1992, and 1993, when it led the counter-offensive of the directors against Gaidar's neoliberal economic policy. In the autumn of 1993 it even tried to dictate the appointment of the key economic ministers. It was also behind the formation of the Civic union, headed by RUIE president A. Volski, masquerading as a sort of 'industrial party'. But after its failure at the general election of 1993 and growing differences within its membership, the influence of the RUIE declined. Nevertheless it remains one of the most important business associations in present-day Russia.

Another organization claiming to be a 'directors' lobby' is the Federation of Producers (FP) headed by Y. Skokov, a well-known representative of the former Soviet elite (as Volski is too). RUIE is one of its affiliated members and both of them have close ties with the Federation of Independent Trade Unions of Russia (FITUR) – an heir to the former Soviet trade union organization. The very title of the FP is meant to emphasize these ties and in fact it is striving to build a united front of producers in their relations with the state. But aiming to preserve the backward industrial structure, it hasn't attracted any real support even among the state-oriented directors and unions and after a short period of publicity in 1993–94 its activity has become less and less noticeable.

Another ambitious attempt to create an influential umbrella-type business association – the Russian Business Round Table – was made in 1993 by a well-known Russian businessman of a new breed, I. Kivelidi. In contrast to RUIE and FP, the main orientation of the Russian Business Round Table (RBRT) has been directed towards the private and privatized section of the economy, and above all towards its commercial and banking sectors. In December 1994 it convened the first Congress of Russian Entrepreneurs, attended by representatives of the most important national and regional business associations (including RUIE), as well as representatives of influential industrial and commercial companies and banks, and top government officials. In contrast to the RUIE and the FP, the Business Round Table is trying to change the government's policy towards a more liberal, free market.

As it emerges from the documents of the RBRT and the statements of its representatives, its influence on the government and the state authorities in general is far less than it wishes. The journal *Biznes i Politika* (Business and Politics), which reflects in general the position of RBRT wrote recently 'the community of Russian entrepreneurs is yet in the process of self-identification and aggregation of its interests, and besides general declarations is unable to elaborate a clear programme of actions' (*Biznes i politika*, no. 1, 1995: 14).

One more organization, which is tying to play the role of a general business association, is the Russian Chamber of Commerce and Industry (RCCI), the heir to the Chamber of Commerce mentioned above. Using the former organization's resources, position and experience, it was able to attract a broad membership and to secure a place in the business community and political circles. Its main influence resides among the commercial and industrial units, involved in the external economic affairs of various kinds. The RCCI is trying to represent both the state-oriented and the market-oriented segments of management, and its political position may be described as centrist. There are now a number of other associations of more or less general character in Russia, including the Small Enterprises Association, the Association of Private and Privatized Enterprises, and the Leaseholders and Entrepreneurs Union, among others. But their influences is substantially weaker. As for their political orientations, they are leaning towards one of those just described.

By the mid-1990s an important place in the business world was acquired by some sectoral or branch business organizations. The most influential among them are those representing the more or less prosperous sectors of the economy (banking, oil, metal producing industries and some others), or the sectors striving for survival (enterprises of the defence sector, old and new agricultural units and so on). A clear example of the former is the Association of Russian Banks (ARB). According to its latest documents, its membership includes 1030 banks (about 70 per cent of all the banks of the Russian Federation), among them a large part of the biggest and most influential ones (Short report on the working of the Council and the Board of Directors of ARB (April 1994 – May 1995), Moscow: ARB, May 1995: 1). The activity of the Association is directed mainly at the promotion of the interests of its members in legislative and executive state institutions. To realise these aims the ARB participated in the preparation of the legislative acts, regulating the activity of the Central bank and of commercial banks, the tax system and so on.

Being representative of financial institutions, most of which belong to the private sector (although the largest of its members – the Savings Bank (Sberbank) and some others are state- or semi-state-owned), ARB is striving to accelerate the building up of a genuine market economy of the Western type in Russia. According to L. Makarevich, an expert of the ARB, 'in the course of the last 5 years the banking sector has become the main generator of market reforms' (*Finansovye Izvestia*, 25 May 1995).

Quite different priorities determine the activity of the League of Defence Sector Enterprises (LDSE) which is a typical representative of the sections of Russian economy, striving for survival and seeking the support of the state. The League's membership includes about a thousand armament-producing enterprises – the remnants of the former almighty MIC.[1] LDSE prefers to act as a coalition of industrial and political forces and it has among its supporters some influential figures in the presidential administration, the government, the Federal Assembly and heads of regional administration. The main aims of the League are to obtain the largest possible amount of state finance to support the defence industry. At the same time a lot of its members want to have large-scale autonomy in the management of enterprises and are opposed to the former, 'ministerial' way of bureaucratic control. Several of the League's members are in favour of a market economy and especially of the right to sell their produce in foreign markets. But the most important priority of the League's membership is to secure state orders for their production and in this way to guarantee their further existence and technological development. Despite strong political support, the influence of the League, especially at the national level, is rather limited. The present balance of political forces in the country and in its political elite is not favourable enough for the strengthening of the MIC and of other 'expensive' parts of the economy.

There are several other relatively influential sectoral business associations, including The Union of Oil Producers of Russia, League of Timber Exporters, Association of Advertising Agencies, Russian Stock Exchange Union, All Russian Council of Collective Farms, and Union of Landowners, but several industries do not have such organization yet. A most obvious example of this is the gas industry, and the reason for this 'passivity' is obvious. The industry is monopolized by a single company, Gasprom, and consequently has no need for an association of that kind.

Despite serious differences between business associations, some of which are mentioned above, they have a principal common feature: their independence from the state and the capacity to act on their own account. Even those which, like FP, RUIE and RCCI, strive for some sort of 'social contract' with the state and the trade unions and actually participate in the first attempts to create such arrangements (some of them being members of Trilateral Commission), are really free from any obligations towards the partners. Taken together, all these associations comprise a substantial element of the new Russian political pluralism, and with some other interest groups (trade unions, ecologists, women organisations, consumers and so on) they constitute an important part of the infrastructure of the emerging civil society. In the absence of a genuine party system some of them are trying to build political parties of their own or to associate with existing ones. The latest attempt of this kind is the formation in April 1995 of the Russian United Industrial Party. Most observers are rather doubtful, however, about its capacity to get past the 5 per cent barrier in order to form a faction in the new parliament.

Despite the growing role of business associations, the most important forces capable of influencing the state economic policy are the big industrial and commercial units mentioned above, and their informal groupings. As business associations they also differ in their political influence and political orientation. Another important difference between them is their relations with the state. Even many of those which are definitely market-oriented are building their relations not only as pressure groups or lobbyists but in more complicated ways. An example of this is the growing intermediation between the biggest banks on one side and the government on another. As experts from the British *Financial Times* wrote, 'a new commercial aristocracy has been born in Russia. And in the society, where laws are not working, it is inevitably interweaving with the structures of the state ... Step by step, unions between new rich and old political power are being forged' (published in *Finansovye*, 13 April 1995). Despite some oversimplification of this statement, it reflects a real process, which takes various forms. Having the vested interest in acquiring solid positions in industry, its most efficient sectors and enterprises (which are predominantly under state or semi-state ownership), banks and credit institutions are striving to enter into close relations with them.

This process is going on mostly at the 'individual' level, but the Spring of 1995 saw a new development. A consortium of six major commercial banks was created which offered to give the government a large credit (worth about two billion dollars) in exchange for the right to manage the state shares in some of mixed-ownership enterprises for five years (*Izvestija*, 27 June 1995, and *Finansovaja Gazeta*, nos. 19–20: 12). Serious discussion between representatives of the consortium and the top government officials, including the prime-minister, were going on at the time of writing (July 1995) with a real chance for the conclusion of a formal agreement.

This consortium is not the first grouping of banks aiming to strike a deal with the government. The enterprises that have the state as one of their major shareholders enjoy much closer and more organic relations with it. Two categories can be identified here. To the first belong the holding companies, concerns and enterprises, which are efficient enough and able to stand on their own feet (Gasprom, Avtovaz and those just mentioned in connection with the consortium, some companies in telecommunication, construction, timber industries and so on). Despite their strength and a large degree of autonomy they are not free from state regulation. To the second category belong companies and enterprises, which are not efficient enough to survive without state aid of various forms. Most of them are state-owned, but many are semi-privatized or owned by their employees and management. Being dependent on the state, their managements are obliged to have their principal decisions vetted by ministerial bureaucracies, and their status is in many cases almost similar to that of the former Soviet enterprises.

In fact, the management of the biggest of them is the slightly reorganized former ministerial structure. Functioning formally as independent joint-stock companies, they have preserved some statist functions. The most significant example of such companies is the concern Roslesprom, heir to the former ministry of timber industry. According to a special decision of the government, the top management of the concern has the right to administer all enterprises of it on behalf of the state.

Almost the same system exists in such giant companies, as Rostextil, Roslegprom (light industries), and there is a tendency to a more close and formal incorporation of them into the system of ministerial authorities. One – among many – manifestation of this is a project, already approved by the second chamber of the Federal Assembly, proposing the reestablishment of the former ministry for the fishing industry, with the aim to restore and modernize its material base and to achieve the former level of its production (*Segodnja*, 7 July 1995). Of course, even if this and other similar suggestions are realized in full, it will not mean a restoration of the old order. The process of 'autonomization' and differentiation of former state industries has advanced too far to deprive company managements of their newly acquired prerogatives, especially because most of the companies are semi-privatized or formally in the ownership of working collectives.

An obvious manifestation of the new kind of relations are the state-supported projects, initiated by industrial units of various kind. Despite the failure of a selective industrial policy in 1993–94, which was aimed at large-scale reconstruction of Russian industry and at reversing the process of deindustrialization, the government has not abandoned this approach. It approved about 30 federal programmes for 1995 (*Nezavisimaja Gazeta*, 19 April 1995). As a rule, the government supplies only a part (25–30 per cent) of the money needed for the projects. The rest is expected to come from the enterprises themselves and external sources, including banks and foreign investors.

Most important projects of this kind are connected with the financial-industrial groups (FIG), the formation of which is one of the first priorities of government's economic strategy. There are a lot of discussions about FIG and many businessmen and bankers are against the attempts by the government to build them on its own terms which would enable it to influence their activities. Because of this restraint only 12 FIG were registered by the middle of 1995. But in reality there are, according to experts of ARB, hundreds of 'unofficial' groups and their role in the economy is growing (*Finansovye Izvestia*, 25 May 1995). Some of them have been created with the participation of foreign partners.

To sum up the processes and relations just described, we stress, first, the heavy inheritance of the state–industry relations carried over from the past; and, second, the importance of new elements, which in fact have destroyed the old model. Although the new system is not yet established and is in the process of formation, it is possible to identify some of its principal features. In reality we can see three 'models' of this new system. The nearest to the old one is the model, based on 'dependency' relations, existing mainly in the weakest parts of the economy. Accordingly, it may be described in bureaucratic corporatist terms, but as it follows from the text above, it is not the same model. The amount of autonomy the enterprises of this sector have, as well as a large part of the national workforce employed here, give many of them the possibility to act as powerful lobbyists or pressure groups. Of course, the element of lobbyism was present in the Soviet system too, but it was not strong enough and functioned as an organic part of the bureaucratic corporatist model, not parallel to it. This difference can be viewed as the reason to describe the new system or model as a mixed, corporatist-pluralist one, with a predominant element of the first.

The second model is emerging mostly in the semi-privatized section of the economy, comprising the 'giants' of former Soviet industries in energy, metal-producing and some other market-oriented sectors mentioned above. According to a recent decision of the government, the most important of them are excluded from the second stage of privatization, which is mainly intended to turn semi-privatized industries and companies into genuine private ones (*Segodnja*, 7 July 1995). Despite some efforts of state authorities to act in an administrative-command way, the real balance of forces and the strong economic and political positions of top management of those companies, as well as close personal relations and mutual business interests compel these authorities to 'consult' them and make this an integral part of the decision-making process. So, here again we have a corporatist system, and the difference between it and Soviet corporatism is even more serious than in the previous case. This can be labelled a 'liberal' version of state corporatism, or a 'liberal-bureaucratic' one. And the word 'liberal' means first of all much more independent and secure social and political positions of the company-side participants. As in the first case, there is also a strong element of lobbyism in their relations with the state, but pluralist elements of state–business relations here are of a more general, political character, based mainly on the social and political activity of the 'giants'.

The third model is functioning in the genuine private sector of the economy, the most important part of which is formed of the big commercial banks, other financial institutions and 'informal' FIGs. Being virtually independent, they are able to exercise a considerable influence on decision-making. This capacity, as well as their general role in the party-political field makes them one of the major parts of the new, pluralistic power structure in Russia. So, we may quite definitely describe the model of their relations with the state as essentially pluralistic. But it is not a genuine pluralistic model. As it follows from the text above, there is a strong element of relations, going beyond the pluralist-lobbyist ones and based on a close intermediation with the state and mutual obligations. They do not determine the bulk of the activity of this section of the economy, but are important enough not to be ignored. So, this third model can be described as a pluralistic one with a strong corporate bias in it. The term 'corporate bias' is borrowed from K. Middlemas, who described in this way the system of 'loose' tripartite relations, which existed in post-war Britain (Middlemas, 1979: 458–63).

There are two main trends in state–business relations in Russia now. One is the tendency to 'recorporatization' which has already led to a system which some observers call 'state-monopoly' (or 'nomenclatura-bureaucratic') capitalism and which I prefer to call state corporatism. Another one is the 'pluralization' of these relations and it is also strong enough to widen the scope of the pluralistic social and political order. These two tendencies will determine economic, and to a great extent, social and political systems of Russia in more or less distant future. The balance between them will depend not only on objective factors, many of which were described above but on the disposition of political forces and the general political development of the country.

Note

1. According to official estimates, the production of the enterprises working for defence fell by 72 per cent between 1991 and 1995 (*Nezavisimaja Gazeta*, 20 March, 1995).

9
Antipodean Exceptionalism?: Australian Farmers and World Trade Reform

Rolf Gerritsen

In the postwar period the agricultural systems of most industrialized countries underwent a similar evolution. Accompanying the decline in the relative economic importance of agriculture, most OECD countries increased the level of market-distorting price and production supports. Against the trend – and anticipating the successful resolution of the Uruguay round of GATT by more than a decade – Australia did the opposite, substantially deregulating agricultural policy and removing virtually all producer subsidies. These reforms were achieved with the active acquiescence of organized farm groups. This chapter seeks to explain why Australian farmer groups pursued policies diametrically different to those pursued by farm groups in most other Western nations.

The postwar development of agriculture

The postwar development of agriculture in most of the industrial nations has featured two interrelated phenomena – the 'capitalization' of agriculture and the growth of agricultural 'protection'. The process of 'capitalizing' agriculture spread from the United States and was a two-phase process initially featuring rapid mechanization (which reduced the agricultural workforce) followed by the 'industrialization' of agriculture, which saw the increased application of scientific inputs to the production process on a constant quantity of land to increase yields and enhance factor outputs (Troughton, 1985). Between 1950 and the mid-1980s, farm total factor productivity tripled in the United States (Gardner, 1992: 69) and increased even more markedly in the EC.

The growing capital intensity of production saw the advent of the vertically-integrated 'agribusiness', with consequent political pressures for subsidies and governmental interventions to preserve 'family' farmers. From the early 1960s governmental inputs accelerated, either through direct expenditure and service provision, regulated consumer subsidies, or through tax expenditures to encourage agriculture's consumption of industrial technology inputs. Notwithstanding these phenomena, declining relative incomes meant that millions of farmers left agriculture. For example, between 1960 and 1983 agricultural employment in the EC declined to seven million from 17 million (Lloyd, 1987: 7). The growing disparity between rural and urban incomes inspired further governmental output subsidies. Assistance measures further interacted with the increased productivity resulting from the new scientifically-based inputs to create large increases in pro-duction and international agricultural commodity surpluses from 1980 onwards (Bouchet *et al.*, 1989). These then depressed international agricultural commodity prices below the long-term terms of trade trend (Lloyd, 1987: 10), in effect increasing the costs of subsidization.

The developments in Australia, despite some delay in mechaniz-ation, roughly followed the US-led pattern. Farm consolidation has been relatively continuous and the rural labor market adjusted in a similar fashion to north American models (Gerritsen, 1987a: 48–9; Lewis, 1990: 209, figure 14.1). In 1950–51 there were 203 350 agricul-tural establishments in Australia; since then farm units have decreased by about 1200 units per annum on average up to the early 1990s (ABARE, 1992: 24). The capital intensity of production grew continu-ously (Ockwell, 1990), with the usual socioeconomic consequences (Gerritsen, 1987a: 48–9). The principal difference between Australian agriculture and that of the US, the EC and Japan was in its export ori-entation (Table 9.3; see also Harris, 1990), the relative unimportance of vertically-integrated agribusiness, and in the high proportion of R&D carried out by government (Jarrett, 1990: 84).

The second, interrelated, feature of international agricultural devel-opment has been the rise of protective subsidies and other such meas-ures. It appears that notwithstanding the variety of political and institutional policy systems amongst the advanced industrialized states, these policy outcomes were almost universal (for example, see Stoeckel, 1985; Skogstad, 1987b; Gardner, 1989). The rate of growth of agricultural protection in the post-War period has seemingly been inverse to the comparative advantage of the subsidizing nations (Anderson and Tyers, 1986), though this effect has been masked by the (originally unintended) export surpluses that protection generated. This protectionist trend accelerated in the years following 1980, when EC surpluses began corrupting world food markets. In the period 1979–87 the average agricultural 'producer subsidy equivalent' for 'developed' countries rose from 30 per cent to about 50 per cent of the gross value of agricultural production (Schmidt, 1991; see also OECD, 1990). Consumer subsidization of agriculture also continued to rise in most developed countries during the 1980s, with the exception of Australia (and New Zealand). This was standard across a range of countries, as indicated by Table 9.1.

Notwithstanding the Uruguay Round of the GATT, agricultural protectionism became pervasive and deleterious for taxpayers and consumers in protectionist nations and efficient producing nations

Table 9.1   Agricultural subsidization (1990 levels)

	Producer subsidy equivalent[1]		Consumer subsidy equivalent[2]	
	Total ($billions)	*% of value of production*	*Total ($billions)*	*% of value of consumption*
Australia	1.3	11	0.4	8
Canada	6.5	41	3	26
Finland	5.3	72	3.5	71
Japan	30.9	68	32.8	48
New Zealand	0.2	5	0.1	7
Norway	3.1	77	1.7	64
Sweden	3.4	59	2.8	63
Switzerland	5.0	78	4.0	56
United States	35.9	30	19.3	19
EC[3]	81.6	48	63.8	41
OECD	175.5	44	133.41	36

Notes:
[1] The value of transfers from domestic consumers and taxpayers to agricultural producers resulting from a given set of agricultural policies;
[2] The value of transfers from domestic consumers to agricultural producers net of the transfers from taxpayers to domestic consumers resulting from a given set of agricultural policies (ie., implicit consumption tax);
[3] Producer subsidy equivalents and consumer subsidy equivalents are not calculated individually for the 12 member states of the EC.
Source: Agricultural Policies, Markets and Trade: Monitoring and Outlook 1991, OECD, Paris, 1991.

alike (as well as developing countries – see Valdez, 1987). An example was the American Export Enhancement Program, which was introduced in 1985 ostensibly to counter growing EC penetration of 'traditional' US export markets. There is little evidence that this expensive American strategic trade 'bluff' contributed to the establishment of the WTO.

The politics of international trade are one reason that agricultural protection and subsidization are rife in developed industrial democracies (see Schmitz, 1988), as international trade conflict interacts with domestic pressures for agrarian protectionism (Mahler, 1991). It was only in 1996 that the American Farm Bill began the process of dismantling agricultural subsidization among the northern hemisphere OECD nations. Simple explanations of agricultural protectionism rely on the observed correlation between economic development and agricultural protectionism. This argument is usually expressed in terms of the existence of a pattern of development where, as a consequence of industrialization, countries move from taxing to protecting agriculture (Anderson and Hayami, 1986; Johnson, 1991; Lindert, 1991). Agricultural protection is thus positively correlated with average *per capita* incomes; that is, capitalist societies appear to have an income-elastic demand for assisting farmers. Yet uniformly in developed countries farmers are only a small proportion of the workforce and agricultural production is a minor part of GDP, as Table 9.2 indicates.

If the agricultural constituencies are so minor, why then has agricultural protectionism been so pervasive in OECD countries? Partly this has reflected inertial development ('institutional persistence') from the historical legacy of measures instituted during the 1930s (or the 1890s in the case of Germany – Hendriks, 1987) to ameliorate price instability and rural poverty (Petit, 1985: chapter 4). Currently, the two (domestic) economic justifications for protectionism commonly advanced by agricultural policy administrators in these countries is that this protectionism is either for the purposes of domestic price stabilization or to supplement the incomes of the rural population (implicitly to provide an incentive against rural–urban migration).

Neither of these arguments is borne out by empirical observation. The effect of price supports is to increase the variability of international market prices, by up to 40 per cent on Johnson's estimate (Johnson, 1991: 151). Also the primary beneficiaries of rural income supplementation are not rural laborers but rich farmers (von Witzke, 1986: 157; for the USA see Cochrane, 1986). Indeed some studies estimate that 90 per cent of the increase in net returns to farm resources

Table 9.2   Agriculture in OECD economies

	Gross value added in agriculture as percentage of GDP[1]			Employment in agriculture as percentage of total civilian employment		
	1976	*1983*	*1991*	*1976*	*1983*	*1991*
Canada	3.0	2.1	1.3	5.9	5.5	4.5
United States	3.1	2.1	1.5	3.9	3.5	2.9
Japan	3.6	2.4	1.8	12.2	9.3	6.7
Australia	4.7	4.4	2.7	6.6	6.6	5.5
New Zealand	10.5	7.1	5.6	10.5	11.2	10.8
Belgium	2.8	2.4	1.8	3.6	3.2	2.6
Denmark	4.3	4.1	3.1	8.3	7.4	5.7
France	4.5	3.7	2.6	9.9	7.9	5.8
Germany	2.3	1.6	1.0	6.7	5.0	3.4
Greece	15.7	13.5	12.5	34.2	29.9	22.6
Ireland	14.5	9.6	6.6	22.1	17.0	13.8
Italy	6.5	5.0	3.2	16.5	12.4	8.5
Luxembourg	2.3	2.4	1.2	7.0	4.5	3.7
Netherlands	4.4	4.0	3.6	5.6	5.0	4.5
Portugal	n/a	6.0	3.5	33.9	23.2	17.3
Spain	7.1	5.3	3.5	22.1	18.7	10.7
United Kingdom	2.3	1.6	1.1	2.8	2.7	2.2
Austria	5.0	3.7	2.7	12.4	9.9	7.4
Finland	4.8	4.2	2.4	16.2	12.7	8.5
Norway	3.2	2.2	1.6	9.4	7.7	5.9
Sweden	1.8	1.3	0.6	6.2	5.4	3.2
Switzerland	3.1	2.7	3.4	7.8	6.4	5.5
Turkey	26.7	18.3	n/a	61.3	53.6	46.6

Notes:
[1] At market prices; n/a not available.
Source: Economic Accounts for Agriculture 1976–89, OECD, Paris, 1991, and the *OECD Observer* no. 176, June/July 1982.

go to land and capital and only 10 per cent to labour (Johnson, 1991: 237; see also Miner and Hathaway, 1992). It could be argued that the protection of agriculture in the EC, the USA and Japan has the primary, if unintended, effect of distorting the price of land and thus lowering the rate of return on capital invested.

Even if the counterproductive consequences of agrarian protection are realized, the advocates of such policies point to the 'need' to preserve domestic agricultural production notwithstanding the economic costs. These arguments are usually couched either in 'national security' terminology – the political and strategic danger of becoming dependent upon foreign food suppliers (very much a factor for Japan) – or in 'nostalgia' terms. This latter case – popular in France – assumes the intrinsic value of maintaining the rural lifestyle and environment, even though agricultural protection is an inefficient means of achieving either (Winters, 1990).

To explain the persistence of inefficient agricultural protection analysts have increasingly turned to the role of political factors, particularly the power of farm interest groups and their ability to dominate the policy settings of agriculture (see Petit, 1985; Rausser, 1990; Schmitz, 1988; Tracy, 1990). An exemplar of this approach, by Anderson and Hayami, has three parts:

1. As incomes grow in developed countries and food constitutes a smaller percentage of consumer expenditure, consumers and industry become less assiduous in seeking lower food prices;
2. The decrease in the number of farmers cheapens the costs for politicians of buying farmer electoral support (Lindert expresses this element by arguing that agricultural decline enhances political empathy for farmer demands – see Lindert, 1991: 66); and
3. Once industrial economies lose their comparative advantage in agriculture and become net food importers, the food security justification gains in net policy importance. (Anderson and Hayami, 1986: 1–3; see also Tyers and Anderson, 1992: chapter 3).

Underlying Anderson and Hayami's postulates is a simple model based on public-choice theories. To put it in Olsonian terms, the reduction in the number of farmers actually encourages their interest groups because of the reduced likelihood of them having to share the benefits of their protectionist rent-seeking activities with 'free-riding' non-contributors.

This model fails to account for the fact that in the 1980s protectionist policies in the EC and the USA (though not Japan) were subsidizing *exports* and hence went further than mere farmer income support and food security measures. Indeed, in the short term the EC will have to reduce its administered domestic prices to a level below world prices to constrain production. To change EC policy would require acceptance of farm production supports being replaced by income transfers. This is difficult if – as in France – agricultural activity is seen as a good in itself. Refinements of this model can be made by applying it to particular countries while taking into account politico-institutional elements peculiar to those countries (for America see de Gorter and Tsur, 1991; for the EC, Schuknecht, 1991, and for Japan, Jones, 1989)

By 1990, agricultural subsidies and transfers in OECD countries were slightly greater than Australian GDP, so the threat to Australian agriculture's export markets was profound. In 1991 the EC's Common Agricultural Policy cost Australian wheat farmers alone Aus$700 million in lower market prices and the American EEP another Aus$175 million. Yet, in contrast to the prevailing pattern in the OECD, the 1980s saw the peak council of Australia's farm sector – the National Farmers' Federation – support market liberalization of Australia's agricultural policy and trade regimes. This chapter seeks to explain the farmers' role in this exceptionalist response to the contemporary international agricultural policy paradigm.

The Australian policy experience

Given that since the Second World War Australia's agricultural industries produced a declining proportion of GDP and employed a shrinking workforce, intuitively it could be expected that the Anderson and Hayami (1986) model would also apply to Australia and be reflected in increasing levels of agricultural protectionism. And for a period after 1945 that appeared probable.

State intervention in Australian agriculture has a venerable history and was further strengthened in the decades following the Second World War. Indeed organizing this intervention was one of the reasons for the formation and early strength of the Country Party in Australia (Ellis, 1963). State support focused on statutory pricing and stabilization schemes and quasi-state organisation of international marketing; various tax expenditures, and publicly-provided underpriced services such as irrigation water, research and quarantine services (Edwards, 1987; Edwards and Watson, 1987). Some arguments for such governmental aid rested on a 'second-best' economic case for assisting exporters to compensate them for the costs imposed by Australia's manufacturing tariffs regime (Harris *et al.*, 1974). From the 1960s there was some decline in public sector support for unconstrained private production decisions, with the 1968 Wheat Industry Stabilisation Plan possibly the seminal indicator that the popularity of open-ended government support for increases in agricultural output was dissipating (Butlin, Barnard and Pincus, 1982: 138). The average effective rate of protection for agriculture peaked at 30 per cent in 1970–71. It soon dropped, as the late 1960s and early 1970s saw significant wheat and dairy policy reversals for the agricultural protectionists (Coleman and Skogstadt, 1995: 250–51), mostly forced by market adjustment to British entry to the EEC.

But there was still a degree of policy inertia favoring farm support programs (Seiper, 1982), especially amongst State governments (Gruen, 1990: 25). The level of support and subsidization varied widely – dairy, sugar, tobacco and canned fruits, for example, enjoying much higher than normal levels of assistance – in ways that can largely be explained by public choice theories about the (geographically) concentrated benefits and diffused costs of such measures (Anderson, 1978; Seiper, 1982). Also, the balance of payments justification for assistance to agriculture under a fixed exchange rate regime was an article of faith for the Country Party's successor, the Nationals, and proved residually popular amongst the rural rumps of the other major political parties.

In 1954 average farm income was 209 per cent of average weekly earnings (AWE); in 1986 it was 86 per cent of AWE (Lloyd, 1987: 4, table 1; see also chart A, p. 8). In the early 1990s it had fallen even further. Similar income trends in the advanced industrial countries had seen an escalation of production subsidies (without solving the relative income disparity problem). Australia could have followed the international pattern of increasing subsidization of agriculture; instead it did the opposite.

In the early 1980s the conventional (Campbell, 1985a; Seiper, 1982) argument was that Australian farmers were not going to allow the overthrow of a system that benefited their short-term interests (Campbell, 1985a: 252–3). Yet, particularly from the mid-1980s, Australian agricultural policy was substantially deregulated and governmental supports reduced – principally by the federal government (Coleman and Skogstadt, 1995). As indicated above, this was contrary to the experience of most OECD countries and occurred within the context of declining export market prices caused by a combination of the major OECD countries' agricultural policies together with deteriorating terms of trade for agriculture. Intuitively, this could have been expected to reproduce the protectionist politics of 'domestic defence' (Castles, 1988) typical of Australia's postwar experience prior to the 1980s. Yet the result was the opposite. In the 1980s Australia's governments responded to the challenge of corrupt world markets by facilitating increased agricultural productivity and infrastructural efficiency. The reform thrust – as sketched briefly below – had three principal, interrelated, elements: the quest for managerial and administrative efficiency, improving economic efficiency, and while reducing it, restructuring agricultural assistance more equitably (Martin, 1990).

'Managerialist' efficiency

The 1980s saw a comprehensive reorganization of the institutional structures of Australian rural policy. Under the post-1983 Labor governments the administrative restructuring of agricultural agencies has been the most corporatist-like of all the governmental policy domains (Gerritsen and Murray, 1987: 10–11; Gerritsen and Abbott, 1988: 19; Gerritsen and Abbott, 1991: 8; Newton, 1990). Above all the traditional commodity marketing, policy making and research councils were 'corporatist' peak councils – like the Rural and Allied Industries Council and the Australian Fisheries Council and later an R&D peak council. These reduced the traditional policy centrality of the intergovernmental Agriculture Council and the Standing Committee on Agriculture (Gerritsen, 1991: 282–3) and introduced trade unions and food processors to the policy advisory process, though in the short term the National Farmers' Federation's power was the most enhanced.

Economic efficiency

The quest for improved microeconomic efficiency was continuous during the 1980s. Reforms focused on deregulating agricultural policy and implementing more cost-efficient structures. During the 1980s there were wholesale deregulatory reforms of Australian agricultural policies. Protection of the dairy, dried fruit and citrus fruit juice, sugar and tobacco industries was drastically reduced (Martin, 1990; Gerritsen, 1992b). From 1990 the Wheat Board's domestic monopoly was removed, though it retained its 'single desk' seller role in the international market (Gerritsen and Abbott, 1991: 10).

Unlike the northern hemisphere experience with subsidized public sector inputs for agriculture, cost-recovery as an instrument of inducing microeconomic efficiency has been broadly implemented in Australia over the last decade. Meat inspection and quarantine services were recast under cost-recovery regimes. Other 'user-pays' initiatives were implemented for the National Agricultural and Veterinary Chemicals Registration Scheme. In some areas, such as horticultural products exports, significant self-regulatory regimes have been instituted.

The pressure for improved economic efficiency has been continuous. One of the reasons for this is the growing policy influence of the Industry Commission, whose reports were increasingly implemented during the 1980s. The Commission was a powerful encouragement to the reform of the dairy industry. Also the government's 'official' rural adviser, the Australian Bureau of Agricultural and Resource Economics, became more assertive in stating its policy positions, to good effect, for example, in opposing restrictions on foreign ownership of cattle stations, abattoirs and feed lots (Gerritsen and Abbott, 1991: 8; Gerritsen 1992b). Both these agencies legitimated and spurred the 'neo-liberal' (Coleman and Skogstadt, 1995) agenda of reduced governmental assistance to the agricultural sector. In this they were (counter-intuitively) aided by the National Farmers' Federation.

Facilitating rural reconstruction

One reason for the excessive subsidization of farmers in OECD countries is those farmers whose cost–price structure is non-competitive in international market terms. The usual OECD reaction is to subsidize output to maintain their incomes (in the process enriching more efficient farmers). Australia, however, adopted a different course, attempting to subsidize only those farmers adversely affected by particular market fluctuations but who would be viable in the long-term at ruling international market prices. The usual instrument of this policy has been the interest rate subsidy on loans. Loans, rather than cash grants, are seen to provide a long-term financial efficiency pressure and so (theoretically at least) not to inhibit rural reconstruction and adjustment.

The government's only expansion of fiscal outlays was in the area of rural welfare, with a variety of schemes designed to improve the access of rural communities to governmental services (Gerritsen and Murray, 1987: 13; Gerritsen and Abbott, 1988: 9; Gerritsen, 1992b). This aspect of policy, subsidizing rural communities rather than rural commodity producers, focused on social equity outcomes.

Why then did Australia reform its agriculture?

Most orthodox political economy analysis would start with the assumption that free trade is theoretically Pareto-optimal. Thus, as Britain industrialized in the nineteenth century it liberalized its agricultural sector by abolishing the Corn Laws. When (perversely, according to orthodox Ricardian economics) measures are implemented that are protectionist or trade-restricting, explanations for this are usually couched in collective action theory terms, of special interests forming 'distributional coalitions' against the interests of the generality of consumers or voters (Olson, 1965) and to the detriment of the nation over time (Olson, 1982). But as the economic costs of such protection grows over time, it could be expected that opposition to protection from groups adversely affected will also increase. In short there should be a long-term tendency for the political equilibrium level of protection to fall.

Intuitively, this would be even more the case if an industry – as is agriculture in Australia – is predominantly trade-oriented and thus subject to the full vagaries of international competition. Australian agriculture is undoubtedly relatively trade-oriented, as Table 9.3 reveals.

Australia and New Zealand are both large exporters and have substantially free market agricultural policies. They can thus be expected to be net gainers from freer agricultural trade (Schmitz, 1988: 997–8). Yet several other OECD countries (such as France, Denmark) are also export-dependent, particularly if the value of intra-EC trade (missing from Table 9.3) was factored into the data. Yet they are not agricultural free marketeers. Canada, an erstwhile member of the agricultural free trade 'Cairns Group' is not so export-dependent and during the 1970s and 1980s increased governmental interventions to protect agricultural markets (Skogstad, 1987a). Indeed, there is a theoretical case to be made that export dependence encourages risk avoidance and market protection policies in agricultural policy makers (Tyers, 1991). So this data – particularly in relation to the position of fixed capital formation – is inconclusive in explaining Australia's agricultural policy liberalization of the 1980s. We need an alternative explanatory framework.

Logically, there are two further, not entirely discrete, sets of explanations for Australia's agricultural trade liberalization; let us label them the 'null-alternative' and 'politico-institutional' sets.

The null-alternative ('that Australia has/had little alternative') set

This set has two aspects: one couched in microeconomic theory and the other in trade politics. Microeconomic explanations justifying eschewing European-style subsidization were advanced by the Industry Commission, the Federal Treasury, academic agricultural economists, and (less-significantly) the Department of Foreign Affairs and Trade. This approach focused on the futility of Australia maintaining any form of strategic trade response to unfair trading practices by the major world traders. In essence it argued that microeconomic efficiency and enhanced productivity was Australia's only possible policy response to such distortions of free trade. Paraphrased the argument runs as follows.

Table 9.3   Trade and investment in OECD agriculture

	Production	Trade[1]			
	Gross fixed capital formation	Exports %		Imports %	
	(% of value of final output)	1989	1982–84 annual average	1989	1982–84 annual average
Australia	2.9[a]	33.3	36.5	4.3	4.7
Austria	n/a	3.9	4.9	6.1	7.6
Belgium	16.4	4.2[b]	7.2[b]	8.6[b]	12.3[b]
Canada	33.0	7.0	11.1	5.7	7.3
Denmark	19.8	22.8	23.1	9.4	13.0
Finland	37.7	3.0	5.3	5.4	7.1
France	17.8	12.8	13.9	9.5	11.5
Germany	34.5	3.5	3.7	9.0	12.8
Greece	9.5	25.5	30.5	10.7	8.2
Iceland	n/a	2.9	3.1	9.4	11.5
Ireland	25.7	24.2	29.9	8.3	12.6
Italy	40.0	5.6	5.6	11.4	12.1
Japan	52.3	0.4	0.6	14.0	13.2
Luxembourg	35.6	4.2[b]	7.2[b]	8.6[b]	12.3[b]
Netherlands	28.0	18.3	21.3	13.3	18.0
New Zealand	14.4	56.7	64.3	7.5	6.8
Norway	43.0[a]	1.4	1.8	6.0	6.9
Portugal	21.9	9.3	13.1	22.3	28.4
Spain	n/a	13.8	12.7	12.0	15.9
Sweden	39.7	2.2	3.0	6.0	7.0
Switzerland	28.3[a]	3.1	3.8	6.8	9.2
Turkey	n/a	24.5	40.3	10.3	4.6
United Kingdom	17.3	6.3	6.5	7.2	11.9
United States	16.6	12.6	18.6	5.2	7.1

Notes:
n/a not available;
[1] Food and agricultural raw materials as a percentage of total merchandise trade (intra-EC trade excluded);
[a] 1987;
[b] Belgium–Luxembourg Economic Union (BLEU).
Source: Agricultural data-base, AGR.

Following the 1980 watershed (with the inevitability of a world awash with EC agricultural produce), plus the 1985 US decision not to hold world wheat stocks and to implement the EEP, the (already corrupted) market situation became one of oversupply, which damaged

Australia (Roberts and Whish-Wilson, 1993). As a small player, with negligible market power, Australia had little alternative but to remain efficient. Strategic trade-style subsidization was not possible because of the general constraints on the Australian economy and limitations of fiscal resources. Trade-strategy driven explanations were based on the fact that Australia (and New Zealand) would be a major beneficiary of agricultural trade liberalization to be organized by the WTO. So Australia had a clear incentive to support reform of world agricultural trade.

Given this, and faced with an increasingly corrupted world agricultural commodity market, plus the threat of the emergence of world trade blocs excluding Australia from market access on quota rather than price grounds – and consequently rendering null any strategy of relying merely on improved productivity to remain competitive – the Australian government had no alternative but to attempt to use diplomatic/trade negotiation leverage (and that was more credible if it confronted the agricultural protectionists from the standpoint of relative virtue). Hence Australia's agriculture policy was a 'signaling device' (Higgott, 1991) of a general policy commitment to a freer world trade order.

In the event, neither of these strategies played much of a part in the relatively successful conclusion in 1994 of the Uruguay round of the GATT. These approaches merely justify the Australian strategy and do not explain why the Labor governments of the 1980s moved to liberalize Australia's agricultural policy regime. The second set here hypothesized provides a better explanatory framework.

The politico-institutional set

This set takes an interactive three-part model variable, of policy-making (Gerritsen, 1992a: 67–70). The three elements of the model are: public and private interest variables, and the politics of agenda management. The three variables require a net positive interaction to produce the result of policy liberalization, and that occurred during the late 1980s.

The public interest variable

This part of the model requires a policy community and for that community to define a generally-accepted 'public interest'. There were two developments here that were of significance: firstly, the farm groups united under one peak body, and, secondly, this body adopted a neo-classical stance with regard to economic policy.

Historically, as in many Western countries, Australian farm groups were organized around commodity production groups. In addition, in Australia (as in other federations), these groups tended to be organized on a state rather than a national basis (see Chislett, 1967). In 1979 Australian farm groups managed to form a national peak council, the National Farmers' Federation (NFF), a group which was well-financed and employed a succession of capable administrators. Accordingly, it was able to engage in what the corporatists call interest intermediation and delegated enforcement. In January 1981 it produced *Farm Focus: The 80s*, the first comprehensive policy document to come from the farm sector. The power of the NFF was demonstrated in the late 1980s when it was not only able to be an effective ally of a reforming agriculture Minister (from a political party to which most farmers were hostile), but also to ensure that other (state and commodity-based) farm groups acquiesced in this *de facto* alliance. So the NFF was able to secure what was effectively a single voice for farmers. This development was unlike that, for example, in both the United States – where observers have noted that the 'farm bloc' is becoming increasingly fractured by single commodity organisations and agribusiness and consumer interests (Heinz *et al.*, 1993: 261) – and Britain (Jordan *et al.*, 1994: 511). The advent of a single organized farmer policy voice became crucial in the early 1980s, when the resurgence of neoclassical economic policy reached Australia.

During the period from about 1980 the farm groups accepted what is now known as 'economic rationalism' (Trebbeck, 1990: 138–9). This broadly meant that the agricultural sector abandoned the policy of 'protection all round' (Butlin, Barnard and Pincus, 1982: 133–8), which historically had seen it get some (still relatively minor by international comparisons) governmental regulatory and fiscal supports in compensation for manufacturing tariffs and national wages policies. The changed approach is demonstrated in the contrast between two policy episodes. During the 1979 price fall beef farmers lobbied for subsidies; in the 1985 wheat price fall the NFF focused on reducing farm costs, in particular those created by governmental regulation (Gerritsen and Murray, 1987: 22).

This development is crucial. In effect it meant that Australian farmers (or, more accurately, their organizations) accepted that their long-term interests lay in economic globalization and trade liberalization. So when, in the mid-1980s, Australian governments became committed to liberalization, deregulation and microeconomic reform of the Australian economy (Easton and Gerritsen, 1996), the farm sector gave its support.

The logical policy alternative, raised by the possibility that OECD countries with relatively liberal manufacturing sector policy regimes and strong manufacturing exports were prepared to subsidize agriculture as an unimportant, lagging sector (and that Australia could do the same in reverse order), was not seriously considered. Even if this was the general OECD case, and a possible course of action for Australia, it was recognised by the Australian policy community in the 1980s that no sector could be allowed to 'free ride' on any other. So, in face of Australia's declining external account, retaining agricultural protection in parallel with manufacturing protection was not an acceptable policy option. Thus the definition of the 'public interest' was uncontested and reform could be implemented with the support of all the major stakeholders, in particular the united farm organizations.

The private interest variable

This element of the model involves the politics of 'partisan coalitions' and pressure groups. In the agricultural policy domain the Labor governments of the 1980s were free of the problem of maintaining the support of its partisan coalition of voters and affiliated interests (such as the trade unions). In other policy fields (for example, labour market reforms) these problems complicated the politics of microeconomic reform after 1987 (Gerritsen, 1992a: 72). But because farmers were electorally hostile to Labor (Gerritsen, 1987: 53–5), there were no internal pressures on the Labor government to mitigate its reforming endeavors in the interests of mollifying partisan supporters. Paradoxically, this meant that farm organizations and the Labor government were able to cooperate once they adopted similar policy directions.

This was especially the case after the May 1988 Economic Statement, when the government developed an informal 'exchange' relationship with the NFF (Gerritsen and Abbott, 1991: 14; Gerritsen, 1992b). The government promised significant, economy-wide, microeconomic reforms, to reduce the costs of farm sector inputs, in exchange for the NFF's agreement to the liberalization of agricultural policy. This bargain was dramatized by the removal of the hitherto sacrosanct superphosphate bounty (Gerritsen and Abbott, 1991: 14). Removal of this bounty was offset by the reduction of tariffs on imported agricultural machinery. The previous Labor government had tried to remove the superphosphate bounty in 1974 and had been forced to back down in the face of a storm of farmer protest (Watson, 1979: 166).

Further microeconomic reforms – reform of transport and communications, reductions of manufacturing tariffs, labour market reorganization, improved efficiencies in public utilities and other public services – promised the farm sector more significant reductions in their input and handling costs. This exchange bargain particularly recognized the strong negative effective rates of protection to agriculture as a result of manufacturing industry protection (Terry, Jones and Braddock, 1988: 283).

That the change was negotiated and consensual made the political process of reform in Australia substantially different from that in New Zealand, where change was unilaterally imposed by government (Lattimore, Ross and Sandrey, 1988), although the policy content of reform was broadly similar (Easton and Gerritsen, 1986).

The politics of agenda-setting and agenda-management

The 'political agenda' concept is intrinsic to analyzing the politics of governmental electoral survival. 'Policy' and 'public' political agendas are parts of a concept developed to explain why issues arise when they do (Cobb *et al.*, 1976) and how governments seek to manage these issues to their electoral advantage (Harding, 1985).

Liberalization of economic policy was a governmental policy agenda of the 1980s with which the principal farm group, the NFF, concurred and to which it contributed. This agenda was created by the 1985 Australian dollar/terms of trade 'crisis' (Gerritsen and Murray, 1987: 18), which eventually led to the response that internationalizing the Australian economy was the best remedial course of action. The policy reforms outlined above were implemented by governmental initiative but with farm groups support. This was because both interests agreed that agricultural subsidization was an inappropriate response to Australia's situation. In this context the government's policy agenda was uncontested because it was synonymous with the public agenda that the agricultural sector had to improve its productivity and competitiveness to weather the international trade storm of the 1980s. The role of the NFF was one of delegated enforcement, to ensure that its affiliates held to the policy line.

The interaction of these three elements ensured that, with the support of the agricultural policy community, the government was able to develop an agricultural policy strategy that was the opposite of those implemented in most other OECD countries during the 1980s.

Conclusion

The postwar development of agriculture and the public policy response of intensified agricultural protectionism was broadly similar in most OECD countries. But Australia (and New Zealand) adopted a diametrically opposite public policy strategy, that of liberalizing their agricultural policy regimes. The reforms of agricultural policy entailed by this antipodean exceptionalism have been outlined.

To explain this perverse (from the comparative international perspective) policy response two explanatory sets are derived: the 'null alternative' and the 'politico-institutional' set. The hypotheses under the former are together found to justify the policy stance Australia assumed. But they do not explain why Australia acted as it did. The politico-institutional set does explain why Australia responded to the international agricultural trade crisis in the manner described above. This was principally because farm groups proposed economic and accepted agricultural policy initiatives unique amongst the industrialized countries and diametrically opposite to those pressed by organized farm sector groups elsewhere.

10
Multitiered Systems and the Organization of Business Interests

William D. Coleman and Éric Montpetit

Functioning in a multitiered arrangement is neither an unusual nor a particularly new activity of business interest associations. Certainly business associations have a long experience with working within the federal systems of Australia, Canada, Switzerland and the United States. They have had over a half century to adapt to the federalism of the Bonn Republic and are now in their fourth decade of accommodating themselves to the European Union. With the growing internationalization of some areas of public policy, we might expect that the challenge of working within multitiered political systems will become even more common. Despite these experiences and the many opportunities to observe the organizational strategies chosen by business associations, there do not seem to be clear and obvious linkages between the constitutional structures of multitiered systems and the organizational structures chosen by business interest associations operating within those systems. One finds some highly-centralized associations in rather decentralized federal states like Canada, while many business associations in more centralized states like France and Japan have rather elaborate patterns of territorial differentiation.

Such complexity will not come as a complete surprise to students of business interest associations. As Schmitter and Streeck (1981) have reminded us, the organizational arrangements chosen by associations representing business reflect the influence of two broad sets of variables. First, the membership of the association brings a variety of attributes to the organization and these can vary greatly from one association to another. Some of the more important attributes include the industrial relations system in which members participate, the nature of the production process common to most members, the market focus – regional, national, international – of the member firms, the relative geographical dispersion of the membership, and the presence or absence of reinforcing cleavages with ethnic and linguistic groups. All of these kinds of variables are subsumed under what Schmitter and Streeck term the 'logic of membership.' And each of these will have implications for whether business interest associations choose an integrated or a differentiated approach to territory.

One might hypothesize, for example, that firms operating in a company-level industrial relations system will have less interest in regional differentiation in their associations than firms operating with sector-wide bargaining at the regional level. Economic sectors where Fordist production structures dominate will have considerably less interest in territorial differentiation in their associations than sectors dominated by diversified quality production (Streeck, 1992) or by artisanal processes. Both of the latter industrial structures demand much more networking at a regional and local level than does Fordist production. We do not in this chapter need to multiply these kinds of hypotheses. What should be clear is that the structural characteristics of the members of business associations will have a direct impact on decisions to develop structures that are more or less differentiated along territorial lines.

Second, by their very functions as intermediaries between their members and the state, associations will respond to the organization of the state itself. Where they are forced to deal with more than one state or with a quasi-state such as they might experience in working within the European Union or under the auspices of an international regime, we can expect that they will respond with organizational attributes that assist them to defend interests and to participate in policy-making wherever it is necessary. It is likely that some of these responses will take the form of internal differentiation to manage operations in different spaces. Certainly, some part of these responses will reflect the particular challenges that come with working within a federal system as opposed to a union state like the UK, or a unitary state like France. And even among federal systems, we argue that functional federations such as that found in Germany will provide a different logic for organization than the jurisdictional federations found in Canada and the United States.

To facilitate the discussion that follows, we will examine the degree of territorial differentiation within business interest associations by employing the following categories (Coleman, 1987: 173–4; Schmitter and Lanzalaco, 1990):

- *Unitary:* No differentiation along territorial lines.
- *Unitary with regional sub-units*: A unitary organization that has created a number of regional branch organizations. The branches depend on the central organization for resources, staff, and direction. They do not have a separate constitution and members belong to the national body.
- *Unitary association with regional sub-units, one or more of which enjoys an enhanced status:* This status might involve the relevant sub-unit having responsibility for dealing on its own with related governments. In Canada, for example, some associations take this form with the special sub-units focusing on the Quebec government (Coleman, 1988). Similar phenomena occur also in Spain with respect to Catalonia (Solé, 1989).
- *Federal association*: Regional organizations have sufficient autonomy to be called associations in their own right. They employ their own staff, administer their own budgets, and may have their own constitution. Members, however, belong to the association as a whole and thus are simultaneously members of the regional and the national association. They pay one set of dues.
- *Confederal association*: This arrangement features territorial associations that are virtually independent in their own right. Their constitutions may differ significantly from that of the national/EU/ international association to which they belong. Distinct from federal associations, business belongs directly to the sub-territorial association and it is this latter organization, in turn, that belongs to the broader body. In short, the national/EU/international organization takes the form of a territorial peak association.
- *Affiliation arrangements*: Although independent organizations in their own right, these sub-territorial associations affiliate themselves to a related association with a more comprehensive territorial domain. This affiliation arrangement facilitates exchanges of information between the two organizations and perhaps occasional political cooperation. But the sub-territorial bodies do not 'belong' to the more comprehensive body nor are they subject in any way to its authority. Business persons or firms may choose to belong to one or both of these associations. Belonging to one does not bring any formal membership tie to the other, however, as in the confederal arrangement.
- *Independent sub-territorial associations*: This structure features a series of autonomous associations representing business from different parts of a space, but with no organizational ties to a more comprehensive territorial association, should one even exist.

This chapter reviews the various arrangements used by business in response to a need to operate in different constitutional and political 'spaces'. We draw conclusions, however, with considerable caution because it is difficult to separate out clearly the respective impacts of constitutional/political arrangements from those associated with the logic of membership. Where data are available that allow us to 'control' somewhat for logic of membership variables, we present them. Otherwise, our conclusions must take more the form of hypotheses at this stage. The chapter is organized into two major sections. First, we examine the 'logic of influence', the relationship between the constitutional features of states and patterns of territorial organization by business groups. Second, we consider the impact of the growing internationalization of public policy on the territorial organization of business interests.

Constitutional and political structures at the nation-state level

The political organization of territory by nation-states can be expected to have an influence on the organizational structures chosen by business in operating within those states. The difficulty empirically comes from distinguishing the effects of constitutional and political structures from those coming from logic of membership factors. We investigate the effects of political structures by first a comparative analysis of economic sectors across different types of state structures. This examination of federalist structures continues with a comparison of jurisdictional and functional federations. The section closes with a consideration of the likely impact of multi-level governance on the formation of regional associational systems.

Market structure and form of state

In beginning to look at the possible impact of different forms of state, we pose a simple hypothesis: the more responsibilities assumed by subnational governments in a political system, the more territorially differentiated will be the organization of business interests. Coleman (1988: 243) investigated this hypothesis. Drawing from data collected by the Organization of Business Interests research project, he examined the territorial organization of business interest systems in four countries: Canada, a jurisdictional federation; Switzerland, a jurisdictional federation; Germany, a functional federation; and the United Kingdom, a union state. He argued that Canada's provinces had cumulated the most responsibilities of these countries, followed by the Swiss cantons, the German Länder and the British regions. Thus the constitutional inducement to territorial differentiation in associations should have been greatest in Canada, followed by the other three countries in the order just described.

This hypothesis was put to test by examining the territorial organization of the principal business associations in six industrial sectors (red meat processing, fruit and vegetable processing, dairy processing, industrial chemicals, pharmaceuticals, and machine tools) and in the construction sector. The test was carried out by framing an alternative hypothesis: business associations are more likely to have differentiated territorial structures, the more their members are small rather than large firms, and serve local and regional markets rather than national/international markets.

The results of this initial look at associational structures are summarized in Table 10.1 and give much stronger support to the alternative

Table10.1   Forms of state and selected industrial sectors

Sector	United Kingdom	Germany	Switzerland	Canada
Large firms; national or international markets				
Red meat (GB,CDN)	1			1
Fruit and vegetable	1	1	1	4
Industrial chemicals	2	2	1	2
Pharmaceuticals	1	1	1	1
Small firms; national or international markets				
Machine tools	2.5	4.5	1	1
Large firms; local and regional markets				
Dairy processing	6	3.7	4	6
Small firms; local and regional markets				
Construction				
(exc. civil engineering)	3.7	5	5	5
Red meat (CH, D)		4.5	5	

Source: Adapted from Coleman (1988: 246). Based on an ordinal scale with unitary = 1, unitary with regional subunits = 2, unitary with (enhanced) regional sub-units = 3, federal = 4, confederal = 5, affiliate = 6. Some cells reflect the average score for several associations occupying the given domain.

hypothesis. It is clear that as one moves down the table for each country from the sectors with large firms and national/international markets that the level of territorial differentiation increased. The difference was particularly pronounced between the first of these categories and the other three. Firm size and market orientation have an obvious impact on the choice of business firms to form more territorially differentiated associations.

If we look within each sector and ask whether territorial differentiation varies by form of state, the evidence from these industrial sectors is very weak. These data would suggest that territorial differentiation of associations tended to be a response more to market structures than to political and constitutional arrangements. Before accepting this conclusion, however, it is useful to look in more detail at how a business sector fits into a given political system.

Table 10.2 presents data where we are able to place the given sector, banking, much more specifically into the political system. Five countries with different forms of state are used: Canada, Germany, France, the United Kingdom and the United States. Beginning with commercial banking, the banks that traditionally served large business and the industrial sector, we see that these banks in all five countries have the same market orientation: they tend to operate at the national and international levels. US banks are a partial exception in that there still exist some small banks with state charters that serve a more local area. In terms of policy arrangements, however, with the exception of the USA, all are regulated at the federal/national level. With market structure held somewhat more constant, then, we see differences in the territorial differentiation of the principal commercial banking associations. Those in the two most centralized states, France and Britain, have unitary structures, the Canadian Bankers Association has regional sub-units, the Bundesverband deutschen Banken a confederal structure, and the American Bankers Association affiliate arrangements with state banking associations.

Complementing this information, then, are related data for cooperative banks. In France and the UK, centralization of regulation appears to override some greater regionalization in market structure, again yielding unitary associations. In Canada, where regulatory responsibilities lie at the provincial level, we end up with highly differentiated arrangements that contrast sharply with the commercial banks' association. The US system shows some similarities with the Canadian, except the stronger federal regulatory presence appears to favor slightly less territorial differentiation. Germany again appears as an anomaly with its confederal arrangement. We come back to a possible

Table 10.2 Forms of states and banking associations

	Canada	Germany	France	United Kingdom	United States
Form of state	Jurisdictional federation	Functional federation	Unitary	Union	Jurisdictional federation
Commercial banking[1]					
Regulatory authority	Federal	Federal	National	National	Shared
Market orientation	National/international	National/international	National/international	National/international	State/national/international
Association structure	Unitary with regional subunits	Confederal	Unitary	Unitary	Affiliate
Cooperative banks[2]					
Regulatory authority	Mainly provincial	Federal	National	National	Concurrent
Market orientation	Provincial	Regional/national	Regional/national	National/regional	Regional
Association structure	Affiliate	Confederal	Unitary	Unitary	Confederal

Notes:
[1] Definition of commercial banking is drawn from Coleman (1996). The principal association representing commercial banks is retained for the analysis.
[2] These vary from country to country. Credit unions are the focus in Canada and the US, Volks- and Raiffeisenbanken in Germany, Banques mutuelles including Crédit agricole in France, building societies in the UK.
Source: Data collected by the authors.

explanation for this when we discuss below the likely different impacts of jurisdictional and functional federations.

Coleman (1988: 242) presents one additional set of information that cautions us to be sensitive to how the domain of a business interest association fits into the political regime. Looking at 'nationally relevant' associations in Canada, he classified these as to whether they came principally under federal jurisdiction, under jurisdictions shared between the federal and provincial governments, and principally under provincial jurisdiction. An average score for the level of differentiation for the associations under each of these categories was computed using the scale in Table 10.1. Those under primarily federal jurisdiction had a score of 1.25, thus close to the unitary mode, those under shared jurisdiction a score of 3.56, thus tending slightly to the federal structure, and those under provincial jurisdiction only a score of 3.00. These latter data may not be as reliable because Coleman's decision to focus on 'nationally relevant' associations means that the sample of provincial level associations is far from complete. For the first two categories, however, primarily federal versus shared jurisdiction, associations did appear to respond with more differentiated structures when their focus had to include both levels of government.

In short, there appear to be some data to suggest that business associations take on higher levels of territorial differentiation when they are working in federal systems where responsibilities bearing on their members are divided between levels of government.

Types of federalism and business interests

In both Tables 10.1 and 10.2, we saw German associations taking on structures that were confederal or close to confederal when we might have expected less territorial differentiation. The German machine tools sector is a world leader in exports and its commercial banks are among the strongest in the world. Over the past quarter century, cooperative banks have integrated their operations in ways that allow them to operate as fully national institutions with growing international ties as well. For the two banking groups, the federal government is clearly the dominant regulator. Given its key export position, machine tools attracts a lot of interest from federal trade and economics ministries. All of these factors would favor more unitary arrangements, but the German associations possess rather high levels of territorial differentiation. This finding directs us to consider whether the type of federalism found in a country might have varying implications for territorial differentiation.

In the analysis thus far, we have focused on the relationship between the degree of cumulation of responsibilities by sub-national governments and territorial differentiation of associations. While useful, this variable does not capture the varying types of divisions of labor between national and sub-national governments in federal systems. Students of federalism have developed a number of concepts to distinguish among the several types of federations. In a dictionary of concepts of federalism, Stewart (1984) identified no fewer than 497 adjectives that are used in the literature to characterize federations! Clearly, this number does not imply that there are close to 500 different types of federations, because Elazar (1995: 15) identifies only 21 federal countries in the world!

We have a particular interest in the distinction between what might be called jurisdictional and functional federations. In a jurisdictional federation, responsibilities are divided between national and subnational governments based on jurisdiction. For example, one level, usually the national level, may have jurisdiction over defense, while another level, usually the subnational level, will have responsibility for education. Responsibility here includes the full range of policy functions – policy design, policy formulation, and implementation and administration of policies. The Australian, US and Canadian federations come closest to this model.

In contrast, in a functional federation, the responsibilities are divided between the national and subnational governments by function rather than policy field. Thus the national level has responsibility for policy design and formulation across all or most policy fields and the subnational level is charged with the administration and implementation of these policies. German federalism tends toward this model, although the Länder do have a few responsibilities of their own. Johnson (1973: 105) writes: 'It is clear that the division of legislative competence under the Basic Law confers the bulk of responsibility for law-making, and *a fortiori* for policy-making in the broadest sense, on the federal authorities. The Länder have effectively a residual competence and their more or less exclusive powers are by subtraction concentrated in three spheres: education (up to university level), police, and the general framework of local government.' In certain key policy sectors such as agriculture, the European Union also operates closer to the functional federalist model (Scharpf, 1988).

Whether or not business associations are operating in a functional or a jurisdictional federation appears to have an impact on their level of territorial differentiation. Generally speaking, in a functional federa tion, it will be less common for business to be able to confine political activity to one level of government. Business associations will normally be very interested in both the policy formulation and the administrative aspects of the policy fields that touch their members. For example, banking policy in Germany is formulated by the federal finance ministry and an associated regulatory agency, the Bundesaufsichtsamt für das Kreditwesen. These policies are administered, however, by branches of the central bank that operate at the Land level, the Landeszentralbanken. Similarly, although the machine tools sector might be very interested in the broad lines of industrial, regional, research and development, and training policies formulated in Bonn and Berlin, they will perhaps be even more interested in how these policies are delivered by the Land governments. Hence, they have an incentive to be highly active and attentive to both levels of government.

Some circumstances in jurisdictional federations will provide incentives like those in functional federations, but others will not. Students of these federations often use the colorful terms, 'marble cake' and 'layer cake' to distinguish between two modes of operation (see Elazar, 1994: 133–41). In the marble-cake situation, both levels of government cooperate and share policy formulation and administration responsibilities in a policy area. Such a mode of operation was quite common and important in the Canadian federation between 1945 and 1965 when the federal government and the provinces cooperated to put in place the core elements of the Canadian welfare state (Simeon and Robinson, 1991). In the USA, the various categorical grants established by the Johnson administration in the 1960s provide a classic example. As in Canada, these categorical grants were the product of an increased fiscal capacity of the federal government following the Second World War. With the federal government willing to play a leadership role and the states being accepting of that role, US federalism was partially and temporarily modified by alleviating the 'concern with the legalistic and constitutional division of governmental responsibilities and functions' (Lazlovich, 1993: 189).

In contrast, in the layer-cake mode, responsibilities are more sharply confined to one level of government or the other. Resistance by Quebec in the 1950s and 1960s led the Canadian federal government to gradually abandon conditional grants. More recently, suffering under serious fiscal pressures, the federal government has offloaded many responsibilities to the provinces. Similarly, in the USA, when Reagan took office in 1981, he proclaimed a 'new federalism' whose main thrust was a massive devolution of responsibilities to the states (Beer, 1995: 226). This shift was to be achieved through general cuts in federal grants as well as through the transfer of monies from categorical grants to block grants. Despite the fact that new federalism was to serve a government expenditure reduction agenda rather than being an end in itself, it is generally recognized that it increased the autonomy of sub-national governments (Wolman, 1988: 429). The newly elected Republican majority in Congress in 1994 took up a similar cry in its Contract with America, again seeking to devolve new monies and responsibilities to state governments.

As policy areas in these jurisdictional federations return to the more classic layer cake or 'separate-houses' model, the incentives for territorial differentiation for business diminish. The more responsibilities for a policy sector are confined to one level of government in a federation, the less strong the incentives for territorial differentiation. As Table 10.2 shows, for example, where both policy formulation and implementation are the responsibilities of the federal government in Canada, there is little incentive from the political structure to differentiate by territory for Canadian commercial banks. Contrary incentives exist for their counterparts in the jurisdictional US federation.

In summary, there is good reason to expect that the type of federalism in place in a country is a variable affecting the degree of territorial differentiation in business associations. Even here, however, the analysis must be sensitive to variations across policy areas within broader types of federations. In jurisdictional federations, both marble cake and layer cake scenarios may coexist but in different policy areas, with varying implications for territorial differentiation of associations. And, in functional federations, some policy areas may be confined to one level of government only.

Federalism and regional associational systems

Thus far, the analysis has focused on the structural characteristics of individual business interest associations. There is another dimension of the organization of business interests that should also be considered: the structures of business *associational systems*. Similar to individual associations, the structures of business associational systems may be distinguished by their degree of integration and differentiation (Streeck and Schmitter, 1985; Coleman and Grant, 1988; Coleman, 1990). The analysis of system integration normally focuses on the presence or absence of comprehensive peak associations and on the relationships between these peak associations and their member associations. System differentiation may concern function – for example, many countries have separate associational systems for employment and industrial relations issues (employer associations) and for other political and economic questions (trade associations). Of course, system differentiation might also take on a territorial or spatial dimension.

When one considers why business associations from a variety of different economic sectors might integrate their activities under the umbrella of a subnational territorial peak association, logic of influence factors would seem to be much more important than the logic of membership. Coleman (1987: 182) and Coleman and Jacek (1989) have hypothesized that the development of integrated associational systems within particular territories of a nation-state is more likely in federations than in unitary states. These subnational associational systems may take on a variety of functions (Coleman and Jacek, 1989; Schmitter and Lanzalaco, 1989). They may promote national market integration in the face of autarkic interests by subnational governments, with Switzerland providing a good example (Kriesi and Farago, 1989). Or they may promote market balkanization through pressure on the subnational government as sometimes occurs in Canada (Cairns, 1986; Thorburn, 1985) and in Spain (Solé, 1989). They may seek to compensate for the activities of subnational governments by promoting support for the national government. Or they may act to thwart the attempts of national governments to promote greater market integration and to reduce internal barriers to trade. Depending on which of these functions is more important, these subnational associational systems may be integrated, in turn, into comprehensive and integrated national associational systems (Switzerland, Germany). Or they may exist as subnational associational systems that function virtually independently of national associational systems – the common finding in Canada and the USA (Coleman, 1990).

The development of powerful subnational associational systems appears to occur primarily in federations. No such systems exist in the United Kingdom, France, or in the more centralized smaller European states of Sweden and The Netherlands. The logic favoring such subnational associational systems when translated into the European Union would suggest that their functional equivalents, national peak associations like the Confederation of British Industry, the Bundesverband deutscher Industrie, the Conseil National du Patronat Français, and Confindustria in Italy should have retained their importance despite growing economic integration in the Community. Certainly, there is scant evidence that these peak associations have gone into decline; if anything, they are more active than ever, usually opening their own offices in Brussels (van Schendelen, 1994). Systematic, significant territorial differentiation in government structures begets a parallel response in the structure of the *associational systems* of business.

Internationalized policy-making and territorial organization

Business firms find themselves increasingly in situations where they must operate outside the often familiar domestic policy arena at a supranational level. Admittedly, these pressures are not new; after all, international trade negotiations which affect vitally business interests have been frequent since the end of the Second World War. Processes of regional economic integration such as those that have led to the development of the European Union, the North America Free Trade Agreement, and the Asia Pacific Economic Cooperation Council (APEC) have added to the international concerns of business. What is new for business is that these international policy exercises have become increasingly frequent and more institutionalized. Evidently not all supranational policy-making has become as institutionalized as in the EU, but the development of what international relations scholars call 'international regimes' does indicate that institutionalization has gone on quietly for some time across a broad range of policy areas.

The degree of institutionalization of supranational governance will obviously affect how business organizes itself into associations. Where institutionalization has progressed further as in the EU, then we can expect and to find that business has set up associations that are devoted primarily to political action directed at the supranational institutions. Where institutionalization has progressed less, business may continue to rely on national-level groups, individual firm lobbying, and on *ad hoc* alliances set up to respond to a single, but key problem at the supranational level.

The impact of internationalization on the territorial differentiation of business associations is difficult to assess at this stage. Based on the European Union example, many new supranational associations appear to take on either the confederal or the affiliate form. Greenwood and Ronit (1994) add, however, that in new sectors where associative action is less developed at the national level and supranational (EU) institutions have a strong governance role, collective action can take a range of forms including highly unitary structures. They stress that policy structures will vary significantly across issue areas.

Hence we might expect to find over time the same plurality of approaches to territorial differentiation at the supranational level that we have described as existing on the national plane.

The significant rise in importance of supranational policy-making will also have an impact on the level of territorial differentiation retained by national-level associations. Existing theoretical work and casual empirical observation suggest that incentives will be high for national associations to become more integrated across territory as policy-making becomes more international. Risse-Kappen's recent work (1995a, 1995b) is helpful for elaborating this hypothesis, because it draws together domestic political structures and supranational policy-making. In his analysis of the EU, he distinguishes between two modes of policy-making, intergovernmental bargaining and multilevel governance.

The former refers to decision processes where policies are made through negotiations, usually by heads of state, with little further involvement by specific supranational institutions. Here the game for business associations is relatively straightforward. They seek to have their national governments take a position as close to their own as is feasible, they may cooperate with associations from other states whose members' interests are similar to their own, and they or some of their members may engage in some classic no holds barred lobbying during the negotiations. In order to play this game well, associations will need to be cohesive and single-minded. If members break ranks, particularly along regional lines, some politicians will move quickly to exploit such divisions. Over time, if intergovernmental bargaining at a supranational level becomes regularized in a policy area, national-level associations that continue to be involved in related policy advocacy will experience strong incentives to reduce internal differentiation by territory in order to enhance their effectiveness.

We hypothesize also that multilevel governance will have a similar effect. Multilevel governance refers to situations where 'private, governmental, transnational and supranational actors deal with each other in highly complex networks of varying density, as well as horizontal and vertical depth' (Risse-Kappen, 1995a: 64). Thus decision-making is not restricted to one set of actors (heads of state) working at the supranational and national levels as is suggested by Putnam's (1988) two-level games model and Moravcsik's (1993) liberal intergovernmentalist model. Rather, it is shared both by governmental and non-governmental actors, drawn from regional, national and supranational levels. In these situations, the game becomes more complex for national-level business associations. Not only might they find themselves working politically with government actors drawn from different levels and from various countries, but also with other associations, some representing business, some not, also drawn from differing political levels (Grande, 1996; Kohler-Koch, 1996a).

Important for our analysis in this chapter, Risse-Kappen relates the likelihood of multilevel governance and the involvement of transnational and transgovernmental actors to domestic political structures. He hypothesizes that the more fragmented are domestic political institutions and the more these are buttressed by relatively strong societal interests, the more likely the interlocking politics of multilevel governance becomes. If we follow on this hypothesis with the assumption that federalist regimes foster more fragmented domestic politics than other more unitary regimes, then we can expect that such regimes will also create more openings for multilevel governance. Accordingly, business associations may have special opportunities to participate in supranational policy-making if their home country has a federal constitution.

If this analysis is correct, then we would expect that domestic-level business associations operating in federal systems may feel considerable pressure to lower the level of territorial differentiation in their own organizations. As more unified actors, they should be better placed to take advantage of the lack of cohesion in their own national political system to carry on politics through various alliances with other actors at the supranational level. In contrast, if they themselves remain fragmented, multilevel governance becomes less likely and policy stalemate may follow as the worst case outcome.

Risse-Kappen (1995a: 70–2; 1995b: 286–7) adds one other observation that implies that multilevel governance will place a premium on association cohesion. In intergovernmental bargaining, policy actors engage in instrumental action, driven primarily by self-interest. In contrast, multilevel governance lends itself more readily to communicative action based on the development and acceptance of common norms and understandings of policy problems. Rather than simply being aware of your own self-interest, communicative action requires those involved in the policy process to have a certain base of knowledge and expertise they can share with other actors in the policy network. They need to be able to enter into a process of value-sharing and problem-solving (Kohler-Koch ,1996a: 369–70; Scharpf, 1989). Both of these requirements are again likely to push associations to act cohesively as an integrated organization, perhaps at the expense of territorial differentiation.

In summary, whether domestic-level business associations become involved in intergovernmental processes or multilevel governance at the supranational level, we expect them to accentuate internal integration at the expense of territorial differentiation. Both situations would appear to favor more strongly those associations that can draw on internal expertise and that can speak with one, clear, voice. As Kohler-Koch (1996: 368) notes, 'Interest groups that are weaker in terms of resources and heterogeneous outlook suffer because there is no longer "the" point of access for efficient lobbying.' She adds (1996b: 218) that big business involved in international markets may be best placed to develop a unified position and that their status as 'trend setters' may enhance further their access to the Commission. If all of these observations are correct, we should find that national associations in settings like the European Union, particularly in federal states following Risse-Kappen, should have become more, rather than less, integrated over the past three decades. This expectation appears to be met in Irish agricultural policy-making circles (Smith, 1996). In the wake of such a process, analysts might also investigate whether this centralization process in national-level associations leaves the door open to the formation of new, renegade groups at the subnational level.

Conclusion

This chapter suggests that the view of space held by business firms will affect critically how much importance they given to spatial boundaries in their associations. Thinking of the logic of membership, business firms that are larger and that operate in national and international markets tend to organize groups of similar scope with relatively little attention to smaller territorial subdivisions. The political and constitutional structure also has an impact on the importance given to territory in business associations. This impact, however, is not obvious and requires fairly detailed understanding of how the policy areas of interest to a given set of business firms fit into political structures. We unearthed some evidence that suggests that federal regimes are more likely to induce territorial differentiation in associations. This likelihood is higher in functional federations than jurisdictional federations. In jurisdictional federations, territorial differentiation becomes more pronounced when policy areas are shared or competed for by both levels of government.

Whatever the traditional view of territory might have been, the internationalization of many key policy domains promises to force business associations to question that view. In their analysis of the European Union, Streeck and Schmitter (1991) note the big change that occurs when groups move from the settled corporatism in some domestic policy arenas to the unsettled, 'competitive federalism' at the supranational level. By definition, once drawn into political action at a level beyond the nation-state, associations will look back on their view of politics with the kind of changed perspective that the astronauts had when they first gazed on earth from several hundred miles out in space. This perspective, we suggest, will push many associations to redefine how spatial divisions are reflected in their organizational structures. As they do, can it be so surprising then that globalization is associated with new voices expressing the views and the resistance of regions within states and of localities within regions (Held, 1991).

11
Global Order and Local Collective Action: The Case of Milan Business Interest Associations

Luca Lanzalaco and Elisabetta Gualmini[1]

The internationalization of markets and politics – globalization – represents a significant challenge for the social sciences. It has led, for instance, to a change in the perspectives of analysis in international relations theory (Keohane and Nye, 1972, Rosenau, 1980), in democratic theory (Burnheim, 1986; Held, 1991, 1995) and in the study of capitalism itself (Amin, 1996). Whilst both political interdependence and commercial transactions across national borders have always characterized the modern state and the capitalist system (Wallerstein, 1974), what is new about the contemporary global system are some of the characteristics of this political and economic interrelatedness. These include: the increasing role of financial capital and its dominance over productive capital; the spread of interconnectedness beyond the borders of the economy and politics into new fields, such as technological, cultural and communication dimensions; the astonishing quantitative diffusion of transnational and international regimes, organizations and institutions aimed at global governance, and a consequent loss of national sovereignty.[2] These changes have in turn created their own research agenda.

Such developments are likely to have an impact on the logics of business interest organization and representation. The process of globalization dramatically alters the conditions of competition and relationships between firms, modifies their opportunities for affecting the political regulation of economic activity, and arouses demand for new types of services from small and medium-sized firms. In general, business interest associations (BIAs) have to cope with these transformations by acquiring new functions and restructuring their organization at different levels of associability. The aim of this chapter is to assess the impact of the process of globalization at the local level by analyzing what BIAs have done in Milan, a large industrial city in Italy widely involved in the process of globalization, during recent years. In the next section our analytical framework will be sketched out and the reasons for focusing our attention on business collective action at the local level will be clarified. The following two sections will be devoted to illustrating and discussing the results of the empirical research, and in the last one some tentative conclusions will be drawn regarding the linkage between global order and local collective action.

Logics of associability, types of firms and levels of analysis

According to Schmitter and Streeck (1981), the organization of BIAs may be conceptualized as a compromise among four competing 'logics' of associability. The logic of membership leads to associative structures that reflect the preferences and characteristics of members. The logic of influence tends to produce more unitary and encompassing structures in response to the demands and traits of their public and private interlocutors. The logics of goal formation, and implementation, determine the association's response to the political problem of efficaciously aggregating member preferences into a relatively coherent programme, and to the administrative problem of scale in efficiently delivering a mix of public, selective, monopolistic, and solidaristic goods and services.

In the light of this framework, we may expect that capitalists, facing internationally integrated markets and transnational mechanisms of governance (for example, international regimes), develop strategies designed to help them adapt. They choose to go on 'experimenting with the scale' of their collective action – as they have been during the last two centuries (Lanzalaco, 1992) – trying also to 'globalize' their associative structures. But this adaptive reaction is not the only one; we may also conceive of a more 'strategic' type of behavior. Instead of adapting the scale of their associative action to the increasing scale of markets and politics, capitalists could be prone to react inversely to these trends, choosing to strengthen – or, more generally, to rely on – national or local structures. There are at least two reasons for this latter course.[3] Firstly, well consolidated structures are better equipped to provide the services and advice needed to compete on the global market. Secondly, the ability of firms to cope with global competition depends to a large extent on public goods such as services and infra-structures which are locally supplied, and this makes political represen-tation vis à vis local authorities very important. Furthermore, these services and goods become crucial to the extent that the globalization of markets and production affects mainly the producer interests of cap-italists rather than their class interests (Streeck, 1988; Lanzalaco and Schmitter, 1992). In sum, the inability to control the transnational political and economic arenas, and the related erosion of state sovereignty and policy capability, might be 'compensated' for by an increasing attention to local dynamics.[4]

These speculations are strengthened if we take into consideration the deep differences which exist among firms of different size. The process of globalization is often seen in relation to the role of multinational corporations, conceived as economic agents able to coordinate their strategies, to (de)localize productive plants and to move financial capital across national borders (Martinelli, 1991). However the internationalization of markets not only affects these active 'globalizer' firms, but also a much greater number of firms that are passive 'market-takers'. These 'market-takers' – small and medium-sized firms (SMEs) – are increasingly led to produce and compete in a global market which they are compelled to accept as given, even if they would prefer more limited (and less uncertain) markets. SMEs, which must be taken into consideration not only because they are much more numerous than the multinational ones, but also because many national economies are based on them, are more dependent on local conditions for being able to compete, if not to survive, under the hard pressure of global competition.

Even if the main effects of globalization shift the sites of economic and political decision-making beyond national borders, and make the location (nation, region, area) of firms insignificant for their strategies, it remains that since firms always compete on the same global market, many businesses engaged in economic transactions with distant coun-tries are dependent on 'domestic' conditions as regards their competi-tiveness and success on global markets. These 'domestic' conditions are likely to be localized rather than state-level, to the extent that the process of globalization tends to erode the sovereignty and policy capabilities of nation-states. As such, we shall focus our attention upon the local prerequisites of global competition in the next sections of the chapter.

Milan BIAs responding to transnational regimes

The presence of BIAs in the city of Milan is particularly concentrated and at the same time capillary. At least eight BIAs are the most important territorial associations representing big industrial firms, small- and medium-sized industrial firms, artisan firms, trade and service companies. In some cases these BIAs promote different political orientations. Each association is organized into sectoral categories, which in Milan often number over a hundred. Milan BIAs also interact with three other groups of associations: national BIAs, either territorial or sectoral, whose base is in Milan; foreign chambers of commerce, of which there are 28 in 1996; and second-level organizations regrouping territorial associations sharing special initiatives or similar intents (see Table 11.1).

It is therefore not surprising, given such an associative network, that Milan is called 'Europe's door', and, since the export-led recovery of the 1960s, has been considered the chief seat of international trade in

Table 11.1   Milan business interest associations (BIAs) analysed

Territorial BIAs (provincial level)
- Assolombarda, Milan association of industry
- Camera di commercio di Milano, Milan chamber of commerce
- API, Milan association of small- and medium-sized firms
- Unione commercianti, Milan association of commercial firms
- Confartigianato di Milano, Milan association of artisan firms
- CNA, Milan association of artisan firms

National sectoral BIAs (seated in Milan)
- Federchimica, the national association of Italian chemistry
- ANIMA, the national association of Italian mechanic industry
- UCIMU, the national association for Italian machine tools

Peak BIAs (seated in Milan)
First order association:
- ANCE, the national association for foreign trade
Second order association:
- Centro estero delle camere lombarde, Foreign Centre of Lombardy Chambers[*]

[*] Italian chambers of commerce are not private associations, but public organizations, being the provincial decentralized units of the Ministry of Industry, where all commercial and industrial companies are bound to enroll as a member. We nonetheless consider them within the BIAs because they perform the same functions and, above all, they are particularly active in the domain of internationalization services.

Italy. In 1995, 17 per cent of Italian direct investments in foreign countries were promoted by Milan companies, and 21 per cent of Italian participation in foreign companies could be attributed to Milan SMEs. The same figures would have respectively grown to 33 per cent and 36 per cent if we had considered Lombardy (CCIAA, 1996).[5]

If, from the 1960s to the 1990s, firms engaged in increasing exports and developing networks of distribution abroad to the extent of commercial and productive joint ventures, in order to face the pressing European integration process and the opening of world markets, the same is not true for BIAs. BIAs reacted to the globalization of markets (that is, to the deep changes and transformations of their member firms) with delay and ambiguity. It was not until the 1980s, soon after the EC directives on Euro-Info Centers (which in Italy were mainly established within organized interests), and definitively in the 1990s, after the introduction of the European common market and the export boom (due to the strong devaluation of the lira) that BIAs were urged to react and to redefine their role and their activities.

On the basis of our research work conducted in Milan during 1996, the relationship between globalization and BIAs appears to be characterized by two different elements. On the one hand, by the gradual disruption of national and local boundaries in favor of alliances and cooperations with foreign associations; on the other by the acquisition of new tasks in order to deal with the new exigencies and claims of the membership. Such a process, still in progress and consequently still not well-defined, has developed through successive sequences, with different implications respectively for territorial and sectoral organizations.

The first step taken by the BIAs, dating back to the 1980s, has been the widening of interest representation through the establishment of representation offices abroad. The main intention was to strengthen the opportunities for lobbying on European decision making processes and to increase the visibility and image of Milan associations abroad. Of the eight largest territorial associations examined, all have established an office in Brussels, either on their own or together with the national association. Milan Chamber of Commerce has recently installed ten representation offices in Russia, one in Brazil and one in New York. Assolombarda has recently promoted the so-called 'Japan, China and India desks', targeted to solicit exchanges, cooperation and joint ventures between those countries and Italian firms. All the other associations have organized at least two annual employers' missions to the ASEAN and NAFTA countries, which have resulted in arranging commercial and productive collaborations involving on average 15 per cent of the total member firms.

The national territorial and sectoral associations based in Milan are part of the international organizations that have become the official reference for EC opportunity programmes and financing. To mention one example, the National Association for Italian Machine Tools (UCIMU) obtained the financial resources to establish a base in India where Italian, German, French and Spanish officers worked in shifts to encourage transnational commercial cooperation in 1994. This was largely due to continuous pressure of its international association CECIMO.

The extension of interest representation that has gradually caused the restructuring of national and local boundaries has involved both sectoral and territorial associations. But it is more the competence of territorial associations to be responsible for representation exchanges, public relations and foreign partnerships, whereas sectoral associations tend to intervene once collaborations already exist but need to be implemented.

The second step, for which the widening of interest representation was the premise, has been the introduction of new activities, such as services supply for internationalization, and globalization processes support. Within the wide field of services allocation, we can distinguish among services for export support, Euro-Info Centers, and services for transnational collaborations support. Services for export mainly comprise tributary and customs assistance. This kind of basic consultancy is provided by all the associations in Milan. Some organizations, such as ANIMA, the National Association for Italian Mechanics, have promoted special institutes for product quality certification. Federchimica, the National Association for Italian Chemistry, has recently developed a special project with ICE, the National Public Institute for Foreign Trade, by 'borrowing' an officer from Rome who is directly responsible for the bureaucratic duties connected to the export legislation.

Euro-Info Centers were introduced by the European Community in 1987. They provide firms with three kinds of information. Firstly, information about EC financial opportunities, especially dealing with technology transfer and innovation projects, structural funds, and cooperation among companies. The second type of information is about EC legislation, which at present mainly concerns product quality and technical norms, security in the workplace, and environmental policies. The third kind concerns information products, such as newsletters, special magazines, and internet home pages, to facilitate reciprocal and regular communication lines with employers. In Milan, only the Chamber of Commerce and the Association of Industrial Firms have their own Euro-Info Center. The Association of Commercial Firms makes reference to its Euro-Info Center located in Rome, whilst all the other interest organizations have at least an office or one person responsible for EC policies.

Services supporting collaboration are the most advanced ones. They provide consultancy and promotion of partnerships with foreign companies through the organization of missions and of fairs, targeted to select the right partners and to give rise to opportunities for business. These services, unlike the others, require a contribution from firms, and are provided with higher intensity by sectoral organizations, which, being more in contact with businessmen and managers, claim to better know the technical and practical needs of companies approaching world markets. In fact, with regard to service supply, the division of labor between territorial and sectoral levels is quite clear. Territorial associations tend to offer general services, that is basic and transversal, such as seminars on foreign countries and EC policies assistance. Sectoral associations, however, are more inclined to offer specific services, that is technical support up to the end of the business. This division of labour is also a consequence of the fact that sectoral organizations do not trust common initiatives with territorial associations, partly because they fear losing their specific know how, and partly because they consider territorial associations less qualified in the field of technical assistance.

The increasing success, according to the opinions of people interviewed for this research, of services for support of internationalization, needs to be placed in the context of the overall activities of BIAs. If we look at the data presented in Table 11.2, the positive trend claimed by the associations still seems to be very limited.

The majority of firms that benefit from the so-called 'global services', even though aggregate data does not allow us to distinguish the kind of service, do not belong to Milan BIA networks. Only at the Assolombarda, the Association of Industry, do 54 per cent of the member firms profit by the new opportunities. Table 11.2 clearly points out that in the associations representing small companies the percentage of firms asking for services for support of internationalization is very low, ranging from 10 to 30 per cent. In addition, in almost all these associations, except for the Chamber of Commerce, a separate budget item for the new tasks does not exist. It is national territorial and sectoral organizations that play the dominant role. The

Table 11.2   Firms asking for internationalization support services

	Total membership	% of firms asking for services
Milan Association of Industry (Assolombarda)	4 700	54
Chamber of Commerce (Camera di commercio)	300 000	10
Milan Association of Commercial Firms (Unione commercianti)	50 000	30
Milan Association of Small- and Medium-sized Firms (API)	2 300	33
National Association for Foreign Trade (ANCE)	600	60
National Association of Italian Chemistry (Federchimica)	1 300	10
National Association of Italian Machine tools (UCIMU)	220	54
National Association of Italian Mechanic Industry (ANIMA)	1 000	50

Source: Statistical information given during personal interviews.

National Association for Foreign Trade, the National Association for Italian Machine Tools and the National Association of Italian Mechanic Industry offer their services to more than a half of their membership (60, 54 and 50 per cent respectively).

Two factors therefore seem to be connected to the diffusion of global services: the size of the firm and the kind of productive sector. Large companies show a structurally higher propensity to internationalize, mainly due to the availability of financial resources and of qualified human resources; productive sectors that were originally conceived with a strong export vocation (like the Italian mechanic sector) show more experience and a greater consolidation in foreign markets.

The inner contradictions of globalization

The process of globalization that has hitherto characterized world market economies has had important consequences for the structure and strategic behavior of employers' associations. BIAs are required to reinterpret their role and to reestablish a new equilibrium between global and local exigencies. On the one hand they strongly feel the need to respond flexibly to the transformations of their membership, for which globalization is already an overhanging reality; on the other hand it becomes more and more important for them, precisely for reasons of globalization, to compensate for the collapsing of territorial identity, and to redefine their national, regional and local ties such that members may strongly recognize them.

This is particularly relevant for Italian BIAs, whose structural characteristics have been traditionally marked by localism, fragmentation, weak coordination and an incapacity to develop long-term unitary actions (Martinelli and Treu, 1884; Lanzalaco, 1990: 104; 1993: 113–5). The key question is, therefore, whether global challenges have allowed associations to implement new strategies and to discover new solutions for old problems, or if they have simply emphasized traditional weaknesses.

From the data we have analyzed, it is difficult to answer this question in a unilateral way. The process of globalization figures out as a very contradictory phenomenon. There are at least three different dilemmas that BIAs need to balance: the trade-off between globalization and localism, the contrasting exigencies of large and small-sized firms, and the role of the new activities performed, in comparison with core activities.

Globalism vs localism

As for the first dilemma, it is true that cooperation between Milan BIAs and foreign associations, as well as the growing importance of international organizations, have encouraged higher interdependence. The number of contacts and the occasions for business have multiplied; but this international interdependence has also had opposite effects.[6] That is, it has not transformed itself into a national interdependence, soliciting more unitary and coherent strategies at the national and local level; on the contrary it has reinforced localism and fragmentation. It is easier for BIAs to keep in contact and develop joint programmes with foreign associations than with other Italian associations, which continue to be viewed as the main competitors.

This is particularly evident in the case of service supply. Similar services intersect and overlap, because each association tends to develop its specific service know-how. The cleavage between sectoral and territorial associations is particularly strong. Vertical (that is, sectoral) associations believe that service distribution is their own task, due to their being directly in contact with firms, and having therefore the possibility to specialize. Contrary to this, territorial associations, also facing the incipient crisis of representation functions, have increasingly invested in internationalization services, considering them to be a profitable opportunity for associative marketing. This means higher segmentation and higher redundancy. Services are modeled to appeal to faithful members, reflecting the very local characteristics of the association where they are distributed.

Big vs medium and small-sized firms

In addition, the process of globalization has produced an ambiguous relationship between the associations and their member firms. At the end of the 1980s and in the first years of the 1990s, because of the associations' delay and inertia in responding to the new challenge, the relationships with companies which promptly reacted to transnational regimes substantially loosened. Big companies in particular were inclined to bypass the associative level. Starting from 1993–94, links became tighter with large firms that decided to try the new services offered by the associations, and with small companies that were unable to exploit the new opportunities on their own, though manifesting the intent to do so.

Nonetheless, since we are observing a phenomenon still at its very beginning, the weaknesses of these small firms have, in a sort of isomorphic process, become the weaknesses of their interest associations. The lack of both financial and human resources, the oppressive bureaucratic duties and the cultural constraints are mentioned both by employers and by their associations as the main hindrances to internationalization.

It is worthwhile to consider these constraints. The lack of financial resources is generally attributed to the difficulty in obtaining loans from banks which tend to privilege bigger firms. Only recently has the National Association of Commercial Firms (Confcommercio) promoted a special agreement with the Ambrosiano-Veneto bank to provide easier credit for SMEs. The blocking of the Ossola law in 1995, (which has now been removed), including financial facilities for export plans, worsened the situation. The lack of human resources is explained in two different ways: the difficulty in hiring people especially qualified to implement internationalization projects; and the quantitative lack of personnel inside small firms. From the results of an inquiry sponsored by Anima, 63 per cent of the difficulties highlighted by companies regarding their efforts to internationalize lay in the lack of adequate human resources. Training and vocational courses, according to employers, are not likely to resolve the problem. Another disadvantage that companies highlight is the huge number of bureaucratic duties companies have to fulfill to obtain the licenses and authorizations for export and for commercial joint ventures. According to the employers, public institutes for foreign commerce and insurance suffer the typical bureaucratic inefficiencies (delays and formalism) and are unable to respond to the firm's contingent needs. The culture of localism is mentioned as the last drawback, very deeply rooted in the history of associations: small firms are accustomed to developing their commercial strategies inside Italy; outwith Italy, the European market, particularly Germany and France, accounts for more than 80 per cent of their exports.

These lock-in effects that small companies have to get through in order to face open markets have combined, and have diminished the pressure on their associations to respond to transnational regimes.

New services vs core activities

The third contradiction, connected to globalization, concerns the very nature of 'global' tasks. According to the people we have interviewed, the difficulties met by BIAs in developing activities for internationalization support lay in the nature of those very functions. Globalization support activities are still not perceived as strategic when compared to core activities, such as collective bargaining. Companies, particularly bigger ones, can easily choose to bypass associations, since there exists no system of specific constraints that bind the membership. Moreover, competition in the field of services is very intense, considering that companies can address themselves directly to public institutes or to private consultants.

Coming back to our key question, it is therefore possible to conclude that globalization has not, up to now, given rise to a full reorientation of the associative role and tasks, since it is still perceived as a process concerning the periphery of the associative system and not its very center. Whether global services and global representation are about to become core functions within Milan BIAs, potentially able to substitute the old ones and to introduce important innovations on the association's structural features, it is probably still too early to say.

Concluding remarks about globalization, scale and the associative order

Of course, a case study is not sufficient either to corroborate or to falsify an hypothesis; what it may help to do is to explore new interpretative hypotheses that can be applied to new case studies. This is what we shall tentatively seek to do in this section.

From the case study of Milan it clearly emerges that the process of globalization has had an impact – even if not as deep as we should expect to find – upon BIAs at the local level. It has led to changes more in the functions accomplished by the associations than in the structure of the associative system. However, the main point is that this impact has not been clear and univocal, rather, intrinsically contradictory. The collective challenge of globalization has not motivated unitary and inclusive forms of collective action to cope with the 'common enemy' (other national economies, other sectors, other firms). On the contrary, it has brought about competition and attrition between and within associations: tensions between territorial and sectoral associations, between local, national and transnational associations, between different types of functions within associations and between small and large sized firms.

The impact of globalization seems to have increased the problems of 'representative dissonance' (Schmitter and Lanzalaco, 1988) and to have given rise to centrifugal forces, reducing the internal coherence of associative relationships at the national and local level. No clear trend is easily identifiable: globalization breeds transnational associative structures but it also involves local associative levels; it requires the development of new functions but it does not make the older ones obsolete; it concerns large firms but it also interests SMEs in a dramatic way; it calls for collective action but it also stimulates conflict and associative competition. How can we explain this disruptive, incoherent and conflictual effect of globalization upon business associations?

A first answer could be that the process is at its beginning, so that this fluidity is a temporary obfuscation of the clear and sharp trends which will emerge as the global market stabilizes and the actors (both firms and BIAs officials) learn to adapt to it. This hypothesis is not a persuasive one, since it neglects the very essence of the process of globalization, namely its capacity for restructuring the nature of economic, political and social relations.

The alternative hypothesis we advance – which must obviously be submitted to further empirical validation – is that this intrinsic

incoherence may become a constant, distinctive and peculiar characteristic of associative action under a situation of global markets and
transnational capitalism. And this clearly emerges if we consider precisely what the process of globalization means for social order.

According to Philippe Schmitter and Fritz Scharpf (Schmitter and
Scharpf, 1986; Schmitter, 1988) the action space within which actors
develop their social and political strategies consists 'of relatively institutionalized collectivities capable of mobilizing/organizing their
members around three generic motives or principles: identity, interest
and authority (Schmitter and Scharpf, 1985).[7] These three 'memberships' – contrary to the assumptions of traditional approaches – are not
usually fused and coherent, rather they have historically tended to
develop on different scales (local, regional, national, transnational).
The only 'historical experiment' in which these three dimensions of
membership, or models of social order, have been almost perfectly
overlapping and reinforcing one another corresponds to the nation-
state. Otherwise – in the feudal era, in the empires and in the absolutist
period – interests, identities and authorities have each developed on a
different scale.

The contemporary situation of transnational capitalism looks, in
comparison to the previous historical ones 'much more complex and
incongruent' (Schmitter and Scharpf, 1985: 7) since interests are
defined on different scales depending on the type of sector, size and
technology of firms considered. New supranational identities have
emerged but they have been paralleled by the strengthening of local
and regional identities. Meanwhile new levels of authorities have
emerged at the transnational level and regional ones have strengthened, eroding the (still existing) nation-state authorities (Schmitter,
1986: 7). The crucial difference between the era of globalization and
the previous ones is that differences in scale are present not only
between the three different dimension of membership but also within
each one of them. Interests, identities and authorities are articulated
along a plurality of scales and domains. So we can no longer speak of
the scale typical of each dimension, but, rather, of its scales. This is
what makes the contemporary situation of transnational markets and
politics complex and incongruent: the 'multilayered scale' of each one
of the three dimensions of membership.

But the intricacies do not finish here. In fact, the last two centuries
have also known another element of novelty, namely the widespread
diffusion of private associations and organizations, and the increasing
importance of the associative model of social order, alongside the state

(authority), the community (identity) and the market (interests) models (Streeck and Schmitter, 1985). One of the peculiar characteristics of this model of order is that it is based on mechanisms such as concertation, pacts, and mutual adjustment by means of which actors attempt to integrate their interests and aspirations and to reduce uncertainty. Hence, associative orders are able to internalize the demands and the properties of their environment according to the logics of associative action and, because of this capability, they can operate as private interest governments (Schmitter and Streeck, 1981; Streeck and Schmitter, 1985).

This means that the complexity and incongruence characterizing the transnational and globalized form of contemporary capitalism are partially absorbed by associative systems, since interest associations 'are always to some important extent dependent on community values, kept in check by economic and political market forces, and subject to hierarchical control, political design and the pressure of possible direct state intervention' (Streeck and Schmitter, 1985: 27–8). Hence, BIAs are going to be overloaded by the multiple, conflicting and incoherent scales of definition of interests, identities and authorities: they have to deal with multiple levels of authority, with various ways of perceiving interests and with clashing identities. Unfortunately, organizational devices to face this turbulent and labyrinthine environment and to create unity from a messy variety of interests and identities are not to be easily found. This could explain not only the uncertain prospect of corporatism in a global economy (Schmitter, 1996), but also the incoherent and centrifugal response BIAs seem to be giving to the challenge of globalization. To organize a capitalist world that, whilst becoming more global, is also becoming increasingly complex and incongruent, is likely to make associative action less clear and 'logical' than it was when identity, interests and political institutions were more coherent and overlapping. In this sense, a loosely structured associative order might be not a temporary phenomenon, rather, a new and relatively stable form of order.

Notes

1. The authors acknowledge the financial support of the Chamber of Commerce, Industry, Agriculture and Artisanship of Milan and they are grateful to Lara Stancich for a careful revision of the English text.
2. So, there exists a difference between internationalization and globalization. In the former process the authorities of each state keep on controlling the national boundaries and decide to establish transactions with the other

states, while in the latter the economic, cultural and political transactions acquire a certain degree of institutionalization and autonomy and the permeability of national boundaries is no longer a choice of national governments, so they actually suffer from a loss of sovereignty. On this point see Yarbrough and Yarbrough (1990: 249, n.52)

3. These two contrasting hypotheses about the Logic of Influence (to imitate vs to compensate the structure of interlocutors) have been originally advanced by Schmitter and Streeck (1981: 94) with reference to the relations between the degree of decentralization of the state and the relevance of territorial structures within peak associations; and they have then been utilized by Lanzalaco and Schmitter (1992) in dealing with the impact of European Community institutions upon business interest associablity.

4. A third reason concerns the difficulties and the dilemmas linked to the transnational organization of business interests (Lanzalaco, 1995). Here we ignore it because it is not relevant to our argument.

5. In 1995, the total amount of Milan companies' exports reached lira 55 860 billion: lira 33 985 billion in European countries, 7542 in American countries, 11 507 in Asian countries and 2267 in Africa. Imports amounted to lira 86 000 billion (Camera di commercio 1996).

6. What is known in the business community's jargon as the problem of 'glocalization'.

7. Of course, the model is much more complex. We are only extracting and highlighting the aspects useful for our argument.

12

Leading and Following: Private and Public Organizations in the Evolution of Global Shipping

Karsten Ronit

Introduction

Shipping has a global character due to the nature of its transcontinental operations. But its global nature is also a factor of the internationalization of ownership, the economic importance of seaborne trade, and the adoption of international conventions regulating the conditions of shipping around the globe. The intention of this chapter is to study the institutionalization of shipping through the formation of private and public organizations as contributors to the emergence of a global policy field for shipping. Particular emphasis will be put on the role of private shipowners and their associations, since they form the economic and political core of business interests. This chapter will not, however, attempt to cover the entire and relatively heterogeneous domain of the sector with all its specialties. As most associational formats have evolved over a long period of time, and before the 'global age' characterizing the last decades (Barnet and Cavanagh, 1994), their historical foundations will also be examined.

One issue in the evolution of the industry concerns whether a set of parallel actors in the private and public spheres has been created. As in other sectors of the economy, shipping interests are not organized out of thin air; they can be seen as responses to market challenges and changes in their political environment, and usually from other collective actors such as international organizations on the global scene. The drive towards collective action in business, however, does not necessarily follow as a straightforward or simultaneous response to particular events or stimuli.

Neo-corporatism correctly stressed the omnipresent role of the state in modern societies and its constitutive role in the organization of group interests (Schmitter, 1974), but this observation can be exaggerated when used to support the thesis that the history and life of associations always follow from and depend upon state action. Thus, in national polities where mature forms of corporatism persist, the existence and thriving of associations *prior* to anticipated or deliberate state action, including the creation of some relevant regulatory agency, is often forgotten. This negligence may be even more problematic at global levels, where state authority through intergovernmental cooperation has been slow to emerge. Although cooperation between nation states may be residual to the market (Cerny, 1995), it should be borne in mind that not only spontaneous forces in the economy, but also intermediary institutions, such as interest organizations, may have a decisive role to play.

Indeed, organized shipping may be the first 'mover' in shaping a global policy field. This may provide it with significant advantages in forming and consolidating traditions, and influence the behavior of relevant regulatory agencies. In other words, business may in some cases and under certain historical circumstances help in structuring state activity rather than vice versa. This is a question which can only be answered empirically for each sector, but behind this perspective lies a more general ambition, namely to understand global politics as not only formed by the interactions of nation states, often within the framework of international organizations, but to see the global scene as inhabited by a variety of public as well as private actors with a capacity to influence global politics.

In sectors where business succeeded in the early formation of global associations, this may suggest that lower territorial levels were either given less priority or were completely superseded. In analyzing associability we cannot take for granted that there is a simple historical trend, according to which still higher and more encompassing associations – representing business from first national, later regional and finally global contexts – are founded. Other patterns are imaginable. Here it seems relevant to draw upon explanatory variables such as the economic and technical properties of an industry. These include issues such as how fast economic operations move beyond different territorial units and are globalized, and the historical traditions surrounding it, such as the time in which industries emerged as global in character, and were affected by contemporary trends in organizing business.

No doubt the order in which private and public organizations appeared is highly relevant in understanding the sector today, but the exchanges between them are, on the other hand, not a simple product of the past. Although the driving force behind the global institutionalization from the early days could probably be found in the private domain, the role of the state level should not be underestimated. One possible impact of state action upon private organizations in shipping is through the encouragement of some associational formats, particularly the selection of actors representing a significant proportion of shipowners. In this way associational fragmentation generated by the various subsectors and specialties within modern shipping, and the national and regional cleavages in membership, could be eased and, where possible, resolved through the creation of a single and more representative association. If the state level, globally manifested through intergovernmental organizations, is unable to create coherent structures for itself, the potential for encouraging greater coherence in industry, becomes rather dubious, and the task of bringing greater coherence may lie with the private organizations. However, there is also the possibility to be discussed that private and public organizations develop independently and do not mutually adapt.

An early start to global associability

The organization of shipowners dates from the beginning of the twentieth century. Underlying the drive towards combined action were important economic and political factors, such as the increase in seaborne trade and the emergence of maritime legislation, which generally confronted all vessels and shipowners irrespective of their national origin. When legislation was adopted by leading maritime powers, notably the UK, this had a strong impact on the climate of shipping world wide, as the UK hosted the bulk of world tonnage and controlled ports throughout its empire. The changing organizational surroundings of shipping also propelled associability. Few challenges, however, were produced by permanent international agencies. In lieu of such bodies, disparate contacts at an intergovernmental level were still predominant, and, in turn, this gave associations a decisive role in globalizing the sector.

The International Shipowners' Federation (ISF) was established in 1909, initially within a narrow European framework, but later becoming a global forum, in 1919. The International Chamber of Shipping (ICS) emerged more than a decade after the ISF, in 1921 (Farthing,

1993). Ever since, these have remained the two key associations in shipping with the federation (ISF) representing employer interests and the chamber (ICS) handling producer aspects. Labour is organized through the International Transport Workers' Federation (ITF), but no single association has managed to unite the different groups of consumers, including those business segments which also belong to the large shipping community. The ICS and ISF have almost always presented themselves as global organizations, the core group of members (in the form of national shipowners' associations) originally came from maritime nations in the industrialized world, in particular from Western Europe and the USA, and this pattern largely prevails today.

Global regulatory bodies emerge

Private interests were faster to organize at the global level than were governments. However, labour market issues were addressed relatively early on at the interstate level by a permanent body, the International Labour Organization (ILO), founded in 1919, and based in Geneva. Placed under the auspices of the United Nations (UN), it is one of the UN's numerous special organizations, but by covering the entire terrain of labour relations, a relatively small institutional framework has been created. Although the ILO is not particularly known for its involvement in shipping, more general issues may spill over into the sector.

As far as the producer side is concerned, the picture is quite the reverse. An intergovernmental organization was founded much later, but its domain was limited exclusively to shipping. Known today as the International Maritime Organization (IMO), its predecessor was established in 1948 as the Intergovernmental Maritime Consultative Organization (IMCO), but was only fully recognized in 1959 as a specialized body belonging to the UN family. Its decade-long birth pangs were due not least to disagreements among shipowners, who found themselves divided between groups which favored a strategy of minimal regulation and saw the advantages of a working relationship with a standard-setting agency which was globally recognized, and groups of free enterprise-minded shipowners, who feared that such a body might be too powerful. Instead other arrangements, partly of a self-regulatory nature in safety and navigation matters were preferred, an example being the Comité Maritime International (CMI), founded in 1897. As a private organization, it had a strong legal orientation, drafted conventions and even convened diplomatic conferences until the early 1970s (Farthing, 1993).

Although the fears of an overly powerful regulatory organization proved unfounded, regulation did increase during the next decades in the form of international conventions which set uniform standards in merchant shipping. Today these conventions amount to 24 with a further 700 codes and recommendations added to the regulatory complex (see IMO, 1995, *A Summary of IMO Conventions*). The conventions aim to enhance safe navigation and address issues from the measurement of ships and tonnage to the prevention of oil pollution. At the same time, the organization has steered clear of sensitive problems in international trade, which has been left to organizations such as UNCTAD (United Nations Conference on Trade and Development), known as 'friendlier' to developing countries, but often paralyzed by conflicts.

From initially being a small forum based on a convention signed by 21 states, the IMO has expanded considerably and today organizes around 150 countries from all continents. From that point of view, it would be correct to speak of an evolution in globalization, rather than a sudden and radical move. However, the limits of globalization are emphasized by the fact that the authority of the IMO, albeit undisputed as the single agency for global regulation of shipping, is weakened by the unwillingness or incapacity of its members to ratify and implement conventions at the national level. In other words, the power of the member states halts the globalization process, although their potential to do so varies considerably, based on different shares of world tonnage carried. Indeed, different status is attributed to the members in internal decision-making. As in the past, some countries play an extremely important part in the world economy and are at the same time strong maritime powers. This is reflected in the governing structure of the IMO, which is led by a council of 40 member states, which includes all major maritime nations. Participation in the numerous committees of the IMO is in principle open to all members.

However, it would be impossible to understand the IMO as an international organization only from the perspective of the relationship between its member states as a form of intergovernmental cooperation. The organization inherited, so to speak, a preexisting organized shipping community. It therefore liaises with a range of global associations in the sector, making it fully operational and providing it with technical advice and political legitimacy. Various ways have been found to formalize cooperation, a key ingredient in its ultimate success.

The granting of public recognition to private associations

In common with many other international organizations, including those belonging to the UN system, the IMO has defined and elaborated the category of 'consultative status'. A number of associations within shipping therefore enjoy privileged access to the organization, its secretariat and its four main committees plus a long list of sub-committees.

'Consultative status' grants associations advisory functions, but the degree to which the IMO exchanges with the selected associations varies a great deal. From the IMO's perspective, the integration into public policy-making gives the IMO an opportunity to draw on associational resources, and to some extent also delegate tasks to them, whereby the aspirations of large sections of organized shipping for self-regulation are adequately met.

Since 1960 the IMO has on various occasions adopted and reformulated these guidelines, most extensively in 1979. Today a significant number of associations – more than 50 – enjoy consultative status, and official links of a looser character are established with a further 20 associations. Indeed, this is an impressive list of associations, but compared to many other special organizations in the UN system the number is relatively small. As mentioned at the beginning of this article, shipping is a relatively heterogeneous sector and cannot be reduced to a few associations of shipowners, although these form the vital core of the sector in both economic and political terms. Therefore, it is no surprise that consultative status is granted to so many associations, representing interests completely beyond the wide domain of the ISF and ICS.

Most IMO-recognized associations are global in their scope. They organize (or at least attempt to organize) members worldwide, but a few of them are of a more limited territorial nature, for example organizing the interests of shipowners of a particular continent. However, none of the recognized players are composed solely of one national origin, and none are single firms. Of further interest is the fact that some groups with broader aims, such as environmental interests, have also been granted consultative status with the IMO in recent years. The overwhelming majority of recognized organizations, however, are business interest associations, mainly related to shipping. A few are of a general nature, as for example the International Chamber of Commerce (ICC), which through its Transport Committee specializes in shipping.

The fact that a variety of collective actors are recognized, and enjoy the same status, does not mean that they are equally recognized and of equal importance to the IMO. By virtue of their territorial coverage, agendas and history, some associations have acquired a more privileged position. This kind of hierarchy was established prior to, and relatively independently, of any IMO recognition, and cemented rather than disrupted the organization, as consultations are first and foremost made to integrate all specialties in shipping, irrespective of the form in which they were already organized.

The impact of recognition on organized shipping

A major objective for many international associations in shipping is to become formally recognized by the IMO. This is partly in order to demonstrate their indispensability in interest representation to their membership, and partly to improve their position in the invisible status hierarchy of associations in the industry. On the other hand, the prestige of associations does not unilaterally hinge on IMO recognition, and as seen from the associations' perspectives the policy of recognition has not been understood as one of selection. Consequently, no powerful strategy has been pursued to rationalize interest representation, although it has been discussed on some occasions in recent years (Middleton, 1993).

Seen from an IMO viewpoint, the granting of recognition has not been designed to structure earlier patterns of associability, as the criteria for consultation has been very broad and without preference for particular types of associations. Although it is not the only international organization with an area of competence in shipping, the IMO does handle a wide range of issues which demand cooperation with all sections in global shipping. However, the overall pattern is one of exchanges between a relatively fragmented associational landscape, and a relatively coherent public authority which integrates a variety of issues from different parts of the sector.

In studies of interest representation at national and transnational levels, it has often been claimed that public and private structures undergo a process of mutual adaptation (for example, Eichener and Voelzkow, 1994). Accordingly, an institutional concentration of regulatory power should gradually be matched by a similar concentration of power in large associations managing internal conflicts by seeking compliance across a broad and heterogeneous membership, ending in the creation of a single encompassing association. To explain the limited associational adaptation in global shipping different factors may be taken into account, and here *the historical dimension* is of par ticular importance. The key actors in organized shipping were founded prior to the IMO, and not in a kind of parallel process. Therefore the IMO was unable to influence the fundamental pattern of organized shipping in its formative stage, and was only in a position to assist in marginal restructuring of the old core actors, and those associations established more recently.

Key associations have reacted to changes in their environment, in particular the increase in intergovernmental cooperation and the growing authority of the regulatory agencies. Thus, the IMO and other international organizations have experienced a gradual extension of their membership to different parts of the world, with intentions to widen it even further. The membership base of the ICS and ISF still only covers around 30 countries, which compares unfavourably with the global coverage of the IMO with its almost 150 member states. There is also a noticeable bias in both associations, as shipowners from Western Europe, North America and Japan are strongly represented, whereas, for example, South America is weakly represented, and Africa, together with Eastern Europe and China, are almost completely missing. Nevertheless important small countries outside the industrialized world, for example Panama and Liberia, are affiliated.

Such a patchwork of membership has led to the creation of regional associations outside the ICS and the ISF. Regional associations such as the dormant Latin American Shipowners' Association (LASA) and the (government-initiated and more ambitious) Islamic Shipowners' Association (ISA) operate outside the framework of the ICS and ISF. However, compared to the ICS and ISF, which together represent half the world's tonnage, LASA and ISA are relatively small players. These regional associations are recognized by the IMO as regional outlets. They do not claim to represent shipping at a global level, rather, these regional associations recognise the ICS and the ISF as global players to which some of their national associations are affiliated.

Another factor which shows that the IMO has not assumed a guiding role in shaping organized shipping can be explained by the *character* of the associations. Few associations in the sector owe their creation and life to the interplay with the IMO, including those of more recent origin. They very much operate independently of global regulatory agencies, to which only a fraction of their activities are related, even if they enjoy consultative status. Instead, they emphasize a strong membership orientation through the production of various services and pay less attention to political institutions. Or, rather, they exploit these relations to produce services which can only be achieved on the basis of profound knowledge of global regulation. These global associations are typically based on direct membership through shipowners, and therefore produce goods which national associations of shipowners cannot produce. They are relevant only for the international operations of shipowners, and are cost-effective only for a wider international membership. Thus, while these service-producing associations are clearly governed by the 'logic of membership' (Schmitter and Streeck, 1981), it is the commercial, rather than immediate political, interests of the members which are decisive in this context. The performance of such functions could, in some cases, also be lifted by international organizations with a public authority, but the sector is recognised for its ability to manage safety matters, for example through private collective action.

The relatively inactive role of regulatory agencies in assisting structural changes in organized shipping may perhaps give an exaggerated impression of associational fragmentation. Several smaller associations specialize in organizing very narrow interest categories, such as lighthouse authorities or classification societies, and it would make little sense for the two peak associations to seek to organize such interests. It would make sense, however, to include branch associations. In global shipping there are a small number of branch associations based on direct membership from individual companies such as the International Association of Independent Tanker Owners (Intertanko) where national interests play a less significant role in determining the association's policy. New global associations covering all sectors could also be created through the integration of all branch associations into the ICS and ISF, but this might reduce the role of national member associations. If the branch principle was actually applied, it would still make the organization of interests problematic, partly because associations do not exist within all branches, and partly because not all branch associations are highly reputable and representative, although they may enjoy consultative status. Some degree of duplication in interest representation therefore seems unavoidable.

Other patterns of cooperation have been adopted. Organized shipping is constituted by a few core associations, and a much larger group of smaller outlets, some of which rarely have direct access to bodies such as the IMO. Cooperation among the major associations, as well as with the small, is generally sought through interorganizational coordination rather than by attempting to create larger, more inclusive units. Even the ISF and ICS, operating as Siamese twins for employer and producer interests, operating from the same premises in London, serviced by Maritime International Secretariat Services Ltd (Marisec), have agreed to operate separately rather than merge. A competitive relationship is not, however, a general feature of organized shipping (although there is evidently some rivalry among shipowners as a whole). This is mainly because of limited overlaps in membership domains, and due to the existence of an established hierarchy which will often decide upon who is the proper representative of a particular interest category.

Conclusions

From national and regional studies we know that there is a trend towards co-evolution of private associations and public authority. Private associations are brought to life to represent interests in exchanges with political institutions, sometimes deliberately assisted by public funding, or formally granted an exclusive right to represent a given interest category. Political institutions may, for their part, be provoked to regulate by different groups in society in order to mediate between various organized interests.

This interdependence can also be identified at the global level, although some reservations should be spelled out. The thesis of co-evolution should not be rigidly applied, but seen in an extended time perspective. Mutual adjustments are often slow or partial, if at all accomplished, and the constitutive role of public authority in shaping private associations and structuring relations is sometimes replaced by powerful private initiatives.

At the global level a political system has generally emerged later than a private associational system and the exercise of political authority is fragile, although strong variation across sectors may be perceived. As far as the business domain is concerned, the discrepancy between private and public action is perhaps the most significant, as there is a trend towards the economy being globalized before politics. In turn, this has an important impact upon when and how business and state action is organized. But the political character of business interest associations is not a given either. Initially, associability may have a fraternal character and, at later stages, mature into political action, including forms of self-regulation.

The specific history of shipping shows that key global associations were neither sponsored nor deliberately encouraged by regulatory agencies. Rather, such associations predated regulating agencies, and were decisive in creating a further institutional framework for global shipping. The role of private organizations is, however, a more general question in the evolution of such global communities. In fact, the creation of global policy communities with more complex actor configurations seems to be a somewhat different story than establishing policy communities at national or regional levels. In national communities it is simply easier for all actors to identify different parts of such a community, or create one by means of personal communication. Moreover, if there is an existing or potential national interest associated with a certain industry, this may also help in building new alliances in business and between business and government. Smaller and national networks with stable sets of actors are easier to organize around and they usually have a more stable origin with comparatively clearly identified aims, which become challenged and vanish in alliance building at global levels. There is also no straightforward line in the evolution of territorial associability in shipping. National associations were not simply followed by regional, and, in a later step, global associations. The national element is still the essential building block in global associations, and in the two key associations of shipowners there are only national affiliates. Most interestingly, perhaps, the regional link is generally missing or inactive, which, for example, the European case illustrates (Ronit, 1995). By the end of the 1950s, the already existing global network of national associations of shipowners within the ISF and ICS provided a useful platform for both considering and forming new and appropriate regional outlets, when the global associations proved unable to solve some of the more specific tasks confronting European shipowners at the dawn of European integration. However, these new and independent associations were for almost a decade kept in a dormant position, and never built into the global hierarchy of shipping associations.

Public authority through international organizations has had a relatively modest impact on patterns of global associability, and the emergence of a single regulatory agency has not led to a greater centralization in organized shipping. A proliferation of new associations with no will to pool their resources has been unavoidable. As far as the granting of consultative status to associations is concerned, it is not really comparable to the recognition of associations which we know from corporatist structures in nation states, where encompassingness is greatly encouraged, and where internal bargaining in large associations is expected to bind members to common interests. Recognition by the IMO is rather a preference given for consultation with a long list of associations, rather than an attempt to deliver coordination or to establish greater global coherence among shipping associations

Indeed, there are limits to expansions into new maritime subsectors by the shipowners' associations, which have always recognized that there are natural boundaries beyond which the organization of interests would be futile.

Whilst the difficulties of establishing greater global coherence between shipping interests – and the difficulties this creates for the development of shipping policy – should not be overestimated, problems pale into insignificance when compared to the problems of overcoming cleavages across the 150 member states in intergovernmental organizations related to shipping. This is perhaps felt less in the context of the IMO, but is more pronounced in structures such as UNCTAD. The exercise of national authority impedes the authority of international organizations, partly through non-ratification of conventions, and partly through their inability to compromise. In other words, the organization of shipping at the global level has been less sprawling than the organization of public interests through intergovernmental organizations in the field, although at first glance fragmentation may appear comparatively stronger in shipping, where many associations address a few regulatory bodies. In the context of an exchange pattern, where private and public organizations are each characterized by specific cleavages, business has been the stronger part and the driving force in creating a global institutional framework in the sector.

13
International Standardization, Corporate Strategy and Regional Markets

Michelle Egan

Although traditional tariffs have been progressively lowered in regional and international trade agreements, the significance of non-tariff barriers has increased dramatically, and assumed greater relative importance in trade negotiations (Baldwin, 1970; Curzon, 1972; Grieco, 1990; Hillman, 1991). These new types of economic protectionism or 'behind the border' issues fall within what is known as the 'reserved powers' of states, and form part of the domestic policies pursued by national governments. However, as international trade has expanded, the impact of these divergent national, and in some cases regional, barriers for agricultural and industrial products have been subject to increased scrutiny by the global trade regime.

Among the most prominent, but hitherto neglected, sources of these existing and potential non-tariff barriers to trade are 'technical barriers to trade'. Technical barriers are the result of divergent standards and testing and certification practices determining whether a product conforms to a particular standard or regulation. The trade-hampering effects of these barriers are difficult to discern. Firms either internalize the specific costs of modifying a product to meet divergent national requirements, or simply forgo market access as exporting to third countries becomes more costly. Instead, they focus inward on their domestic market and may divert themselves to exploiting captive home markets by lobbying to keep trade barriers in place, rather than engage in dynamic corporate strategies.

The extant and proposed policy responses to deal with technical barriers include multilateral and regional cooperation to harmonize these diverse market entry requirements. This creates both opportunities and risks for firms. On the one hand, common standards can lower production costs through economies of scale in production, increase the level of competition through coordination and compatibility and lower transaction costs by lowering information costs (Kindleberger, 1983; Farell and Saloner, 1987; Walters and Toyne, 1989). In this sense, standards are critical for both firm and state competitiveness, assisting efficiency in production and distribution, as well as information and technology transfer across firm and country boundaries. On the other hand, common standards, by easing market access can increase competition and threaten the viability of some firms that have become accustomed to the protection offered by divergent standards and regulations.

Given the wide-reaching implications of standards for economic competition, more and more trade in regional markets is being defined in terms of specific standards. Among the most significant developments is the emphasis given by the European Union in the EC-92 programme to the removal of technical barriers. The development of European-wide standards at the regional level has a number of positive effects for market access, domestic and international competitiveness and the liberalization of trade. Through their impact on the cost of production, price and consumer perception, 'common standards' can create new marketing opportunities and strategic opportunities for European firms to capitalize on a unified market.

With European standards affecting the global business environment, what does this mean for their competitors, particularly American and Japanese firms? This chapter examines this question by looking at the structure and impact of European standards networks and the implications for Japanese and American firms. The first section provides an overview of the European standardization process and institutional framework. An initial focus on Europe is important, as European standards bodies and firms have been the driving force in most areas of international standardization. The second section takes a closer look at problems of collective action facing European firms in the standardization process, and how this influences European behavior at the international level. The third section then examines two areas: the degree to which the European network creates a barrier to entry for non-European firms and the regional response of Japan and the US through APEC.

The development of European standardization

The completion of the single market by the end of 1992 committed member states to maximize economic welfare by removing constraints on cross-border economic activity within the European Community. Surveys of business perceptions about the most important barriers to trade ranked the different categories barriers to trade in terms of the Community market as a whole; diverging technical standards and regulations were ranked as the most important obstacle to intra-EU trade by German, French, British and Danish firms.

Recognizing that the barriers created by different product standards and regulations distorted production patterns, discouraged business cooperation, and frustrated the creation of a common market, the EU attempted to replace these national standards and regulations with Euro-norms. This policy of harmonization, once widely accepted as a solution to regulatory differences was widely regarded as inefficient, excessively uniform, and ultimately ineffective, since new national regulations were introduced at a rate that exceeded the establishment of European-wide regulations (Pelkmans, 1987). Negotiated harmonization under conditions of relative symmetry in bargaining power produced relatively few results in the European Community. The EU sought new policy solutions as differing national regulatory environments, whether designed for protection or not, became major impediments to implementing the common market.

The 'new approach' to standardization introduced in 1985 provided a new template for removing national restrictions to the free movement of goods (Figure 13.1) (see Strawbridge, No Date; Pelkmans, 1987). Its main purpose was to ensure that only those regulations that were 'essential' or 'genuinely necessary' to protect health, provide consumers with adequate information, ensure fair trading and provide for necessary public controls would fall under Community harmonization legislation, leaving specific standard-setting to private standard-setting bodies. Instead of a centralized model of market liberalization through painstaking harmonization, the new approach adopted mutual recognition as a norm. As such it required an unprecedented degree of trust between member states to accept each other's extraterritorial authority.[1] In cases where national regulations are not mutually equivalent, and European harmonization is necessary, considerable power to set standards has been delegated to private standard-setting bodies.

This delegation of regulatory functions to non-governmental organizations owes much to the perceptions of a serious mismatch between

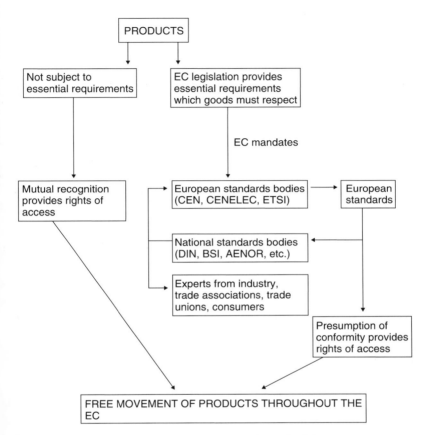

Figure 13.1   Free movement of products throughout the EC

existing institutional capacities and traditional styles of administration such as harmonization on the one hand, and the public reaction and growing complexity of policy problems on the other (Majone, No Date; Breyer, 1982). The willingness to delegate important policy-making powers is in some sense an attempt to reduce the transaction costs and improve the efficiency of collective political outcomes. This shift towards a more contractual view of policy-making is in large part a reflection that regulation is not achieved by simply passing the law, but requires involvement of the regulated firms. Regulation does bear the risk of being influenced by the activities of special interest groups, leading to 'regulatory capture'. Because regulators lack information that only regulated firms have, regulators and regulated firms constantly bargain over the precise obligations of the latter.

By agreeing to the delegation of regulatory authority, member states are allowing private standard-setting bodies to coordinate collective outcomes, thus incorporating private actors into the policy process. Rather than view this as regulatory capture, the EC's approach acknowledges the role of distribution of powers between public and private actors which is a central feature of European 'mixed economies' (Pelkmans, 1982). As a result, European standardization takes place predominantly in three institutions: the Comité Européen de la Normalisation (CEN), the Comité Européen de la Normalisation Electrotechnique (CENELEC), and more recently the European Telecommunications Standards Institute (ETSI) created in 1988 (Egan, 1994; Besen, 1990). These three standards bodies are private associations of the EC and EFTA member states' national standards bodies.

While these three standards bodies are formally independent organizations, they have established closer ties with the European Commission. Though the detailed operation of each of these standards is slightly different, the operating norms are similar. Standards are set through a consensus process which often requires trade unions, consumer groups, local governments, government departments, as well as individual firms and trade associations to work together. Large firms and trade association play the dominant role in the process. Significant barriers are erected against the intermittent participation that may be feasible from small or medium companies, or trade unions and consumer groups. Because of their size, SMEs often lack the financial resources and necessary expertise to influence the pace and direction of standardization at the European level. To ensure a more balanced representation of interests, the EU provides direct support to weaker interest associations, such as the European Trade Union Confederation (ETUC). This alleviates the collective action problems with respect to the advocation of general interests which are even more extensive at the European level than within the member states (Olson, 1993).

Creating standards is the essential but humdrum task of an army of committees (Batchelor, 1993). These committees are assigned the task of framing the issues to reach accommodation in such diverse fields as information technology, textiles, biotechnology, shipbuilding, banking and financial services. CEN, CENELEC and ETSI provide the framework within which this voluntary collaboration takes place, although these organizations do not set standards themselves. They are the 'peak associations' that coordinate the activities of over 25 000 participants at the European level.

Corporate strategy and bargaining over European standards

Because the demand for standards has grown due to the single market, the pace of standardization has increased rapidly, and Europeanization of standardization is now proceeding at a much quicker pace than before. Although firms and trade associations are requesting more pan-European standards so that products and services can cross borders more easily, the process is time-consuming and complex. Even though there are benefits to cooperation, overcoming collective goods problems is difficult as firms often disagree about the most appropriate standard that will ease market entry barriers. Since standards are adopted by consensus, there is a need for participants to agree on joint policies in the face of their individual and varying interests and goals. Under these circumstances, even though there may be gains from cooperation, such cooperation is difficult to implement since there are numerous potential paths that provide a multiplicity of policy outcomes (Krasner, 1991).[2]

Product standards are critical for the corporate strategy and competitiveness of firms, as they can influence both market access and market advantage. Decisions about corporate strategies and products are made not only on the basis of calculations about the European market, but, for many manufacturers, the global market. As national markets have opened up, competition on a European scale has grown steadily more intense. Firms cannot react simply to market signals but must make strategic choices about their product design, development and production processes.

In order to understand the corporate strategies of firms, it is essential to explore their role as policy participants. This does not just mean looking at the pressure group activities of businesses; it means understanding how the choice of firms shapes the policy environment. Clearly, involvement in the standards setting process provides a means for competing firms to cooperate, collaborate and share information in shaping the rules for market entry. *De jure* standardization, no less than strategic alliances and joint ventures, represents a way to combine the dynamics of market-based competition with the requirements of coordination. With high pre-development costs and shorter product life-cycles, firms in vastly changing environments are increasingly paying critical attention to standardization.

In such a context, analysis and deliberation are important for identifying collectively advantageous solutions. This enables active networking and enhances the ability of firms to make informed choices as to their future corporate strategies, as well as providing information on competitor companies. But collective decision-making through consensus can entail high transaction costs (Scharpf, 1988; 1991). Unanimity or consensus means that one single interest can dominate the agenda and exercise veto power. British firms, for example, have sought to scotch plans for a standard Euro-plug, claiming that European standards would cost about £20 billion to rewire domestic and commercial properties in Britain (*Financial Times*, 1993, 1994). For 18 years, British firms have maintained national standards as a means to insulate themselves from increased competition.

To overcome the excessive decision costs, the European standards bodies have altered their decision-making style in response to EU pressure; qualified majorities can now be used for positive collective action. In the absence of unanimous agreement, the default condition is no longer the maintenance of the status quo. This enhances efficiency and increases the incentives for participants to create minimum winning coalitions. The implications of such changes mean that firms and trade associations involved in standardization may 'pressure' as well as be 'pressured'.

How a firm perceives the policy options proposed will often depend on its economic position, and in particular its international competitiveness, as well as its ability to undertake market strategies to adjust to the post-1992 single European market. Since the market position of firms may be significantly affected by the particular standard chosen, intense bargaining and negotiation precludes the adoption of a particular standard. It is unusual for standards to be developed quickly; in fact a period of several years is common. New standards may sometimes cause an upheaval of certain segments of the market, given their influence on relative costs or even the production process. Broad market acceptance of a standard, between competing possibilities, may enable a single firm to achieve a competitive advantage in the manufacturing process. Conversely, a particular standard may be thought to worsen the competitiveness of certain firms *vis-à-vis* others. Hence, significant changes at the European level can impose adjustment costs disproportionately across industrial sectors.

Cooperative activity is not costless, so that private standards organizations are a partial solution to the collective action problem. By creating a standards-setting body, firms contribute to the financing, and each firm receives a net benefit from participation. However, it is important to distinguish between the costs and benefits of passive membership and the costs and benefits of active participation (Grant, 1989). Not all firms are standards developers, many are standards users. Since standards are public goods and once developed are available to anyone, a firm can benefit from the existence of a standard without incurring the costs of participation (Stigler, 1974; Olson, 1965).[3] Even though trade associations provide some selective incentives or positive inducements, standard-setting organizations tend to rely on a firm's desire to stay abreast of developments and present their points of view as an adequate incentive. This motivates the entrepreneurial firms and highlights the differences between the logic of membership and the logic of influence.

As a result, standard-setting is a complex and multilayered set of corporate networks. Yet the establishment and maintenance of these corporate networks is in itself complex, and requires a significant degree of policy entrepreneurship on the part of individual firms. Pushing standards through the process is often the work of a few firms that are willing to commit resources and time. Much of their entrepreneurial activity is aimed at creating a constituency of support, while simultaneously trying to persuade and bring together disparate economic interests. Thus, not only will a small number of firms exercise leadership and agenda setting, but these entrepreneurial firms will also build a consensus about how the problem should be defined, and broker compromises with diverging interests in the standards setting process (Zito, 1995).

Although this provides entrepreneurial firms with a window of opportunity to push forward new solutions and policies, the significance of their ideas in shaping the debate, clarifying objectives, and in helping to select a particular outcome depends on persuasion and evidence (Kingdon, 1984; Goldstein, 1993). This is an integral part of the standards process, as the adoption of certain policies cannot be understood solely in terms of power, influence and bargaining (Majone, 1989). Even though firms are seeking to promote their own goals, they must justify their position by appealing to the merits of the case (Majone, 1989; Kingdon, 1984). The standards community is thus characterized by policy participation, not policy advocacy. The norms of standard-setting means that firms that refuse to negotiate and adjust their positions are often considered 'outsiders' in the policy process. Unfamiliarity with the norms of the network can reduce bargaining power and leverage, as a set of mutual expectations governs the relationship among those involved in standardization activities.

This market-driven response selected by the EC has drawn many firms and trade associations into a complex array of transnational networks. The increased role of private economic agents reflects a shift in the substance of policymaking in the EU. The increased willingness to delegate important policy-making powers to technocratic bodies (such as CEN) enjoying considerable political independence reflects not only the growing complexity of public policy, but also the growing importance of corporate strategies for shaping the rules of market governance. Moreover, this negotiation and adaptation at the EU level has enabled firms to engage in collective political action, providing the norms and prescriptions for policy action that they have transferred to the international level.

The international implications of European standardization

European standardization is not only affecting trade prospects in Europe, but is increasingly affecting trading relations in the global market. Building on the relationship between standards and competitiveness, the European Union is using standards as both a marketing device and a means of technology transfer to sell their products in Eastern Europe and developing countries. Recognizing that once a standard is in place, trading relationship become locked in, the European Union and European standards bodies have fostered extensive ties through foreign aid programs and other cooperative schemes to assist in the adoption of European standards (Interview, CEN; EC Commission, 1990). To stimulate trade, the EU and the European standards bodies have reinforced their position and interests by providing technical assistance to firms, governments and standards bodies in Mexico and India as well as ASEAN countries. European policy-makers and firms recognized that European standards could be used as a component of industrial policy for greater political and economic leverage to promote their standards in the international arena (Hayes, 1989).

In addition, European firms have recognized the economic advantages of promoting their European standards as international ones. After years of watching American and Japanese firms dominate consumer electronics, a turnabout has taken place in communications technologies. European companies are racing ahead, largely because cellular phone companies across Europe agreed to a common standard known as GSM in the mid-1980s. As more than 70 countries have already adopted the European standard, European equipment makers have pushed to have the standard adopted at the international level

(*Business Week*, 1994). In other areas, European activity at the international level through the international standards organizations (International Standards Organization and International Electrotechnical Commission) has placed Japanese and American firms under pressure, as certain international management and environmental standards are starting to make inroads into the American and Japanese market, complementing and even possibly replacing traditional manufacturing strategies and production processes.

Increasingly, international standards are being viewed more favorably for both political and economic reasons. The impetus from regional standardization in Europe has pushed both Japan and the United States into reconsidering their attitudes towards international standards (Egan and Zito, 1995). Although European members are keen to promote more effective international standards organization, Japan and the United States have not traditionally seen the international standards organizations as a suitable arena for promoting their own domestic standards. The USA and Japan with their larger, homogenous markets had less need to join the move towards greater harmonization. Japan has traditionally used its standards as a means to promote its industrial strategy and insulate its markets (Lecraw, 1987), and the style of Japanese standard-setting has led to many complaints from foreign-owned firms about the difficulty of getting into the Japanese market due to lack of transparency (Coccodrilli, 1984). In contrast to the voluntary, market-driven approach to standardization in Europe and the United States, Japanese standards are often the result of the pervasive interconnections between government and business. This has meant that national standards have been developed under the supervision, direction and control of government, particularly MITI and the Ministry of Agriculture.

Often viewed as governmental-extended bureaucratic structures, Japanese standards committees are characteristic of the network of contacts and liaisons between government, industry and trade associations. Foreign firms have expressed confusion in understanding the distinction between 'voluntary' and mandatory standards, as well as determining the role played by the government and private sector in drafting standards. In fact, Japanese standards are drafted by committees of selected firms, subject to government approval. Membership is critical since it confers the distinction between insiders and outsiders – as well as providing firms with crucial information.

The system of standards-setting in Japan has been a source of trade friction, as product standards are both stricter and more detailed than those in Europe. Unlike Europe, where there is an emphasis on flexibility under the new approach, in Japan literally thousands of products must be tested before they can be legally sold. Moreover, while European standards are usually based on performance criteria, Japanese standards tend to be detailed specifications of production design; the latter frequently favoring a particular Japanese product or process. On the surface, and from the vast amount of publicity that Japanese trade barriers have generated, it may not appear that external pressures have had any effects on Japanese standardization. However, two things should be noted. First, the Japanese strategy of closure to foreign firms has significantly shifted over the past 15 years. The restrictions on standards, testing and certification practices have been modified as a result of international pressures. In that time, Japan has committed itself to the GATT Standards Code adopted in the Tokyo Round to ensure non-discriminatory access. As a result, the Japanese allow products certified in third countries to be sold on Japanese markets. Until then, Japanese agencies were reluctant to accept the results of products tested outside of Japan, so that foreign firms incurred higher marketing costs in having their products subject to additional approval and inspection to ensure market access.

Second, the Japanese, for all their well-earned reputation for manufacturing quality, have been responsible for drawing up only 2 per cent of international standards. In light of the changes in Europe, efforts to internationalize Japan's economy in 1985 through the Action Programme for Improved Market Access focused extensively on standards and certification. The Action programme increased transparency in the domestic standards setting process and eased market entry for foreign firms by accepting their product test and approvals as much as possible. In 1991, the Japanese standards system introduced new long-term strategic and policy objectives which focused on implementing more international standards at the domestic level (Japanese Standards Association, 1994).

American participation in international standardization activities has fluctuated over the years (Congressional Hearings, 1966; Congressional Hearings, 1976). Serious but unsuccessful Congressional attempts to support US participation in international standardization have highlighted the trade effects of European dominance of international standards organizations, as well as the trade implications that regional efforts such as CEN and CENELEC pose to US exports. However, the EC-92 programme has been the most significant impetus to change. EC-92 has not only raised the profile of industrial standards in the

USA, but also generated intense debate about the need for improvement in public–private cooperation in standards development to enhance present and future export opportunities. American firms were initially able to 'exit' from the international arena, thereby weakening their political impact in shaping international standards activities. This was because of several factors: (1) a large domestic market, (2) a dominant economic position in global markets, and (3) the postwar dominance of American standards in third country markets. Yet with the changed status of the United States in the world economy, American firms can no longer impose their product designs on the rest of the world, especially in sectors and industries where it has no credible presence.[4]

US firms have argued strongly that there was little incentive for them to participate at the international level since the Europeans (EC and EFTA) can outvote them 18–1. In the American view, the voting arrangements provide the EC and EFTA countries with a strategic advantage in terms of setting international standards. This reinforced the American tendency to dismiss international efforts, instead concentrating on national standards for their domestic markets. As one trade association noted, 'international standards still need more recognition by United States corporate political leaders. We see progress in moving standards from the backroom to the boardroom. However, many of our corporate leaders… still do not recognize the crucial effect international standards has on our competitive posture' (Mazza, 1994: 85).

American efforts to influence international standards activities have also been hampered by collective action problems. The political impact of American activities have been hindered by the competing organizations that set standards in the USA. These standards organizations range from those serving particular sectors, to trade associations, professional societies and general membership organizations that bring together a wider spectrum of participants. These differ in size, resources and organization. While trade associations such as the American Petroleum Institute, the American Society for Testing and Metals, and the American Gas Association, are important in structuring political choices and have developed a significant number of American standards, there are also highly specialized, small trade associations such as the Diamond Walnut Growers Association that have a more limited influence. With over four hundred standards setting organizations, the overall pattern is characterized by high differentiation and low integration of the various associations which are involved in setting standards.

Even though many trade associations and professional societies are affiliated to the 'umbrella' organization, the American National Standards Institute (ANSI), the relationship between the different organizations is rather tenuous. This is a source of weakness as competition among these organizations for membership hinders collective action. The picture is similar at the international level. Although ANSI represents the American 'voice' at the international level, its effectiveness is often undermined by competing domestic standards organizations with divergent policy positions. But the external challenges from Europe have prompted intense discussions in the USA about greater coordination and even the possibility of a radical overhaul of American standardization. While many trade associations have supported greater coordination, they are extremely reluctant to alter their unique, pluralistic standards system.

Given the new landscape, American policy-makers and trade associations have increasingly recognized that they must work in concert and 'revisit the way that they set standards' (IFAC, 1991). In this vein, American policy-makers and industry have begun to cooperate to promote standards as a trading tool to open up markets in Russia and Middle East for their products. Much like earlier European efforts, American firms are seeking to use their standards as a means to lock in and capture third country markets (Interview, National Institute of Standards and Technology, 1995).

European networks: a barrier to entry?

A key question for American and Japanese business executives and policy-makers who have been closely monitoring developments within the EU is whether European standards activities are a barrier to entry for outsiders. For a barrier to entry to exist, firms must make strategic decisions that exclude certain industries and sectors (Barney, 1991). European firms must possess strategically relevant resources such as information or membership that excludes American and Japanese firms. Network theory suggests that a firm entering a network must position itself among established members of the network, in order to gain information, establish close contacts and be able to pursue their policy goals (Thorelli, 1986).

Although American and Japanese firms often circumvent the problem of market access through foreign direct investments, many firms initially saw their outsider status as a barrier to entering the corporate networks established by European standardization activities.

Although there were originally fears of a protectionist slant emerging in Europe, this has partially been replaced by exporters' perceptions of the attractiveness of the post-1992 single market. Yet much uncertainty existed in the late 1980s among the American and Japanese business community in particular about: (1) reciprocity, and (2) restrictive European standards testing and certification requirements. In this context, US companies questioned the attractiveness of the post-1992 market as they assessed entry barriers, market characteristics and competitiveness in the new Europe. Focusing on potential restrictive trade practices, a flurry of Congressional hearings in the late 1980s and 1990s emphasized concern about product standards, testing and certification, and public procurement laws that could potentially make it more difficult for American firms to meet European requirements (Congressional Hearings, 1989). Those firms that testified called on US policy-makers to ensure that the EC-92 programme and other concomitant policies were favorable to US business.

Fears among American trade associations that the EC's unwillingness to improve transparency and fairness into its standards activities was placing American exporters at a competitive disadvantage led to the establishment of a US–EC dialogue in 1989. Product standards were given international visibility and, for the first time, made a focus of bilateral negotiations. Despite EU assurances that foreign exporters will benefit from the economies of scale inherent in being able to produce for a large market in the same way as EU firms do, American firms contended that there remained significant handicaps for US exporters.

In particular, the EU's initial requirement that testing and certification take place within Europe generated concern that this would place exporters at a competitive disadvantage given the costs involved. A more substantial problem concerned EU calls for 'reciprocity'. While American firms can take advantage of a single product standard, testing and certification process, European firms were faced with a plethora of standards, testing and certification practices at the state, local and federal level. This creates, in the view of many European firms and trade federations, tremendous difficulties in penetrating American markets. European policy-makers, supported by European industry, wanted assurance of 'balanced access' for their own products in American markets.

To ease problems, the EU and the USA have been trying to promote regulatory cooperation though establishing mutual recognition arrangements. These initiatives have led to certain agreements over mutual acceptance of testing and certification practices so that both

European and American firms avoid any additional costs or discriminatory barriers to market entry. The aim of such agreements is to enhance market access on a reciprocal basis. Trade associations in telecommunications, pharmaceuticals and medical sectors have been actively supporting such developments. These industries view this cooperation as particularly valuable given the wide range of products and the rapid technological developments, resulting in new products entering the marketplace. In addition, American firms complained about the way European standards were adopted in CEN and CENELEC. This led to trade friction as the USA requested a 'seat at the table' in these institutions. Although the EU refused Americans direct access, agreement was reached on regular expert level consultation between the USA and the EC on the development of standards. American firms were provided with the opportunity to comment on draft European standards, thereby having an indirect influence on the process.

Moreover, American concerns that standardization efforts in Europe would distract firms from international activities and duplicate work unnecessarily led to significant changes in European policy. The European standards bodies pledged to work in close cooperation with international standards bodies, and concluded several agreements to use international standards as the basis of their activity where appropriate.[5] Closer coordination of international and European activity has clearly increased the commercial incentives for both American and Japanese firms to renew their commitment and participation at the international level. American and Japanese interest in international standards is also likely to grow because exporters from third countries to the EC are more interested in using international standards as a prerequisite to penetrate the European market.

In contrast to American firms, Japanese firms have been visibly more cautious in their reaction to European standardization. Rather than lobby directly, or via their national government, Japanese firms have frequently sought information from the European standards bodies (personal correspondence, CEN, 1995). On other occasions, Japanese firms have commented or raised questions about European standardization through their national organization, the Japanese standards system. That said, the European standards bodies are under no obligation to modify their standards, although Japanese and American firms have found it useful on occasion to make their position known early on.

In addition, Japanese firms based in Europe have been able to take advantage of their corporate networks and strategic alliances with European firms in order to gain information about European standards.

If a Japanese and American subsidiary in Europe is a member of a national or European trade federation, they can in principle participate and express their views via the trade association. Through these corporate networks, non-European firms can play an important role in influencing the shape and pace of standardization efforts. Here, size of the firm makes a difference as large firms are more likely to undertake unilateral political activity. Such firms have greater resources and often control larger amounts of investment and employment, making them important political constituents (Camerra-Rowe, 1994). In a few cases, working groups involved in standardization have invited non-European experts in such areas as medical and road transport infomatics to provide additional technical expertise.

Clearly, American and Japanese firms have been able to reduce barriers to entry by seeking to minimize the uncertainty of the environment in which they operate. In order to ensure the availability of information and the conditions of market access, Japanese and American firms have adopted several strategies: lobbying via their national governments, engaging in bilateral dialogue with European standards bodies, exchange of information and requesting information on European market entry requirements. With some success, access to the European standards bodies has been improved, albeit American and Japanese firms still feel that the policy differences that survive may produce some disadvantages in the short run.

The regional response to Europe: APEC's role in standardization

Responding to developments in Europe, both Japan and the United States have focused their attention on using APEC as a means of aligning their standards to reduce costs and increase trade. Aiming to enhance trade and productivity in the Asia-Pacific region, APEC began in 1994 to promote the alignment of the national standards of the 18 APEC members with international standards (APEC, 1995). The objectives of APEC'S work in standardization is to identify trade problems created by divergent standards, so as to reduce the negative effects on trade and investment flows due to the differing standards, testing and certification arrangements in the region and to ensure that standards and regulations are not adopted or applied with the effect of creating unnecessary obstacles to trade.

As part of the trade policy role of APEC, the Committee on Trade and Investment has outlined a framework for harmonized standards and common testing and certification arrangements, largely based on existing multilateral agreements on technical barriers to trade such as the General Agreement on Tariffs and Trade (GATT)/World Trade Organization (WTO), World Health Organization and Codex Alimentarus. Although APEC at this stage is focused on infrastructure issues, the increasing institutionalization of this regional trade bloc is likely to foster further cooperation that will ease the market restrictions and cost raising entry barriers from divergent standards, testing and certification practices. Government delegations in Japan and the US have solicited opinions from private sector interests about the most restrictive barriers to trade through existing industrial advisory committees. So far, American firms have indicated their priorities for mutual recognition of standards, testing and certification requirements in telecommunications and information technology, while Japanese firms have voiced their priorities to be alignment of standards in the areas of electronics and electrical equipment.

In comparison to the EC-92 programme, however, there has not been the same level of interest mobilization among Japanese and American trade associations with regard to APEC's activities. Some firms have relied on the National Association of Manufacturers (NAM) and ANSI, to closely follow the developments in APEC committees. This is because APEC is concerned at the moment with setting the institutional framework for what is essentially 'interorganizational diplomacy' between member states. Firms are likely to formalize their cooperation in this new collective fora as member states establish ties to organized interests in order to meet the functional demands arising from the new tasks agreed upon. This may be difficult, as even within a single sector, firms may have different market positions and different policy preferences making the costs of collective agreement high. As the available evidence in the European case indicates, this multilateral coordination in the standards arena is a complex and time consuming task. Notwithstanding the information needs and the costs of non-membership, particularly where the business environment is increasingly complex, and in many respects unfamiliar, increased patterns of business association may be more difficult to forge given the greater differences in national regulatory environments and business cultures among the APEC member states.

Conclusion

This chapter underscores the significance of standards in international trade as well as the importance of studying corporate strategies in shaping the rules of market governance.

First, the strategic implications of standards for firms has led many of them to participate at both the regional and international level. While European firms have recognized the importance and relevance of standardization as a strategy that effectively uses private resources to strengthen their competitiveness, American and Japanese firms have focused instead on developing national standards for their domestic markets. The European standards bodies have effectively promoted their institutional advantages at both the regional and international level. By tying their European standards development to an international framework, the EC and EFTA countries have raised the visibility and importance of setting standards in both the United States and Japan, prompting serious consideration about the need to participate more vigorously at the international level.

Second, setting standards has enabled firms to advocate their preferred positions, but the dynamics of collaboration and association still lead to collective action difficulties. This, in turn, has significant consequences for trade as firms often find it difficult to aggregate preferences. While standards setting has drawn many firms into a complex array of transnational corporate networks, the norms, rules and procedures facilitating cooperation that are critical to reach accommodation and agreement should not hide the often disparate economic interests involved.

Third, the overriding goals of standardization to increase competitiveness and enhance market access opportunities has resulted in spillover and policy-borrowing. The significant challenges from European regional organizations such as CEN, CENELEC and ETSI has served as a focal point for the development of cooperative solutions in other regional markets. The spillover from the European to international arena has increased the number of participants, and given Japanese and American firms an indirect 'voice' in the European policy process. In addition, as APEC has sought to establish a regional standards regime to counteract European influence, it has borrowed from the EU the pattern of regulatory rapprochement by advocating mutual recognition of product standards and testing to help facilitate trade.

Notes

1. Mutual recognition is thus a voluntary surrender of sovereignty. Regulators lose control over some of the transactions that occur within their territory, but will gain extraterritorially.
2. In game-theoretic terms, even though there may be gains from cooperation, it is often difficult to discriminate between different potential outcomes in terms of their efficiency. If multiple Pareto-efficient equilibria outcomes are

possible, then reaching an agreement or durable bargain may take longer. See Stephen Krasner (1991).

3. Olson and Stigler discuss the importance of selective inducements to encourage participation in an activity whose output is a public good available to all, including non-participants. George Stigler, 'Free Riders and Collective Action: An Appendix to Theories of Economic Regulation' *Bell Journal of Economics and Management Science,* vol 5, 1974: 359–65; Mancur Olson, *The Logic of Collective Action: Public Goods and the Theory of Groups,* Cambridge, Mass: Harvard University Press, 1965.

4. One trade official noted, 'many of our products used to set de facto global standards by virtue of the fact that we were dominant in those markets' private interview.

5. It is estimated that 90% of European standards will be of international origin.

14
Global Economic Governance by Private Actors: The International Chamber of Commerce

Volker Schneider

Introduction

The proliferation and growth of international organizations during this century is one of the most significant transformations in modern world politics. A new level of world politics has emerged, with these entities transcending the conventional sphere of nation-states and intergovernmental relations. The broad social and political effects of these transformations, however, are still unsatisfactorily reflected in the theory of international relations. Whereas realists tend to treat these new entities as either irrelevant for global politics or as mere instruments of governments of intergovernmental coalitions, 'transnationalist' or 'globalist' approaches still appear to be too immature to offer convincing theoretical explanations about the role and capacities of international organizations in global politics.[1]

Most studies on international organizations or international networks concentrate on governmental relations, thus neglecting the importance of private actors. This has similarities to the conventional conceptionalization of political processes at the national level in which private actors have only lately received attention. However, today in global politics the private dimension is almost completely absent. As a matter of fact, the involvement of non-state actors in world politics is neither new, nor negligible. The first forms of private action were witnessed in the early nineteenth century, but it is this century that has seen a particularly large growth in these new political forms. The decades following the Second World War, in particular, saw an explosive increase in the population of private, non-governmental organizations, some of which are related to specific intergovernmental or supranational arenas, some also to particular issues or events. Similarly to national patterns of public policy-making, the role of private organizations at the international level is not restricted to lobbying and interest representation, but also includes various contributions to the governance and self-regulation of societal sectors.

International private actors are particularly numerous in the trade and business domain, since the business sector has always been one of the major forces in expanding socioeconomic relations beyond national boundaries. The current wave of globalization has shown that actors representing economic interests appear to be the quickest to adapt to this accelerating trend. This chapter will highlight, and study in some detail, one of these private business organizations at the international level. We deal with one of the most influential non-state actors in international politics: the International Chamber of Commerce (ICC). Although the actions of this international body do not have a high profile in public discussion, its statements and services are well-known to governments and other international organizations. Just as the national Chambers of Commerce have a long history in their contribution to the development of institutional infrastructures for commercial and industrial undertakings in national markets,[2] the ICC as an organization translates some of these national activities to the global level.

While some of its member associations have a quasi-public status in different countries, the ICC essentially is a non-governmental organization composed of thousands of companies and business associations in more than 140 countries. The ICC is engaged in a broad array of activities. On the one hand, it is the major pressure group and lobbyist of global business, whilst on the other, and perhaps even more interesting, are its contributions to the governance of international trade and business. In order to substitute state regulation which is either impossible or undesired, the ICC tries to promote self-regulation in a number of areas ranging from the formulation and promotion of economic rules and standards over the monitoring of commercial crime to the development of self-regulatory codes in environmental protection.

Foundation

The ICC was established in June 1920 in Paris as a result of decisions taken at an international trade conference in Atlantic City (USA) in

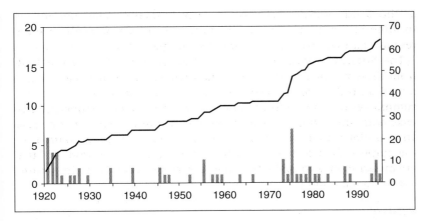

Figure 14.1 National committees (foundations per year and cumulated numbers)

1919. The initiative for this foundation came from the major national chambers of commerce in the USA, UK, France and Belgium. The principal motives were to help those countries in need of economic reconstruction after the First World War, to boost world trade, and to promote the free market system which, at the time, was being challenged by the Bolshevik revolution and related social upheavals in continental Europe. During the 1920s most European countries joined this organization but its growth rather stagnated during the 1930s until the end of the Second World War (see Figure 14.1). In the late 1940s the ICC was reestablished and registered by the French Ministerial Decree of 24 January 1949, Paris. In the postwar period the large expansion of world trade contributed to the increasing globalization of the ICC as it expanded its constituency – especially during the mid 1970s – into the so-called Third World. Currently, it has members in almost all economically relevant regions and countries throughout the world.

Organizational structures and policy resources

The organizational core of the ICC is based at its headquarters in Paris, which contains a staff of almost 100 permanent employees. The second pool of resources on which the ICC can draw is the national committee staff in some 64 countries and the support of member associations and firms, enabling the combination of specialized knowledge by thousands of experts. The comparatively small budget, amounting to some $12 million a year, is therefore only a fraction of the overall resource bases on which the whole ICC complex can call.

The financial contributions to the budget come to a large extent from these national committees. Their contributing shares are determined according to the economic importance of the countries the committees represent. Other sources of income rest on commercial services and publications. The increase in this commercial component is an important trend in the organizational development supported by the current chief of the ICC, who wishes to raise the profile of the organization and to make the chamber more businesslike in nature, that is, to make money (Jack, 1995).

Organization

The formal structure of the organization displays the principal elements of international organizations. In a similar way to the UN, it has very roughly comparable, legislative, executive and judicial elements. The members of the organization are grouped into national committees, which either regularly participate in, or send delegates to, plenary organs such as the Congress, the Conference and the Council. The executive domain is composed of; the presidency, the executive board, and above all, the administrative staff. In addition to these classical organs, there is also a long list of 'working bodies' providing the important communications links between the executive and legislature. Finally, the ICC International Court of Arbitration provides a kind of judicial component to the organization. The *national committees* enable the representation and intermediation of business interests via national groupings in Europe, North and South America, the Middle East, Asia and the Pacific, and Africa. Most of the members of the ICC – about 7000 companies and business associations – are grouped into National Committees, which are formally established associations representing all parties within a particular country who have an interest in the issues of international business. This is accomplished through regular participation within the ICC, particularly through attending ICC Council sessions and the support of various technical commissions, policy-making committees and services. National companies and organizations joining the ICC automatically become members of a national committee or group if one exists in their country. In countries where there is no national committee, subnational chambers, business associations or firms may become direct members.

In approving the foundation of a national committee and the ratification of its constitution, the ICC's Council applies the following criteria: (1) the members of the committee must represent the main economic forces in the country concerned; (2) the relevant country should adhere to the principals of the market economy; and (3) the working organization must be able to regularly and effectively participate in the work and the meetings of the ICC.

Conferences and congresses

The plenary components of the organizations are the Conference and Congress. Congresses are open to all members, and are held every three years on a subject of general interest to businesses. A Conference is then held between two Congresses.

Council

The key legislative body of the ICC is the Council, which meets twice a year and determines the major policy lines. Its composition reflects the different financial weight of the various national committees. Each may nominate one, two or three members according to the proportion it pays of their national committee's total contribution to the central budget.

Presidency

The presidency of the ICC represents the business organization to other national and international organizations. It consists of the president, the vice-president and the immediate past-president. It meets on an *ad hoc* basis and possesses no formal organizational structure.

Executive board

The executive board is responsible for the implementation of the policies decided by the 'legislative' organs just described. It consists of 15 to 21 members elected by the Council on the recommendation of the president. Members serve for a three-year term, and in order to guarantee a certain continuity a third of them must retire at the end of each year. There are seven ex-officio members: beneath the president, vice-president and past-president, also the chairpersons of important working bodies. The secretary general has the role of the secretary of the board which meets at least three times a year, twice in conjunction with Council sessions.

Secretary general and international secretariat

The secretary general is elected by the Council and ensures the general management of the organization. For this, he is supported by an international secretariat, fulfilling preparatory and follow-up tasks for all ICC work in particular, coordinating the activities of different organizational components and of the different commissions. The international secretariat is based in Paris, whilst the publishing activities are provided by a separate organization with the ICC publishing company producing and publishing practical works of business reference.

Central working bodies and discussion forums

Most of the ICC's activities take place within specialized working bodies, that is, particular commissions, services, bureaux or forums. There are 16 commissions – themselves composed of more than 70 subgroups (committees, working parties and standing groups) – covering almost every aspect of contemporary business from energy and the environment to international trade policy, from banking technique and practice to financial services, from competition law to marketing. Commissions are composed of some 500 senior business executives and business experts, specialized in the various aspects of corporate business, and delegated by member companies and organizations. They meet regularly to formulate recommendations on a broad range of issues affecting business and commerce. The various commissions are listed in Table 14.1.

In addition to those bodies that are primarily concerned with policy formulation, there are a number of organizational units which primarily have implementation functions, providing important services and quasi-public goods to their members and the global business community. Altogether, they provide important contributions to governance and self-regulation of international business. Among these units are:

- The *International Court of Arbitration* as the leading body for the resolution of international commercial disputes by arbitration;
- The *International Maritime Arbitration Organization* engaged in maritime arbitration;
- The *International Centre for Technical Expertise* acting as broker for the specialized expertise essential for investigations, findings, recommendations and arbitration;
- The *International Council on Marketing Practice* which administers various ICC codes of marketing practice; and
- The *Institute of International Business Law and Practice* which deal with the legal problems of international trade.

Table 14.1 Commissions of the ICC

Name	Activities
Commission on Air Transport	Forum and spokesman for commercial parties of airline industry to tackle common problems.
Commission on Banking Technique and Practice	Provides international banking industry with uniform rules and positions regarding financial transactions.
Commission on Computing, Telecommunications and Information Policy	Promotes technical guidelines and standards on IT, computer security and telecommunications.
Commission on Energy	Concerned with the role of business and the market economy in the production, conservation, and allocation of energy resources.
Commission on Environment	Works for common position of global business toward environmental problems including self-regulation.
Commission on Financial Services	Monitors and discusses developments in international financial services and their implications for business.
Commission on Insurance	Provides an international forum for insurers and users of insurance services.
Commission on Intellectual and Industrial Property	Promotes protection of patents, trade marks and industrial property rights in general.
Commission on International Arbitration	Promotes arbitration as a means of settling international business disputes.
Commission on International Commercial Practice	Supports development of commercial practice required by progress in transport and information technologies, and market instability.
Commission on International Trade and Investment Policy	Monitors and studies international trade and investment issues at both policy and technical levels.
Commission on Law and Practices	Aims to influence national and EU competition policies with particular reference to the merger control regulation.

Table 14.1   Continued

Name	Activities
Commission on Maritime and Surface Transport	Covers all aspects of maritime and surface transport industries.
Commission on Marketing, Advertising and Distribution	Promotes standards of business behaviour by fostering codes of conduct and self-regulation in the marketing sectors.
Commission on Taxation	Concerned with the harmonization of taxation systems and the resolution of international tax conflicts.
Standing Committee on Regulation of Contractual Relations	Develops international rules for contractual performance.

The different units of the Commercial Crime Services monitor all kinds of economic fraud and crimes, and cooperate with related national law enforcement agencies. The various units are the Commercial Crime Bureau (dealing with commercial fraud in general); the International Maritime Bureau (concerned with all types of maritime crime, including fraud, cargo theft and piracy), and the Counterfeiting Intelligence Bureau which helps companies to prevent faking of their products. The Centre for Maritime Cooperation, also based at the Commercial Crime Services, is promoting merchant fleet development in developing countries.

The International Bureau of Chambers of Commerce (IBCC) provides a world forum for the exchange of ideas and information between the national chambers of commerce. The IBCC is the center of a cooperation network linking chambers of commerce on every continent, and its special mission is to transfer know-how and experience from established chambers in the industrialized countries to chambers in developing countries or the countries in transition to a market economy. The IBCC is also heavily engaged in professional training (for example through instructional books issued by ICC Publishing, the organization of practical seminars on the techniques of international trade, and training programmes). The ICC's Institute for Business Law and Practice organizes regular seminars on negotiating, drafting and exe cuting international contracts. These seminars are mainly organized for business people and lawyers from developing countries and economies in transition.

Another type of organizational sub-unit are the forums being established to facilitate information exchange amongst the various member organizations. The principal example here is the World Business Council for Sustainable Development which resulted from a merger of the World Industry Council for the Environment, and the Business Council for Sustainable Development which had been founded several years ago. The Council encourages discussions on environmental problems and attempts to elaborate the common position of world business toward this issue area.

Activity patterns: between lobbying and self-regulation

In general, the ICC's activities have never attracted great public attention. Only when it acts in global policy arenas playing the role of the spokesman for global business, such as in international trade negotiation at the former GATT or current WTO level, or in the frame of large environmental conferences, does the ICC get some media coverage. The major work of this international organization, however, takes place in rather closed technical commissions, whose conclusions only reach a small circle of experts. However, it is this type of activity in which the ICC provides a major contribution to the governance of international economic relations. Such activities include the making and provision of rules on international financial and non-financial transactions, the rules on temporary duty-free imports, and, most significantly, the arbitration of international trade disputes by the work of the International Court of Arbitration. Further activities in self-regulation are the voluntary codes in the domain of business ethics, marketing and environmental protection.

Representing business in the global policy arena

One of the principal functions of the ICC is interest-representation and lobbying for the global business community. For this function it has an almost unique position, in that it represents the interests of all the main business sectors (including banking, financial services, manufacturing, marketing, communications, air, sea and surface transport) and all world territories and regions. It is therefore no exaggeration to say that the ICC is the only encompassing organization speaking for business in every part of the world. This quest for territorial universality had been a deliberate goal of ICC's policy during the 1990s. As its 1995 activity report says:

> ... the ICC must be seen to be truly representative of companies and business organisations in every part of the world. This means that the ICC must be strong on every continent – not just in the industrialized nations, but also in the former Communist countries, in the Middle East, in Africa, in Latin America, and especially in Asia.

The functional and territorial universality of the organization gives it a distinct authority in dealings with governments and other international actors. It is recognized by the major actors in world politics and has access to all important global arenas ranging from the UN system, the OECD and the EU to the Group of Seven (G7) summits. For instance, each year on the eve of a G7 summit, an ICC delegation calls on the host government leader to present proposals on behalf of international business for consideration at the summit. In its statement to the Naples summit in 1995 for instance, the ICC urged for swift ratification of the Uruguay Round agreements so that the World Trade Organisation could start work on schedule.

The ICC is engaged in intense information exchange and strong working relations with a large number of intergovernmental and non-governmental international bodies concerned with economic and legal affairs. In a special consultative body (the ICC–United Nations–WTO Economic Consultative Committee) the members of the Executive Board and the heads of the major international agencies involved in economic matters meet regularly to discuss the key issues of world trade. Amongst these are the newly formed WTO, the OECD, and a number of UN agencies. These meetings provide an opportunity structure for business leaders and intergovernmental organizations to develop contact at the highest level and promote cooperation on important policy issues.

Within the UN system the ICC has consultative or observer status with the major UN institutions and specialized agencies and other main intergovernmental organizations (IGOs). These are:

- The UN Economic and Social Council (ECOSOC);
- The Food and Agriculture Organization of the United Nations (FAO);
- United Nations Industrial Development Organization (UNIDO);
- World Intellectual Property Organization (WIPO) (Observer Status);

- International Maritime Organization (IMO); and the
- Council of Europe (CE).

In addition, the ICC has intensive cooperation relations with a large number of other IGOs concerned with business issues, and also a huge number of NGO (non-governmental organization) relations. In the environmental area the ICC has broad access to governmental decision-makers and key international bodies. It enjoys official consultative status with the United Nations and UN specialized agencies dealing with the environment, like the UN Environment Programme (UNEP) and the UN Commission for Sustainable Development (UNCSD).

An example of the global representation of business interest is the role it plays in environmental policy. In the preparation of the Earth Summit in Rio de Janeiro in 1992, the ICC and other international business associations founded the World Industry Council for the Environment (WICE) in order to forge a common position for global business toward environmental issues. In the meantime, this council – to which more than 90 major companies belong – has become the foremost business spokesman on environmental issues at the international level. The council mainly organizes conferences in which representatives of companies and business organizations try to counterbalance the worldwide spread to 'green ideologies'. The principal message of business here, is that greater environmental regulation tends to restrain international trade and economic growth, and that solid economic growth is the only way of providing the resources needed for environmental protection on a global scale. Lobbying and policy influence is not the only function of this international body as it is also engaged in private self-regulation, an activity that will be described later on.

Economic governance and global self-regulation

Besides interest representation toward the 'outer actor world' within the global policy arena, there are also important activities of the ICC directed to the provision of 'goods and services' for the internal global business community itself. As has been shown by existing social research on national associations, these activities have a long history. In many countries, the chambers of commerce have played an important role in the construction of the social and institutional preconditions of market economies.[3] Prominent neo-institutionalist studies in economics and social sciences have shown[4] that markets are not the natural state of economic relations but presuppose complex

combinations of institutional elements, ranging from ethical foundations of economic behaviour restricting opportunism, to measurement
and quality standards, to rules and norms regulating contractual performance. Market exchanges involve a host of uncertainties, meaning
that market relations will only flourish and expand if the parallel
development of supportive institutional rule systems succeed through
which these uncertainties are mitigated or, at least, 'governed'.
Because of the enormous political and cultural heterogeneity around
the globe, immense communications problems, and immature institutional mechanisms enabling 'second and third party enforcement'
(North, 1990) on a world scale, the transactional risks involved in
international exchanges is still considerably greater than in national
settings.

In this context, the ICC fulfills important governance functions by
which international market transactions are facilitated. This includes
the making and promotion of norms and standards facilitating cross-
border exchanges, the monitoring of global business behaviour, the
quick diffusion of information on commercial crime, the participation
in the resolution of economic conflicts, and, finally, its contributions
to the mitigation of negative externalities (such as environmental
pollution) in international economic actions.

The making of rules and standards

One of the ICC's main activities is the setting-up and promoting of
rules and standards which decrease the costs of international transactions. Probably the best-known rules complex in this regard are those
of the International Commercial Terms (Incoterms). These terms are
internationally agreed definitions of contractual clauses and key words
frequently used in international trade relations. These rules were issued
for the first time by the ICC in 1936, and have been revised several
times since. Most current ones are perhaps standard clauses such as
FOB (free on board) or CIF (cost, insurance and freight) in international contracts (Hülsemeyer, 1996). From a theoretical perspective
these definitions are 'micro institutions' which reduce transaction costs
(that is, the cost of making and enforcing contracts) through the provision of standardized contractual elements. The ICC also provides complete model international contracts for all principal commercial
relations such as sales of goods, agency, distributorship and franchiz-
ing. The model contracts can be used directly by the parties – thus
economizing in treaty-making costs – or as a reference during negotiations. All in all, these institutional arrangements help to mitigate

divergent contractual interpretations, thus increasing legal security. The diffusion of these standards is supported by the ICC through books, pamphlets, seminars and lectures. The rules are periodically updated to ensure they conform to changes in international practice and new technology, and the latest version came into force in 1994.

From paper-based transactions to electronic trading

As mentioned above, one of the most broadly used 'micro-institutions' developed by the ICC are the 'Uniform Rules and Practice for Documentary Credits' which are also known as letters of credit, or abbreviated as 'L/Cs'. Letters of credit are promises for local banks to pay an exporter once evidence of the exchange of goods (that is, shipment) is provided. Documentary credits thus provide a means whereby exporters are assured of payment by a bank and importers know that the bank will not make payment unless the seller presents the documentary evidence that the goods have been shipped. This system is accepted throughout the world as the mechanism of financing trade that is used by banks. The system is most used in trade with developing countries where credit and country risks are of particular importance.

For some time the ICC has attempted to adapt the old paper-based system to the new possibilities opened up by technological developments in the information and communications sector. Since the document-based nature of the old system often causes delays in payment and collection of goods, and improvements in photocopying and reprographic techniques increase the risk of fraud, it is expected that some of these problems can be solved by the introduction of new technologies. In cooperation with other international organizations, the ICC, therefore, plans to set up a system based on electronic trade credits (ETC).

This idea of creating an electronic alternative has been talked about for a number of years. Banks have automated parts of their L/C processing procedures, and the Swift network allows for the transmission of L/C details between banks. However, the heart of the operation – the checking of documents – still depends on manual procedures. Moreover, modern transportation technologies lead to the problem that goods often arrive quicker than the covering documents. It is expected that this could change rapidly with the spread of corporate telecommunications networks (Schneider 1994). EDI techniques are increasingly applied at all stages of the production and distribution chain, such as stocktaking, ordering supplies and customs procedures. It is expected that electronic trade credits will be just a natural prolongation of this trend, thus leading to a completely new approach to international trade financing.

Another rule system facilitating international trade and global business contacts which will shortly have to be mentioned, is the ATA Carnet system. A 'carnet' is the passport of merchandise which allows temporary duty free imports of it into a foreign country for up to one year. This facilitates, for instance, the presentation of goods and products in foreign fairs, and the system is jointly administered by ICC's IBCC and the World Customs Organization.

Monitoring international fraud, corruption and piracy

Another important contribution to the self-governance of international trade is provided by the ICC's commercial crime services which assist its member companies in the fight against all types of international commercial crime. These services are comparatively recent and started with the International Maritime Bureau in 1981. The ICC Commercial Crime Services, based in London, has bureaux specializing in fraud, maritime crime, and the fight against commercial counterfeiting. There is also a regional office in Kuala Lumpur, which focuses on piracy and other maritime infringements. All these services dealing with commercial crime worldwide are facing growing calls on their resources, and have expanded rapidly during recent years.

An example of international crime inhibiting world trade is that of the persistence of piracy in Southeast Asia and East Africa. The ICC advises ships to take particular care in transiting waters between the South China Sea and the Java Sea. Relatively heavy weaponry, such as mortars and rocket propelled grenades, are being used against vessels sailing in East African waters. In recent incidents, pirates in the coastal regions of Somalia have sometimes misrepresented themselves as coastguards. Their deception often begins with voice warnings, followed by firing with automatic weapons. It is believed that some attacks are aimed at gaining control of a ship in order to seize others, because the pirates' own craft are often too small and slow to be effective. One of the latest incidents saw pirates attacking a British racing yacht off the coast of Somalia. A small craft fired a mortar at the *Longo Barda* in the Gulf of Aden, and some of the crew attempted to board the yacht. However, they quickly fled when a container ship and a Canadian Navy vessel came to the yacht's rescue. Problems in Brazil have recently been highlighted by observers increasingly concerned about armed gangs attacking vessels in the country's ports.

Less violent, but economically much more costly, are commercial crimes such as fraud in trade of raw materials. A recent fraud in the sugar trade, concerned a vessel having berthed at a Brazilian port to pick up a cargo of sugar for India. Unknown to the vessel's owners, a second (false) bill of lading had been drawn up by some criminals, which also showed a sugar cargo being loaded onto the vessel at the same port at about the same time and for the same destination. However, the cargo specification was completely different. The fraudsters then attempted to sell the phantom cargo to the National Trading Company of Nepal, but were caught when this company checked out the documents first with the Commercial Crime Bureau in London.

A further type of fraud is related to the abuse of the documentary credit system where sellers, buyers and banks can all be cheated. Under this system, an importer's bank gives an irrevocable undertaking to pay the exporter against presentation of shipping documents. Provided the documents appear correct, the bank is obliged to hand over the money and its customer has to reimburse the bank. Sometimes, this results in dishonest sellers obtaining full payment for non-existent or low-quality goods, while the buyer still has to pay. An example of this is the Bulgarian trading company who paid out $3.8 million under a letter of credit to buy 12 500 tons of Brazilian refined sugar from a Brazilian trader. But the boat on which the sugar was said to be loaded never arrived and the money was disbursed into five accounts in Switzerland.

In other instances, fraudulent buyers tricked exporters by forging worthless documentary credits. The criminals usually request that goods be shipped by air freight, and in some instances false bank drafts are also presented. Then, when the exporting company claims the payment, it discovers that the bank which is said to have issued the L/C knows nothing about the transaction. An importer who discovers that he may have been defrauded after the credit has been issued and the goods have been shipped, usually has little chance of stopping the bank from paying. This is because courts in most countries have held that bankers' irrevocable payment undertakings are essential to the conduct of international trade. In most instances, the buyer will be left with no remedy other than to sue the seller for the return of the money. Because of the difficulties in stopping or recovering international letters of credit (L/C) payments, preventive steps such as the consultation of the Commercial Crime Services sometimes provide the only effective safeguard.

From a theoretical view, the role of the Commercial Crimes Services of the ICC seems to have a function comparable to the role of medieval law merchant several hundred years ago, at a time when modern nation states did not yet exist and there was no central authority able to enforce contracts. Therefore, other institutional arrangements had to be invented in order to mitigate fraud and cheating, and to protect the merchants from pirates and brigands. As Milgrom *et al.* (1990) convincingly show, the old law merchant and its court of law provided such a mechanism whose effectiveness did not rely on authority but on a reputation system. The law merchant system provided a structure for communication within which information on the behaviour of other traders and particular risks had been transmitted. The monitoring system of commercial crime coordinated by the ICC seems to provide some similar elements of private governance.

Rule-enforcement and arbitration

Another governance mechanism that is closely related to the monitoring system is the ICC International Court of Arbitration, one of the best-known of the ICC's services. Since disputes arise even amongst honest merchants, there needs to be a system for hearing and settling these disputes. Created in 1923, the ICC Court ranks first in the world among institutions organizing and administering international commercial arbitration. It is a neutral and independent body composed of 56 legal experts from about 50 countries and is responsible for the worldwide administering, supervising and resolution of international business disputes by means of arbitration under ICC Conciliation and Arbitration Rules. The Court of Arbitration also acts as appointing authority in *ad hoc* arbitrations. The chairman of the ICC Court appoints referees under the ICC Pre-arbitral Referee Procedure Rules which provide for nomination of a referee empowered to rapidly order provisional measures in matters of urgency during the course of a contract.

A very famous case that has been dealt with at the ICC's Court of Arbitration was a FFr 20 billion claim by Eurotunnel, the operator of the channel tunnel link between France and Great Britain, against the British and French railway companies. The dispute related to the railway usage contract signed in 1987 between the railways and Eurotunnel, the company contracting and operating the channel tunnel. Eurotunnel claimed that the contract would no longer deliver the balance of benefits envisaged by the parties at the time it was agreed, and that some terms should be modified, whereas the railway companies wanted to stick to the original contract (Peston 1993).

Mitigation of negative externalities of industrial activities

Another component of the global economic governance takes the form of institutional devices that help to alleviate some of the negative externalities created by industrial activities worldwide, such as environmental pollution. The organizational units of the ICC dealing with these kind of issues are the Commission on Environment and the World Council on Sustainable Development. The Environmental Commission is one of the 16 specialized commissions that have been outlined above: it includes representatives from enterprises such as Allied Signal, British Petroleum, Dow Chemical, Gerling, ICI, Shell, Texaco and Volkswagen.

The Environmental Commission and the World Council are also, as mentioned above, engaged in private self-regulation. The most noticeable example here is a business charter in which initially about 200 firms and associations committed themselves to environmentally sound operations and environmental management. Mounting concern about environmental issues motivated the ICC to formulate and promote a voluntary code which is known as the 'Business Charter for Sustainable Development'. At the latest count, more than 2000 companies worldwide – including more than a hundred members of the Fortune 500 – have signed to follow the Charter's 16 principles of environmental good conduct. The problem, however, as it is in most international agreements, is that the Charter is dependent on the voluntary spirit within business, and stands or falls depending on how well companies themselves translate their commitment into action, and communicate the progress they are making. The ICC does not even assume a monitoring role, but helps the companies to exchange experiences and to learn how other Charter supporters are tackling implementation.

Conclusion

This case study has aimed to contribute to the growing literature that is inspired by 'transnationalist' or 'globalist' approaches, emphasizing that beside nation-states, private actors such as global business organizations also play an important role in world politics. It was shown that the ICC, as one of the most influential organizations in this sector, not only performs the function of interest representation and lobbying, but also works as one of the global institutional governance devices in the area of commerce and trade. Important activities of the ICC are directed to the provision of 'quasi-public goods' or 'club goods' to the global business community. Major contributions are supportive institutional arrangements including ethical foundations of economic behaviour, measurement and quality standards, rules and norms facilitating the making and enforcing of contracts, monitoring of global business behaviour, effective diffusion of information on commercial fraud and crime, the participation in the resolution of economic conflicts, and, finally, its contributions to the mitigation of negative externalities in international economic actions. Many of these activities would be genuine public tasks and prerogatives within existing nation-states. In a global setting, where effective supranational authority has not yet evolved, it fulfills an indispensable role in the regulation and control of global economic relations.

Notes

1. A short and concise overview on the range of competing theories in this area is given by Willetts (1990).
2. For the history of national chambers of commerce in general and their role in socioeconomic self-regulation see Fischer (1964), Huber (1958) and Magliulo (1980).
3. The German chambers of commerce, for instance, play an important role in vocational education. The chambers are responsible for the administration of apprenticeship examinations through which they can act as 'quality controllers', thus contributing to the 'pool of highly skilled workers in the German economy' (Streeck, 1992), which for a long time was one of the major elements of Germany's competitive advantage.
4. See North (1990), Streeck and Schmitter (1985) and Williamson (1991). A German collection of this kind of studies is provided by Kenis and Schneider (1996).
5. The contract says that 50 per cent of tunnel capacity should be made available to the railways against payments related to volume of traffic and operating costs. This would allow the railways to carry 17.4m passengers and 8.1m tons of freight each year. However, railway usage in the early years of tunnel operation was far less than at the time the contract was signed – and therefore Eurotunnel's revenue from the railways was less. This shortfall was partly due to the late arrival and slow build-up of scheduled passenger train services, according to Eurotunnel (Peston, 1993).

15
Conclusion

Justin Greenwood

There is a long-established and rich tradition of the study of political action involving business interests in domestic environments, and an emergent analysis of business interests in some transnational regional environments, of which studies addressing the EU-level are by now well-instituted. Yet at the global level, and in transnational regional environments beyond the EU, discussion of the role of non-state actors in world politics has been at best patchy, largely dependent upon the popularity of artificially contending camps of international relations. Where mainstream concerns of international relations with states and security have dominated scholarship, so the recognition of non-state actors in global politics has suffered. When international relations has focused on non-state actors, most notably in the first instance during the 1970s (see the branch of 'transnational relations' studies, exemplified by Mansbach *et al.*, 1976), and more recently through international political economy (for example Strange, 1996), so its ability to explain global economic governance has been enhanced. Yet, as Underhill argues persuasively in this volume (Chapter 2), the juxta-position of *either* states *or* transnational actors as the explanatory focus of transnational governance is not a helpful one, in that any credible study of international relations needs both elements. As Levy *et al.* (1996) contend, whether non-state actors contribute is now passé; the issue is what form it takes.

Yet even the very phrases coined by international relations of 'non-state actors', or 'societal interests', belies its failure to adequately address the role of corporate interests in world politics. Indeed, within 'alternative' international relations, studies of business interests have lagged behind study of the role of institutions and regimes, or, where the focus is upon actors, to those of non-governmental organizations such as environmental and wider public interests (see for example Pei-Heng, 1981; Willetts, 1982 and 1996; Princen and Finger, 1994; Williams, 1997). Even where the focus is upon business, the tools of international relations tend to be applied more to the role of multinational firms in the market place, or the political implications of market hegemony, than to the role of business as political actors (see, for instance, Grunberg, 1994; Strange, 1994; Kozul-Wright, 1995; Krasner, 1995; Hirst and Thompson, 1996).

Serious study of political action by, and organization of, key business interests has been left more to comparative political economy, with analysis of the role of firms and organized collective business. Beyond analysis of business actors as political players, comparative political economy and international relations have each offered sustained analysis of the structures within which actors are embedded, and the ways in which these structure and socialize the political response of firms and organized business. Both international relations and comparative political economy are strong in the analysis of the ways in which institutions and regimes structure the responses of business interests to their environment, whilst international political economy has a particular strength in demonstrating how market relations structures political activity. Rather than using one of these traditions, it is the task of this concluding chapter to use insights from each of these perspectives in conjunction with the contributions to this volume and beyond, starting with an analysis of the role of business interests in global liberalization.

Interests and global liberalization

Whilst the thesis of 'globalization' has been questioned as an overstatement (Hirst and Thompson, 1996), no one disputes the growing internationalization of production and finance. The increasing volume of trade in manufactured goods has been particularly marked between industrialized countries. Technological change, transborder communications and mobile capital are all responsible for the internationalization of production, which in turn requires international regulation in the same way as international trade demanded an international law of the sea. Alongside the internationalization of production has been the growing internationalization of finance (Lanzalaco and Gualmini, Chapter 11), particularly since the 1970s. However, much of this is concentrated in the developed world, whose countries represent 95 per cent of the sources of foreign direct investment, and the host of 80 per cent of such flows (Grunberg, 1994). If not 'globalization', there is unquestionably an emerging international economy, where the most important relationships remain those between members of the Organization for Economic Cooperation and Development (OECD) (Hirst and Thompson, 1996).

Growing economic internationalism has both created the need for international systems of regulation of production, exchange and distribution, and responded to it. Large firms have been key factors in all of these processes. At the regional transnational level, the EU and NAFTA are both preferential, transnational marketplaces which have largely been constructed in response to the needs and articulated demands of large-scale business interests, while APEC follows the logic of GATT 1994 in seeking to construct non-preferential, liberalized systems of market exchange in a form of 'open regionalism' best suited to the diversity of the APEC region (Vines, 1997). Much of the 'hyperliberal globalization' thesis which drove significant aspects of the Uruguay Round of GATT was constructed by or with the crucial support of big business interests; indeed, public policy initiatives are not possible without a significant degree of consensus on the ideas on which such initiatives are based. 'Hyperliberal globalization', and its incorporation into the agreements of GATT 1994, represented a triumph of ideology over competing claims of protectionism.

For instance, agreement over GATT 1994 would not have been possible without agreement for the removal of significant protectionism over agricultural subsidies, or without the EU interpreting APEC as the regional (and competing) alternative to a world trading system if the Uruguay Round had not been concluded. Amongst other reasons, the balance between the countries seeking liberalization of agriculture (the 'Cairns group') and those seeking protection (led by the EU and Japan) was resolved through the entry into the arena by new interests seeking to control agricultural support programs. Needless to say, the respective positions of the Cairns countries versus the EU and Japan were very much informed by the interpretation of interests by the farming lobbies in these countries (see, for instance, Gerritsen, Chapter 9). On the other hand, as a *quid pro quo* to other agreements under the auspices of GATT 1994, developing countries insisted on liberalization elsewhere such as textiles and clothing, against the interests of key manufacturers (Hoekman and Kostecki, 1995). Clearly, no one is seeking to lose sight of states as key actors during the focus in this volume upon non-state interests; rather the contributors to this volume argue for recognition of the interdependent world of states and markets.

Basic political economy dictates the business players lining up behind competing claims for liberalization, and protectionism. Those firms in a strong competitive position argued for liberal unregulated market conditions. These are almost always multinational firms, and certainly export-dependent firms, although there are some regional variations, with EU firms less likely to favor protectionism than are American of Japanese firms. Where these firms are unable to achieve multilateral trade agreements, so they are likely to pursue scale economies through existing multilateral trade arrangements (Busch and Milner, 1994). Those facing large losses from such a system have a much greater incentive to organize against liberalization. These respective pressures can account for the ways in which the preferences of states are constructed. For Hoekman and Kostecki (1995: 24), 'the WTO is somewhat analogous to a mast to which governments can tie themselves so as to escape the siren like calls of various pressure groups.' Key amongst these are multinational firms.

Internationalization of markets, finance and politics has resulted in the concentration of firms. This process has been underway for some time, but has been accelerated by the growth of regional transnational markets as firms seek to place themselves in the best competitive position to take advantage of expanded transnational markets and the forces of 'globalization'. Thus, the European single market completion project witnessed a wave of take-overs, mergers and strategic alliances (Jacquemin and Wright, 1994) as firms sought to secure economies of scale, the ability to move into newly-opened marketplaces, enhanced abilities to provide customer services, and restrict competition. Recent years have witnessed considerable global concentration of firms in key economic sectors, such as information technology, telecoms, automobiles, chemicals and pharmaceuticals, banking and financial services, energy and airlines. The result of concentration has been the consolidation of corporate power, with British, Dutch, German, American, Japanese and Swiss firms in particular showing signs of significant orientation beyond their homebase (Hirst and Thompson, 1996). Some of the 7000 multinational corporations with subsidiaries in other countries have more resources at their disposal than even major source countries have (Risse-Kappen, 1995), and are bound therefore to be major agents in the structuration, operation, distribution and regulation of global markets and politics. While states can be undermined by the activities of multinational corporations (MNCs), so too can they be enhanced by them, such as the ways in which oil firms have built up some of the Middle East economies (Krasner, 1995). Some firms possess more independence than do states; and most are deeply involved in the construction of preferences which states bring to global and transnational political arenas.

The influence of business interests in transnational politics has been well-documented outside of this volume. Haufler shows how the activities of private organizations can be similar to the activities of states in shaping international regimes (Haufler, 1993). More recently, based on observations about international cooperation among competing firms, Haufler has claimed that 'one of the most significant and growing sources of international governance is the private sector' (Haufler, 1998: 14). These forms of cooperation range from informal industry norms governing the behavior of participants on a global basis, through cartels, to transnational business associations and private international regimes. These latter structures are forms of global governance, enabling firms to achieve efficiency, stability and power. Typical amongst these are self-regulatory structures. From a survey of these, Haufler has concluded that forms of self-regulation are growing at the international level, and in particular the goals of establishing international standards, and ensuring the security of transactions.

The first of these results from the globalization of commerce, and has principally involved technical standards and codes of conduct. International quality and environmental standards developed through the framework of the International Organization for Standardization (ISO) have become requirements for business transactions, although they are now subject to competition from associations as alternative would-be providers. Regimes to improve security of transactions have also been developed by the business participants themselves, such as the alliance between the major credit card providers and those providing software for the World Wide Web to improve the security of internet shopping. Typically, codes of conduct also emerge from business providers to govern transactions, although often as a means of forestalling governmental regulation. Rule-making, however, often develops beyond business participants alone, and self-regulatory arrangements are displaying signs of increasing complexity at the transnational level (Haufler, 1998). In turn, As Haufler remarks, 'all private regimes raise questions regarding the legitimacy of their goals and decisions' (*ibid.*: 17), which in turn may develop into demands to regulate self-regulation. In the UK, for instance, the Office of Fair Trading maintains a register of the most controversial self-regulatory codes.

There is no lack of evidence of the impact of business associations upon global governance. Cowles has convincingly shown how the

European Round Table of Industrialists (ERT) played a considerable part in the 'Europe 1992' project as a response to their needs to compete in the twenty-first century in the global marketplace. Where states faltered in their commitment, the ERT was there prompting, providing support, and where necessary threatening to switch investment (Cowles, 1995). At the European level, states have been complicit in the transferring of authority from individual nations to specialist policy communities (Underhill, 1997). At the global level, the Multilateral Agreement on Investment concluded under the auspices of the Organization for Economic Cooperation and Development (OECD) continues to be interpreted by some commentators as a shift of power away from governments towards firms, and evidence that the OECD is a prisoner of corporate interests (Walter, 1997).

At the sectoral level, agreement for tariff free trade in pharmaceuticals under GATT 1994 can be attributed to the preferences of the global pharmaceutical industry, and their role in national governments and transnational authority systems. In another GATT case, Sell (1997) has shown how 12 US-based corporations succeeded in getting their interests in intellectual property protection met in public international law, with agreement reached for Trade Related Intellectual Property Systems (TRIPS) under the Uruguay Round of GATT 1994 to be part of the World Trade Organization (WTO) system. For some commentators, TRIPS had become the highest priority in the Uruguay Round of GATT because of the losses American businesses were sustaining from patent infringements in the global marketplace, either through piracy or because of the inadequacy of the previous global regulatory system administered under the UN framework, the World Intellectual Property Organization (Hartridge and Subramanian, 1989). In the first instance, the Pharmaceutical Manufacturers of America had been instrumental in getting the US government to impose $40 million of tariffs on Brazilian imports because of Brazil's continuing refusal to extend product and process patent coverage to pharmaceuticals (Abbott, 1989).

Following this, chief executive officers of 12 US-based multinationals, principally drawn from the chemicals, pharmaceuticals and IT/electronics sectors, formed an *ad hoc* committee in 1986 which sought, and obtained, changes in US domestic laws; performed a whistle-blowing role where violations arose in other countries; and the pledge of the US government to seek a multilateral intellectual property agreement in GATT. The committee successfully urged European (national and European level) and Japanese industry groups to lobby their own governments directly, resulting in both the Europeans and Japanese tabling proposals for intellectual property protection in the GATT negotiations. The US firms thus formed a powerful worldwide coalition of intellectual property owners with organizations such as UNICE, the Union of Industrial and Employers Confederations of Europe, UNICE affiliates, and Kaidenren, the Japanese Federation of Economic Organizations (Reichman, 1989).

Sell comments that 'the transnational leadership of these US based corporations was decisive in the achievement of the TRIPS accord' (Sell, 1997: 4). Sell's explanation for the success of the grouping emphasizes not just their power but because 'ideas matter', and in particular that they were able to build consensus under their idea of hyperliberal globalisation in world trade, particularly in response to mounting protectionist pressures. The theme that 'ideas' matter run through most of the chapters in this collection, and are particularly important to the analysis of Australian agricultural support (Gerritsen, Chapter 9), Mexican banking (Wood, Chapter 4)), product standardization (Egan, Chapter 13), and in assessing the growing contribution of international political economy (IPE) (Underhill, Chapter 2).

This collection has shown conclusively that non-state actors, and in particular business interests, are deeply embedded in structures of governance at the global level. Schneider's study of the International Chamber of Commerce (ICC) (Chapter 14) shows that the role of private organizations at the international level is not restricted to lobbying and interest representation, but also to governance and self-regulation, ranging from economic rules to environmental protection. Apart from lobbying national governments for a swift ratification of the Uruguay Round, recognition in the UN system, the OECD and G7 summits, and acting as spokesman for business in the World Trade Organization, its work has included the construction of rules on international financial and non-financial transactions, the arbitration of international trade disputes, and standards in the monitoring of commercial crime.

The ICC fulfills an indispensable role in the regulation and control of global economic relations. Indeed, Egan (Chapter 13) shows how the lack of institutional capacities at the global level has led to the delegation of regulatory functions to NGOs. CEN, CENELEC and ETSI do not set standards themselves, but provide the framework for voluntary collaboration, with 25 000 participants at the European level alone constructing agreement on transnational product standardization. This 'grassroots' level of transnational integration, built around private and public interests, has developed sophisticated procedures to match those in some of the most advanced transnational institutions, such as qualified majority voting. These structures have been largely developed by business interests, although the presence of these institutions has undoubtedly created a 'pull' factor in integration. In shipping, however, business has undoubtedly been the driving force in creating a global institutional framework (Chapter 12). Here, Ronit finds little evidence of an 'institutional pull', and does not locate mutual adjustment between the International Maritime Organization (IMO) and the main business associations. In standardization, trade associations have been the main players active in trying to promote regulatory cooperation through the establishment of mutual recognition arrangements.

At the transnational regional level, business has been a key driving force in the integration process. In the European Union, where the political role of business has been analyzed most, business shares with states and trans national institutions the responsibility for the achievements of the most advanced regional integration project in the globe (Chapter 5; see also, *inter alia*, Greenwood, 1997). But Gallant and Stubbs (Chapter 6) show that, in Asia, business has led regional economic cooperation rather than governments. Business strategies to seek out low-cost production centers in Southeast Asia led to more foreign direct investment, and more trade, within the region. But rather than governments responding to the activities of business, business has also been the lead player in forcing governments to consider ways of regularizing economic relations, and in seeking the institutionalization of regional economic relations (Chapter 6). Across regions, the story is not dissimilar. For instance, the EU and the USA, already mutually trading goods and services worth more than ecu355 billion (19 per cent of each other's trade in goods), have engaged on a New Transatlantic Marketplace plan with a package of measures to liberalize transatlantic trade. This involves removing trade barriers in four key areas: greater mutual product recognition and/or harmonization; a political commitment to eliminate industrial tariffs by 2010, provided a critical mass of other trading partners also agreeing to do so; a free trade area in services; and further liberalization of investment, public procurement and intellectual property. According to EU sources, proposals to liberalize EU–USA trade could result in benefits to Europe of 150 billion Euros after the first five years (European Commission London, 1998). Whilst the US and EU administrations have been closely involved in establishing the Trans-Atlantic Business Dialogue between American and European firms, EU and American trade associations have taken the agenda forward enthusiastically and meaningfully. Thus, in fields such as telecoms, pharmaceuticals and medical devices, business trade associations on each side have been trying to promote regulatory co-operation through establishing mutual recognition arrangements (Egan, Chapter 13).

In regional integration both 'push' and 'pull' factors can be identified. 'Push' factors include not only pressure for seeking transnational solutions, but in socializing the ideas and preferences of member states to seek transnational solutions. Whilst business is almost always present in 'push' factors for regional economic integration, the institutional 'pull' factor is only clear in the cases of the EU. Indeed, Gallant and Stubbs conclude that APEC has had little impact on business activity in the Asia Pacific region (Chapter 6). Even where business groups have been established to address the APEC level, such as the Pacific Basin Economic Council (PBEC) and APEC's Business Advisory Council (ABAC), such organizations tend to be underdeveloped and have been able to make little impact (Walter, 1997). Coleman and Montpetit, on the other hand, conclude that the EU and NAFTA have led to the increasing internationalization of business (Chapter 10). In the case of the EU, institutional pulls have clearly contributed to the shifting of loyalties, expectations and political activities (amongst business) towards a new center, the key factor in Haas's definition of political integration (Haas, 1958). European-level interest groups are the most numerous and developed of all transnational groups. Whilst there has clearly been a 'magnetic attraction' of the EU in drawing business interests to Brussels, it is worth noting that, although most firms established political operations in Brussels after the Single European Act, most EU-level groups were already well-established there beforehand (Greenwood, 1997). Thus, most of the 600+ EU-wide business interest groups did not form and set up shop in Brussels in response to the Single European Act and the ensuing program, but to a wider set of 'institutional pulls'.

Coleman and Montpetit show how the architecture of states and their institutions deeply influences the architecture of business interest associations, arguing that federal regimes induce territorial differentiation in associations (Chapter 10). Beyond the architecture, they also deeply influence their character and responses. This is clearly the case in respect of the EU, where positive 'pulls' can be identified (Chapter 5); while in the case of APEC (Gallant and Stubbs, Chapter 6), MERCO-SUR (Diaz de Landa and Carola Sajem, Chapter 7) NAFTA (Jacek, Chapter 3), the absence of transnational institutions is a factor responsible for the lack of development of meaningful transnational business interest associations. While special circumstances clearly apply in the case of Russia, the changing architecture of institutions may also be a factor in the rather fledgling state of Russian level business interest associations (Peregudov, Chapter 8).

Institutional pulls include: funding incentives to groups provided by the EU institutions; the chance to assist the overloaded EU institutions in their integration work, both through the provision of information and self-regulatory capacities, and through the provision of physical support to political structures to operate, such as resourcing inter-groups of the European Parliament; and, the power of ideas and social-ization, provided by the participation of interests themselves in the structures of the EU institutions, ranging from informal policy net-works to formal advisory committees. As Egan remarks (Chapter 13), citing Majone (1989), politics cannot be understood purely in terms of power, influence and bargaining, but just as much in terms of policy-oriented learning through participation in institutional structures, and through the power of ideas. Just as with the TRIPS issue, and with the cases of agricultural deregulation in Australia (Chapter 9) and product standardization (Chapter 13), building consensus around an idea was crucial in building support for NAFTA regional trade liberalization (Jacek, Chapter 3). Interestingly, institutional pulls are not present in the NAFTA context and NAFTA-level business associations have not developed, even though US and Mexican business exercised 'push' for trade liberalization in the early 1980s (Jacek, Chapter 3).

Whilst the absence of institutional pulls upon business interest inte-gration can help explain the lack of development of regional transna-tional business interest associations, sometimes the vacuum means that opportunities arise for business interests to undertake tasks not done elsewhere, thereby performing an enhanced role in the integra-tion process. This is certainly the case at the global level, where the lack of institutional capacities has led to the delegation of regulatory functions to NGOs (Egan, Chapter 13). Something similar has also applied in the NAFTA case with issues of trade dispute resolution (Jacek, Chapter 3).

NAFTA has led to some predictable and unpredictable intraregional effects. Of little surprise to observers was the impact of the trade agree-ment in aligning and acting as a change agent upon Mexican business standards, such as the enactment of comprehensive patent and copy-right laws in 1991 during the negotiation of NAFTA (Singleton, 1996). Similarly, Wood shows the significant impact of NAFTA upon the

Mexican Banking Association (Chapter 4). NAFTA led to increasing foreign participation in the banking system, giving the Mexican Banking Association new technical resources and regulatory priorities, and providing it with a central role in new legislative approaches to the financial sector. As was the case with TRIPS, this 'export' factor is not limited to countries within a region. Egan shows how APEC has 'policy borrowed' the concept of mutual recognition from the EU on product standardization (Chapter 13). The 'export' mechanism also works upwards from countries to regions to the global level, in that a generalized disputes panel mechanism for trade conflicts was 'exported' via CAFTA through NAFTA, and from there adopted by the World Trade Organization. Jacek remarks that 'although ostensibly the disagreements are between national states, often governments are merely surrogates or agents of organized business interests' (Chapter 3, p. xx), particularly in the context of public sector downsizing where states have become dependent upon business for the machinery of settling disputes.

But perhaps of greatest interest from the NAFTA experience has been extent of attitudinal convergence from south to north as well as north to south within NAFTA, illustrated by Jacek's study of environmental and labor standards (Chapter 3). Whilst business leaders expected a change of Mexican values to those north of the Mexican border, what was unexpected was that US and Canadian opinion would also start to incorporate Mexican perspectives on labor standards. Although Jacek does not claim NAFTA to be the independent variable in this process, a convergence of politics, problems and ideas similar to those identified by Kingdon (1984) have created an agenda setting climate for once cherished ideas to go into the melting pot. The mixture of problems, politics and ideas was not dissimilar to the pressures which led to the creation of NAFTA itself. Nonetheless, business still has some way to go to triumph with the trade liberalization idea in the face of substantial domestic opposition, and there has been no attempt to forge a common legal framework for North American trade or to allow general labor mobility between the countries involved. Without new trade initiatives, dramatic business interest association integration seems unlikely.

Whilst recognizing the obvious differences between the EU and NAFTA, the growing interaction amongst the North American business community, evidenced in attitudinal change and increased commercial transactions, is in some ways reminiscent of the development of 'spillover' in low politics domains in the European Union. NAFTA lacks the institutions of the EU to add to the agents of states and interests in the development of the integration process. But it is clear from this collection that more than passing reference is required to the role of business interests in the integration process. Indeed, Underhill rightly is bolder: 'An international relations theory which fails to conceptualize the role of non-state actors in general and of organized business in particular is not an international relations of the real world' (Chapter 2).

Transnationalisation and the organization of business interests

Apart from the dynamics exerted by institutional pulls, an open question from the contributions to this volume is the extent to which the transnationalization of business and politics impacts upon the organization of business interests. The issue is addressed directly in the chapters by Coleman and Montpetit (Chapter 10), and by Lanzalaco and Gualmini (Chapter 11). Taken together, these authors raise a number of theses. Lanzalaco also argues that globalization 'stimulates conflict and competition within and between associations; between territorial and sectoral associations, between local, national and transnational associations, between small and large firms' (Chapter 11). This effect arises because globalization disrupts national and local boundaries because of the new alliances forced with associations in other territories, and through the acquisition of new tasks to satisfy the membership. National trade associations, for instance, need to be networked at regional levels to meet the needs of their members. This is a point pursued by Coleman and Montpetit through examining how associations redefine how they are organized territorially when organization beyond the nation-state occurs. Federal regimes, in particular, are held to induce territorial differentiation in associations, whilst the fragmentation which arises from the multilevel governance so typical of transnational regional and global regimes places a premium on associational cohesion.

Lanzalaco and Gualmini (Chapter 11) note a trend in globalization for large firms to bypass associations. Certainly, there has been a recent trend in Brussels for firms to establish their own public affairs operations to address the EU. Whilst the weakness of global institutions means that such a development is unlikely in the cities where these are based, firms remain central as actors in global politics. One example of this concerns their use as a resource by states and the EU in global negotiations. For instance, EU officials chose to take with them personnel from chocolate firms, rather than from the EU chocolate trade association CAOBISCO, to GATT negotiations, because staff from firms are invariably better informed about technical issues than are trade association officials.

Collective action in a transnational context has most recently been examined in an edited collection hosted by Greenwood and Aspinwall (1997), in a study directed at the organization of European-level interests. Most transnational business interest organizations are primarily federations of national associations.[1] In associations of national associations, associability is not so much a collective action question because member organizations are politically active in the first instance. Whilst contributors to the Greenwood and Aspinwall volume placed more emphasis upon the social construction of political behavior than upon Olsonian type economic incentives, the importance of information to transnational associability was highlighted in the context of associations of firms, as corporations moved beyond their national environments into a more uncertain transnational context. Whilst formal and informal information may not act as a direct membership incentive calculus for firms, it may well form part of the calculation of the potential costs of non-membership. That is, whilst it may not be possible to conceive of a firm using positive information as part of the calculus as to whether to join a Euro group, the possibility of missing out on potentially vital information about market or political conditions may create a form of bounded rationality of membership. Similarly, the need for a large firm to join and retain membership of a group to avoid a collective bad may be more important than a contribution to the collective good. This type of membership decision does owe more to Olson than to explanations couched in the social construction of behavior, because the need to avoid a collective bad is an excludable commodity. Seemingly, then, for firms a type of bounded rationality applies to membership of transnational business groups, whilst for associations, membership of transnational federations may be almost automatic.

Some important qualifications need to be made to this tentative conclusion. For large firms as well as for associations, associability may also be semi-automatic behavior. Firstly, firms work so closely together in a variety of national contexts, whether for political or economic reasons, that anti-trust legislation is needed to keep them apart. Large firms are constantly working together in markets, either in particular contexts such as shared research and development, or where market conditions encourage cartel-like behavior (see, for instance, the record levels of fines handed out by DG IV of the European Commission in recent years). Secondly, expanded markets have encouraged concentration through strategic alliances or mergers, easing collective action and creating possibilities for powerful coalitions of political actors. At the European level, large firms work together in key formal groups like the European Round Table of Industrialists, or in a growing number of informal collective structures which are deliberately designed to be free from formal organizational structures. These range from semi-permanent 'clubs' such as the Ravenstein Group (a private and exclusive fora of large firms), to issue-based alliances, such as the European Business Agenda which provided British firms with the ability to respond to the need to influence the climate of opinion within the British government in the run up to the 1996/7 EU intergovernmental conference, dissolving once the need had passed (Greenwood, 1997). There is every sign that these types of structures are developing beyond the regional context, as Sell has shown in the case of intellectual property. Similarly, the Trans-Atlantic Business Dialogue (TABD) has created a framework for large American and European firms, and associations to be closely involved in the construction of market conditions (Chapter 5).

A third qualification to the idea of firms operating with a bounded rational calculus in collective action contexts is the recognition within large-scale enterprises that without their contribution political action may be impossible. Indeed, the annual financial contribution to a trade association is often the only aspect of a firm's range of activities which is never closely scrutinized, because exit is not a realistic option if sectoral political action is to go ahead. Thus, even for business interest organizations which are direct membership organizations for firms, there are reasons to doubt the economic basis of political behavior. Given that most transnational and global business organizations are federations of national associations, the issue of a collective action 'problem' does not seem to arise. The absence of business interest associations at the global level, and in some regional transnational contexts, can thus be explained more by the lack of institutional pulls than by reference to collective action theory.

Regimes, institutions and interests

'Institutions matter' is a clear contention of most of the contributors to this volume. Regime theory's contention that institutions are a necessary ingredient to any theory of world politics provided a direct challenge to neo-realist claims. Institutions use rules, procedures and programs to alter patterns of influence and interests, guide actor behavior and construct actor preferences, and foster learning, identity and collective understanding among participating actors; in Keohane's terms, institutions are 'persistent and connected sets of rules (formal and informal) that prescribe behavioral roles, constrain activity, and shape expectations' (cited in Risse-Kappen, 1995: 29), which can, in the most developed institutions, alter the actors' conceptions of their own self-interests. Institutions and interests can increase their legitimacy by interacting with each other (Willetts, 1982). International institutions can mediate the policy impact of transnational actors by legitimizing demands for changes in national policies, and lower state boundaries allowing for flourishing transnational relations and lowering the costs of coalition building (Risse-Kappen, 1995). Variations in the development of regional (transnational) and global institutions seem to account for the different roles which business interests play in these different settings.

Hoekman and Kostecki usefully make the distinction between different phases of international agreements as a way of conceptualizing the contribution which private interests make to these. These phases are catalyst, pre-negotiation, negotiation, and post-negotiation (Hoekman and Kostecki, 1995). The catalyst stage requires a visionary stance, whether private interest, think-tank or governmental; the European Round Table of Industrialists provide the clearest example of this role performed by private interests in transnational affairs in the context of the EU (Chapter 5), although private interests can also have key relationships with think tanks, which have performed important roles in both the EU and ASEAN contexts (Stone, 1997). The pre-negotiation stage involves the setting of agenda parameters, and, where necessary, constructing rules for how negotiations will be conducted; in international agreements, there is less scope for the role of non-state actors in this phase as procedures tend to be either prescribed, or involve the negotiating parties – usually states – in seeking to limit or delimit the agenda, although sometimes on the basis of a 'game plan' constructed by private interests.

A more withdrawn role for private interests often occurs during the negotiation stage, involving formal governmental actors, although it is conducted with interest (group or otherwise) participation and representation. At one level, this can involve the provision of information about adopting particular courses of action. Sometimes, private and public interests can form part of the official delegations in international summitry. For instance, 150 official delegations to the 1992 UN Conference on the Environment and Development had NGO representatives (Princen and Finger, 1994). In some international organizations, however, interest groups have formal consultative status during the passage of international agreements. Article 71 of the UN Charter provides for consultation with non governmental organizations through the Economic and Social Committee. Category I recognized interests are principally sectional economic interests, although there has been a tendency for these to become incorporated within the machinery of the UN rather than as initiators or independent critics, and many have become over-dependent upon the support of member states and the UN secretariat for their presence (Pei-Heng, 1981). More recently, ECOSOC has undertaken a two-year study on its relationship with non-governmental organizations (NGOs) after more than 22 000 NGO representatives traveled to the 1992 UN Conference on the Environment and Development (Princen and Finger, 1994).

The World Bank has also expanded its formalized links with NGOs, although there is a more mixed picture with the other two pillars of the international economic order, the World Trade Organization (WTO) and the International Monetary Fund (IMF). The IMF has somewhat selective relationships with NGOs, concentrating primarily upon trade unions who are viewed as a potential social partner (O'Brien, 1997). Different interpretations have been provided of the role of the WTO with NGOs. Williams concludes that the WTO remains relatively closed to NGOs (Williams, 1997), while O'Brien has identified specific points of development since NGOs attended the 1994 Marrakech meeting disguised as reporters. Provisions were made for NGO observers at the 1996 Singapore meeting of the WTO, and there are signs that the WTO is forming alliances with NGOs to help secure the support of key states for further liberalization (O'Brien, 1997).

The post-negotiation stage involves implementation. Like the EU, multilateral agreements have to be transposed into domestic law before they can take effect. Where arrangements are wholly within the jurisdiction of international or governmental organizations, so the possibilities for private interest influence may be restricted to the roles of monitoring and 'whistle-blowing'. Where responsibility for implementation is parceled out, private interests may assume complete responsibility through instruments such as self-regulation. Typically, the last scenario happens in contexts where institutional capacities are weak, and in these contexts the post-negotiation stage can afford the greatest role for private interest input.

Each of these stages – from agenda-setting through to negotiation and implementation – therefore involves private interests, although to a greater or lesser extent depending upon the institutional capacities through which negotiations arise, are concluded, and arrangements made for implementation. Taken as a whole, however, the role of private interests in international agreements seems to be greatest in agenda-setting issues and in promoting ideas which require states to work towards solutions (Levy, Young and Zürn, 1996). This is some way from the realist assumption that states always set the framework within which other actors operate.

Risse-Kappen points to the artificiality of the debate between the 'two worlds' of international relations; the idea that 'states dominate' or that 'societal actors and transnational relations prevail'. It is not a question of 'statist realism' or 'societist liberalism'; both perspectives are clearly key elements to an understanding of global economic governance (Risse-Kappen, 1995). International and transnational institutions, too, are clearly key to the structuring and perceptions of interests of state and societal actors. Comparative political economy, and international relations, each emphasize the importance of the structures within which actors are embedded, and the ways in which these structure and socialize the political response of firms and organized business. Whilst international political economy (IPE) shows how market relations structures political activity, this volume has demonstrated how IPE needs also to draw upon the tradition of comparative political economy in focusing upon the actors themselves, in this case business interests, and their political behavior. The conclusion to this volume is therefore that the interplay between 'structure' and 'agency' matters a great deal.

Note

1. At the European level, there has been a tendency in recent years for federations to accommodate large firm interests directly within their structures. However, there is no evidence that direct firm membership organizations are replacing federated structures, in that the peak period for formation of direct firm membership organizations at the European level was the 1970s (Greenwood, Stancich and Strangward, 1999).

Bibliography

Abalkin, L. (1991) *Neispolzovannyi shans*, Moscow: Politisdat.

ABARE (1992) *Commodity Statistical Bulletin*, Australian Bureau of Agricultural and Resource Economics, Canberra: AGPS.

Abbott, F. (1989) 'Protecting First World Assets in the Third World: Intellectual Property Negotiations in the GATT Multilateral Framework', *Vanderbilt Journal of International Law*, vol. 22, no. 4, pp. 691–746.

Adams, R.J. and Singh, P. (1997) 'Early Experience with NAFTA's Labour Side Accord', *Comparative Labor Law Journal*, vol. 18, no. 2, Winter, pp. 161–81.

Aggarwal, V.K. (1985) *Liberal Protectionism: The International Politics of Organized Textile Trade*, Berkeley, Cal.: University of California Press.

Aggarwal, V. (1994) 'Comparing Regional Cooperation Efforts in the Asia-Pacific and North America', in A. Mack and J. Ravenhill (eds), *Pacific Cooperation: Building Economic and Security Regimes in the Asia-Pacific Region*, St Leonards, New South Wales: Allen & Unwin.

Almeida, H. (1996) 'Cambia el perfil del sector automotor', *Gazeta Mercantil Latinoamericana. Suplemento Especial*, vol. 1, no. 37, December, pp. 15–21.

Almeida, H. (1996) 'Fiat inauguró otra fábrica en Argentina', *Gazeta Mercantil Latinoamericana*, vol. 1, no. 38, December, pp. 22–8.

Amin, S. (1996) 'The Challenge of Globalization', *Review of International Political Economy*, vol. 3, no. 2, pp. 216–59.

Anderson, K. (1978) 'On Why Rates of Assistance Differ Between Australia's Rural Industries', *Australian Journal of Agricultural Economics*, vol. 22, no. 2, August.

Anderson, K. (1992) 'Agricultural Trade Liberalization and the Environment: A Global Perspective', *The World Economy*, vol. 15, no. 1, January.

Anderson, K. and Hayami, Y. (eds) (1986) *The Political Economy of Agricultural Protection: East Asia in International Perspective*, Sydney: Allen & Unwin.

Anderson, K. and Tyers, R. (1986) 'Agricultural Policies of Industrial Countries and Their Effects on Traditional Food Exporters', *Economic Record*, vol. 62, no. 179, December.

Andrea, M. (1995) 'Negocios en alza', *Revista do Mercosul*, vol. 35, December.

APEC Secretariat, (1995) 'Joint Statement. Article 16', *Selected APEC Documents: 1989–1994*. Singapore: APEC Secretariat.

APEC Subcommittee on Standards and Conformance, 4 April.

ARB (1995) *Short Report on the Working of the Council and the Board of Directors of ARB (April 1994–May 1995)*, Moscow: ARB, May.

Areous, G.B. (1994) 'The Mexican Model of Labour Regulation and Competitive Strategies', in M.L. Cook and H.C. Katz (eds), *Regional Integration and Industrial Relations in North America*, Ithaca, NY: Institute of Collective Bargaining, New York State School of Industrial and Labor Relations, Cornell University, pp. 52–65.

ASEAN (1991) *ASEAN–Japan Statistical Pocketbook* Tokyo: ASEAN Centre.

ASEAN (1996) *ASEAN–Japan Statistical Pocketbook* Tokyo: ASEAN Centre.

Asociaciòn de Banqueros de Mexico (1996) *Anuario Financiero de la Banca en Mexico, Ejercicio 1995, Volumen LVI* Mexico: Asociacion de Banqueros de Mexico.

Aspinwall, M. and Greenwood, J. (1997) 'Introduction', in J. Greenwood, and M. Aspinwall (eds), *Collective Action in the European Union: Interests and the New Politics of Associability*, London: Routledge, pp. 1–52.

AUSPECC (1990) *Fourth Report by the Australian Pacific Economic Cooperation Committee to the Australian Government*, Canberra, AUSPECC.

Axline, W.A. (1994) 'Comparative Case Study of Regional Cooperation among Developing Countries', in W.A. Axline (ed.), *The Political Economy of Regional Cooperation: Comparative Case Studies*, Madison, New York: Fairleigh Dicksenson University Press, pp. 7–33.

Axline, W.A. (1994) 'Cross-Regional Comparisons and the Theory of Regional Cooperation: Lessons from Latin American, the Caribbean, South East Asia and the South Pacific', in W.A. Axline (ed.), *The Political Economy of Regional Cooperation: Comparative Case Studies*, Madison, New York: Fairleigh Dicksenson University Press, pp. 178–224.

Baldwin, R. (1970) *Non Tariff Distortions of International Trade*, Washington: Brookings Institute.

Ball, A. and Millard, F. (1986) *Pressure Politics in Industrial Societies*, London: Macmillan.

Baran, P. and Sweezy, P. (1966) *Monopoly Capitalism*, New York: Monthly Review Press.

Barkai, A. (1988) *Das Wirtschaftsystem des Nationalsocialismus*, Frankfurt: Fiseker Tasekenbuok.

Barnet, R.J. and Cavanagh, J. (1994) *Global Dreams, Imperial Corporations and the New World Order*, New York: Simon & Schuster.

Barney, J. (1991) 'Firm Resources and Sustained Competitive Advantage' *Journal of Management*, vol. 17, no. 1, pp. 99–120.

Basáñez, M. (1995) *'Public Opinion: Political Issues of NAFTA in Mexico'*, Paper prepared for presentation to the conference NAFTA: A Three-Way Partnership for Free Trade and Growth, University of Connecticut, Storrs, Connecticut, 7 April 1995.

Batchelor, C. (1993) 'Standard Bearers' *Financial Times*, 25 May.

Beer, S.H. (1995) 'Federalism and the Nation State: What can be Learned from the American Experience?', in K. Knop, S. Ostry, R. Simeon, K. Swinton (eds), *Rethinking Federalism: Citizens, Markets, and Governments in a Changing World*, Vancouver: UBC Press, pp. 224–49.

Bergsten, F. (1996) 'The Case For APEC: An Asian Push for World-Wide Free Trade', *The Economist*, 6 January, p. 62.

Bermudez, I. (1994) 'Las inversiones vienen del Norte', *Clarín-Suplemento Económico*, 18 September.

Besen, S. (1990) 'The European Telecommunications Standards Institute: A Preliminary Analysis' *Telecommunications Policy*, pp. 521–30.

Bielschovsky, R.A. and Stumpo, G. (1995) 'Empresas Transnacionales y cambios estructurales en la industria de Argentina, Brasil, Chile y Mexico', *Revista de la CEPAL*, 55, April.

Biznes i politika, no. 1, 1995, p. 14.

Boeva, I., Dolgopolova, T. and Shirokin, V. (1992) *Gosudarstvennye predprijatija v 1991–1992*, Moscow: Institute Economicheskai Politiki.

Booth, K. and Smith, S. (eds) (1995) *International Relations Theory Today*, Cambridge: Polity Press.

Borthwick, M. (ed.) (1994) *Pacific Economic Development Report 1995: Advancing Regional Integration*, Singapore: PECC Secretariat.

Bouchet, F., Orden, D. and Norton, G.W. (1989) 'Sources of Growth in French Agriculture', *American Journal of Agricultural Economics*, vol. 71, no. 2, May.

Braidot, N. (1996) 'El cambio cualitativo de la oferta', *El Cronista. Suplemento Agropecuario*, vol. 2, no. 44, May, p. 31.

Brea, José Luis (1996) 'Las Multinacionales ingresan por Argentina', *Gazeta Mercantil Latinoamericana*, vol. 1, no. 43, June, pp. 23–9.

Breyer, S. (1982) *Regulation and its Reform*, Cambridge, Mass.: Harvard University Press.

Brown, S. (1974) *New Forces in World Politics*, Washington DC: Brookings.

Bull, H. (1977) *The Anarchical Society: A Study of Order in World Politics*, London: Macmillan.

Burnheim, J. (1986) 'Democracy, Nation States and the World System', in D. Held and C. Pollit (eds), *News Forms of Democracy*, London and New Delhi: Macmillan, pp. 218–39.

Busch, M.L. and Milner, H.V. (1994) 'The Future of the International Trading System: International Firms, Regionalism, and Domestic Politics', in R. Stubbs and G. Underhill (eds), *Political Economy and the Changing Global Order* London: Macmillan, pp. 259–76.

Business Week, 'Wireless Terriers' May 23, 1994. pp. 66–7.

Butlin, N.G., Barnard, A., and Pincus, J.J. (1982) *Government and Capitalism: Public and Private Choice in Twentieth Century Australia*, Sydney: Allen & Unwin.

Buzan, B. (1991) *People, States, and Fear*, 2nd edn, Boulder: Lynne Rienner.

Buzan, B. (1993) 'From International System to International Society: Structural Realism and Regime Theory meet the English School', *International Organization*, vol. 47, no. 3, Summer, pp. 327–52.

Cairns, A. (1986) 'The Embedded State: State-Society Relations in Canada', in K. Banting (ed.), *State and Society: Canada in Comparative Perspective*, Toronto: University of Toronto Press, pp. 53–86.

Camerra-Rowe, P. (1994) '*New Roads of Political Influence. The Response of German and British Road Haulage Firms to the 1992 Single European Market*'. Paper presented at the Conference for Europeanists, Chicago.

Campbell, K. (1985a) 'Prospects for Deregulation of Australian Agriculture', *Australian Quarterly*, vol. 57, no. 3, Spring.

Campbell, K. (1985b) 'Changing Institutions, Processes and Issues in the Formation of Australian Agricultural Policy', *Australian Journal of Agricultural Economics*, vol. 29, no. 3, December.

Cardoso, F.H. and Faletto, E. (1969) *Dependency and Development in Latin America*, Berkeley: University of California Press.

Carr, E.H. (1939) *The Twenty Years' Crisis 1919–1939: an Introduction to the Study of International Relations*, London: Macmillan.

Carter, C. and Schmitz, A. (1979) 'Import Tariffs and Price Formation in the World Wheat Market', *American Journal of Agricultural Economics*, vol. 61 pp. 517–22.

Castles, F.G. (1988) *Australian Public Policy and Economic Vulnerability*, Sydney Allen & Unwin.

Cawson, A. (1992) 'Interests, Groups and Public Policy Making: the Case of the European Consumer Electronics Industry', in J. Greenwood, J. Grote, and K. Ronit (eds), *Organized Interests and the European Community*, London: Sage, pp. 99–118.

Cawson, A. (1995) 'Public Policies and Private Interests: The Role of Business Interests in Determining Europe's Future Television System', in J. Greenwood (ed.), *European Casebook on Business Alliances*, Hemel Hempstead: Prentice Hall, pp. 49–61.

CCIAA (1996) Milano Produttiva, rapporto dell' Ufficio Studi della Camera di Commercio, Industria, Artigianato e Agricoltura della Provincia di Milano.

Cecchini, P. with Catinat, M. and Jacquemin, A. (1988) *The European Challenge: 1992: The Benefits of a Single Market*, Aldershot: Windowed House.

Cerny, P.G. (1990) *The Changing Architecture of Politics: Structure, Agency, and the Future of the State*, London: Sage.

Cerny, P.G. (1995) 'Globalization and the Changing Logic of Collective Action', *International Organization*, vol. 49, no. 4, Autumn, pp. 595–625.

Chase-Dunn, C. (1989) *Global Formation: Structures of the World Economy*, Oxford: Basil Blackwell.

Chislett, G.D. (1967) 'Primary Producer Organisations', in D.B. Williams (ed.), *Agriculture in the Australian Economy*, 1st edn, Sydney: Sydney University Press.

Claude, I.L. (1962) *Power and International Relations*, New York: Random House.

Claveloux, D. (1993) *'Talking to the EC: Consultation, Lobbying and Openness: A Background Briefing for the June 15 1993 Conference at the Palais des Congres in Brussels'*, Brussels, Forum Europe.

CNBV (1996) *Plan Estrategico, 1997–2000* Comision Nacional Bancaria y de Valores.

Cobb, R., Ross, J.-K. and Ross, M.H. (1976) 'Agenda Building as a Comparative Political Process' *American Political Science Review*, vol. 70, no. 1, March.

Coccodrilli, F. (1984) 'Dispute Settlement Pursuant to the Agreement on Technical Barriers to Trade: The United-States Metal Bat Dispute' *Fordham International Law Journal*, vol. 7, pp. 137–67.

Cochrane, W.W. (1986) 'Rural Poverty: The Failure of National Farm Programs to Deal With the Problem' *Policy Studies Journal*, vol. 15, no. 2, December, pp. 273–8.

Colbert, E. (1986) 'ASEAN as a Regional Organisation: Economics, Politics and Security', in K.D. Jackson, S. Paribatra and J. Soedjati Djiwandono (eds), *ASEAN in Regional and Global Context*, Berkeley: University of California Press, pp. 194–210.

Coleman, W. (1987) 'Federalism and Interest Groups', in H. Bakvis and W. Chandler (eds), *Federalism and the Role of the State*, Toronto: University of Toronto Press, pp. 171–87.

Coleman, W. (1988) *Business and Politics: A Study in Collective Action*, Montreal: McGill, Queen's University Press.

Coleman, W. (1990) 'State Traditions and Comprehensive Business Associations: A Comparative Structural Analysis.' *Political Studies*, vol. 38, pp. 231–52.

Coleman, W. (1996) *Financial Services, Globalization, and Domestic Policy Change: A Comparison of North America and the European Union*, London: Macmillan.

Coleman, W. (1997) 'Associational Governance in a Globalizing Era: Weathering the Strom', in J.R. Hollingsworth and R. Boyer (eds), *Contemporary*

Capitalism: The Embeddedness of Institutions, Cambridge: Cambridge University Press, pp. 127–53.

Coleman, W. and Grant, W.P. (1988) 'The Class Cohesion and Political Influence of Business: A Study of Comprehensive Associations.' *European Journal of Political Research,* vol. 16, pp. 467–87.

Coleman, W.D. and Jacek, H.J. (1983) 'The Role and Activities of Business Interest Associations in Canada', *Canadian Journal of Political Science,* vol. 16, no. 2, June, pp. 257–80.

Coleman, W. and Jacek, H. (1989) 'Capitalists, Collective Action and Regionalism: An Introduction', in W. Coleman and H. Jacek (eds), *Regionalism, Business Interests and Public Policy,* London: Sage Publications, pp. 1–12.

Coleman, W.D. and Porter, T. (1994) 'Regulating International Banking and Securitites: Emergingin Cooperation among National Authorities', in R. Stubbs and G.R.D. Underhill (eds), *Political Economy and the Changing Global Order,* London: Macmillan, pp. 190–203.

Coleman, W.D. and Skogstadt, G. (1995) 'Neo-Liberalism, Policy Networks, and Policy Change: Agricultural Policy Reform in Australia and Canada', *Australian Journal of Political Science,* vol. 30, no. 2, July.

Commission of the European Communities, (1990) *Cooperation in Science and Technology with Third Countries,* Luxembourg, Office of Official Publications of the European Communities.

Corwin, E.S. (1978) *The Constitution and What it Means Today,* revised by H.W. Chase and C.R. Ducat, Princeton, NJ: Princeton University Press.

Cowles, M.G. (1994) *The Politics of Big Business in the European Community: Setting the Agenda for a New Europe,* PhD thesis, Washington DC: The American University.

Cowles, M.G. (1995a) 'Big Business and Two Level Games: Conceptualizing the Role of Large Firms in EU Affairs'. Paper prepared for presentation to the Fourth biennial International Conference of the European Community Studies Association, Charleston, South Carolina, 11–14 May.

Cowles, M.G. (1995b) 'The European Round Table of Industrialists: The Strategic Player in European Affairs', in J. Greenwood (ed.), *European Casebook on Business Alliances,* Hemel Hempstead: Prentice Hall, pp. 225–36.

Cox, R.W. (1986) 'Social Forces, States, and World Orders: Beyond International Relations Theory', in R.O. Keohane (ed.), *Neorealism and its Critics,* New York: Columbia University Press, pp. 204–54.

Cox, R.W. (1987) *Production, Power, and World Order,* New York: Columbia University Press.

Cox, R.W. with Sinclair, T.J. (1995) *Approaches to World Order,* Cambridge: Cambridge University Press.

Cram, L. (1995) 'Business Alliances in the Information Technology Sector', in J. Greenwood (ed.), *European Casebook on Business Alliances,* Hemel Hempstead: Prentice Hall, pp. 23–37.

Cuesto, R. del (1997) CEO of Banco Nacional de Mexico and Vice-President of the ABM, speech given to the 60th Banking Convention, Cancun, Quintana Roo, March 7/8, 1997.

Curzon, G. and Curzon, V. (no date) *Global Assault on Non-Tariff Barriers,* Thames Valley Essay no. 3, London Trade Policy Research Centre.

Davey, W. J. (1996) *Pine and Swine: Canada-United States Trade Dispute Settlement-The FTA Experience and NAFTA Prospects,* Ottawa, Ontario: Centre for Trade Policy and Law, Carleton University.

DiMaggio, P.J. and Powell, W.W. (1993) 'The Iron Cage Revisited: Institutional Isomorphism and Collective Rationality in Organizational Fields', *American Sociological Review,* vol. 48 (2), pp. 147–60.

Doern, B.G. and Tomlin, B.W. (1991) *Faith and Fear: The Free Trade Story,* Toronto: Stoddart Publishing.

Dougherty, J.E. and Pfaltzgraff, R.L. (1990) *Contending Theories of International Relations,* 3rd edn, New York: Harper & Row.

Dowbiggin, T. (1996) Bank of Montreal, interview conducted 17/03/96, Toronto, Ontario.

Easton, B. and Gerritsen, R. (1996) 'Economic Reform: Parallels and Divergences', in F. Castles, R. Gerritsen and J. Vowles (eds), *The Great Experiment. Labour Parties and Public Policy Transformation in Australia and New Zealand,* Sydney: Allen & Unwin, pp. 22–47.

Ebbinghaus, B. and Visser, J. (1994) *'Barriers and Pathways to "Borderless" solidarity: Organized Labour and European Integration',* paper prepared for presentation to the Economic and Social Research Council conference on 'The Evolution of Rules for a Single European Market', University of Exeter, 8–10 September 1994.

Economist, The (1995) 'Latin America in the Fallout Zone', 7 January.

Economist, The (1995) 'No Action, No Agenda', 25 November.

Economist, The (1997) 'Banking in Emerging Markets Survey', 12 April.

Eden, L. and Hampson, F. O. (1997) 'Clubs are Trumps: The Formation of International Regimes in the Absence of a Hegemon', in J. Rogers Hollingsworth and R. Boyer (eds), *Contemporary Capitalism: The Embeddedness of Institutions,* Cambridge University Press, pp. 361–94.

Edwards, G.W. (1987) 'Agricultural Policy Debate: A Survey', *Economic Record* 63: 181, June.

Edwards, G.W. and Watson, A.S. (1987) 'Agricultural Policy' in F.H. Gruen (ed.), *Surveys of Australian Economics Vol. 1,* Sydney: Allen & Unwin, pp. 189–239.

Egan, M. (1994) *'Regulatory Strategies and European Market Integration',* Paper presented at the Conference for Europeanists, Chicago.

Egan, M. and Zito, A. (1995) *'European Standards Networks and the Formation and Integration of Global Markets',* Paper presented at ISA annual conference, Chicago, April 1995.

Eggertson, L. (1997) 'Marchi a new breed of trade minister: The former environment minister says putting social concerns alongside business matters will be his trademark', *The Globe and Mail,* Toronto: 8 July 1997, pp. B1 and B4.

Eichener, V. and Voelzkow, H.. (1994) 'Europäische Integration und verbandliche Interessenvermittlung: Ko-Evolution von politisch-administrativem System und Verbändelandschaft', in V. Eichener and H. Voelzkow, (eds), *Europäische Integration und verbandliche Interessenvermittlung,* Marburg: Metropolis, pp. 9–25.

Elazar, D. (1994) 'Cooperative Federalism in the United States', in D. Elazar, *Federalism and the Way to Peace.* Kingston: Institute of Intergovernmental Relations, pp. 133–59.

Elazar D. (1995) 'From Statism to Federalism : A Paradigm Shift' *Publius*, vol. 25, pp. 5–18.

El Economista (1995) 'Las inversiones son el motor de la integración económica en el MERCOSUR', 20/01/95, Buenos Aires.

El Economista (1995) 'Las empresas argentinas recién miran a Brasil', 24/11/95, Buenos Aires.

Ellis, U. (1963) *A History of the Australian Country Party*, Melbourne: Melbourne University Press.

Eminent Persons Group Report (1995) *1995: Implementing the Vision*, Singapore: APEC Secretariat.

EUROCHAMBRES (1996) *'The Active Partner for European Enterprise'*, Brussels: EUROCHAMBRES.

European Commission (1996) Directory of Interest Groups, Luxembourg, Office for Official Publications of the European Communities.

European Commission (1992) *An Open and Structured Dialogue Between the Commission and Special Interest Groups*, SEC (92) 2272 final, Brussels: Secretariat of the European Commission.

European Commission London (1998) *The Week in Europe*, 12 March 1998, London, European Commission Office.

European Round Table of Industrialists (ERT) (1996) *The European Round Table of Industrialists*, February 1996, Brussels, ERT.

Evans, P. (1992) 'The State as Problem and Solution: Predation, Embedded Autonomy and Structural Change', in S. Haggard and R. Kaufman (eds), *The Politics of Economic Adjustment: International Constraints, Distributive Conflicts and the State*, Princeton, New Jersey: Princeton University Press, pp.163–166.

Fagen, D. (1997) 'U.S. group files NAFTA lawsuit: Says dispute settlement is unconstitutional', *The Globe and Mail*. Toronto: January 17, p. B7.

Falkner, G. (1995) *'Social Europe in the 1990s: After All an Era of Corporatism?'*, paper prepared for presentation to the Fourth biennial International Conference of the European Community Studies Association, Charleston, South Carolina, 11–14 May 1995.

Far Eastern Economic Review, 1 February 1996. p. 47.

Far Eastern Economic Review, 12 October 1995. pp. 54–60.

Farrell, J. and Saloner, G. (1987) 'Competition, Compatibility and Standards: The Economics of Horses, Penguins and Lemmings', in H. Landis Gabel (ed), *Product Standardization and Competitive Strategy*, Amsterdam: North Holland, pp. 1–21.

Farthing, B. (1993) *International Shipping*, 2nd edn, London: Lloyds of London Press Ltd.

Fecser, P. (1996) Director, Rulings and Compliance Division, Office of the Superintendent of Financial Institutions, interview conducted 19/03/96, Toronto, Ontario.

Financial Times 17 October 1994.

Financial Times 10 December 1993.

Finansovaja Gazeta, no. 19–20, 1995, p. 12.

Finansovye Izvestia, 13 April 1995.

Finansovye Izvestia, 25 May 1995.

Fischer, W. (1964) *Unternehmerschaft, Selbstverwaltung und Staat. Die Handelskammern in der deutschen Wirtschafts- und Staatsverfassung des 19. Jahrhunderts*, Berlin: Duncker & Humblot.

Friedrich, C.Y. and Brzezinski, Z.K. (1956) *Totalitarian Dictatorship and Autocracy*, Cambridge (Mass.): Harvard University Press.

Galtung, J. (1971), 'A Structural Theory of Imperialism', *Journal of Peace Research*, vol. 13, no. 2, pp. 81–118.

Gardner, B. (1989) 'Economic Theory and Farm Politics', *American Journal of Agricultural Economics*, vol. 71, no. 5, December, pp. 1165–71.

Gardner, B. (1992) 'Changing Economic Perspectives on the Farm Problem', *Journal of Economic Literature*, vol. 30, March, pp. 62–101.

GATT (1989) *GATT Trade Policy Review Mechanism – Australia*, Geneva: GATT Secretariat.

Gerritsen, R. (1987) 'Why the "Uncertainty"? Labor's Failure to Manage the "Rural Crisis"', *Politics*, vol. 22, 1 May 1987, pp. 47–59.

Gerritsen, R. (1991) 'Rural Policy', in B. Galligan, O. Hughes and C. Walsh (eds), *Intergovernmental Relations and Public Policy*, Sydney: Allen & Unwin, pp. 277–292.

Gerritsen, R. (1992a) 'The Politics of Microeconomic Reform: Structuring a General Model', *Australian Journal of Public Administration*, vol. 51, no. 1, March, pp. 66–79.

Gerritsen, R. (1992b) 'Labor's Final "Rural Crisis"?: Australian Rural Policy in 1990 and 1991', *Review of Marketing and Agricultural Economics*, vol. 60, no. 2, August, pp. 95–111.

Gerritsen, R. and Abbott, J. (1988) 'Shifting to Certainty?: Australian Rural Policy in 1987', *Review of Marketing and Agricultural Economics*, vol. 56. no. 1, April.

Gerritsen, R. and Abbott, J. (1991) 'Again the Lucky Country: Australian Rural Policy in 1988 and 1989', *Review of Marketing and Agricultural Economics*, vol. 58 no. 1, April, pp. 7–23.

Gerritsen, R. and Murray, A. (1987) 'Rural Policy Survey, 1986: The Battle for the Agenda' *Review of Marketing and Agricultural Economics*, vol. 55, no. 1, April 1987.

Gill, S. (1990) *American Hegemony and the Trilateral Commission*, Cambridge: Cambridge University Press.

Gill, S. (1993) *Gramsci, Historical Materialism, and International Relations*, Cambridge: Cambridge University Press.

Gilpin, R. (1975) *US Power and the Multinational Corporation: the Political Economy of Foreign Direct Investment*, New York: Basic Books.

Gilpin, R. (1977) 'Economic Interdependence and National Security in Historical Perspective', in K. Knorr and F.N. Trager (eds), *Economic Issues and National Security*, Kansas: Regents Press of Kansas/National Security Education Programme, pp. 19–66.

Gilpin, R. (1987) *The Political Economy of International Relations*, Princeton: Princeton University Press.

Glazjev, S. (1993) *Teorija dolgosrochnogo tekhniko-economicheskogo razvitiya* Moscow: Vla Kar.

Goes, F. (1996) 'Fábricas para acortar distancias', *Gazeta Mercantil Latinoamericana*, December 1996. pp. 8–14.

Goes, F. (1996) 'Se dinamiza el comercio de carne', *Gazeta Mercantil Latinoamericana. Suplemento Especial*, vol. 1, no. 37, December 1996, pp. 15–21.

Goldstein, J. (1993) *Ideas, Interests and American Foreign Policy*, Ithaca: Cornell University Press.

Gordon, L. and Keopov, E. (eds.) (1993) *Noviye sozialniye dvisheniya v Rossii*. Moscow: Progress-Komplex.

Gorter, H. de and Tsur, Y. (1991) 'Explaining Price Policy Bias in Agriculture: The Calculus of Support-Maximizing Politicians', *American Journal of Agricultural Economics*, vol. 73, no. 4, November, pp. 1244–54.

Gourevitch, P. (1978) 'The second image reversed: the international sources of domestic politics', *International Organization*, vol. 32, no. 4, pp. 881–912.

Gourevitch, P. (1986) *Politics in Hard Times: Comparative Responses to Economic Crises*, Ithaca: Cornell University Press.

Grande, E. (1996) 'The state and interest groups in a framework of multi-level decision-making: the case of the European Union', *Journal of European Public Policy*, vol. 3, pp. 318–38.

Grant, W. (1987) *Business Interests, Organizational Development and Provate Interest Government: An International Comparative Study of the Food Processing Industry*, Berlin: Walter de Gruyter.

Grant, W. (1989) *Government and Industry*, Aldershot, Hants: Edward Elgar.

Grant, W. (1990) *'Organised Interests and the European Community'*, paper prepared for presentation to the 6th International Colloquium of the Feltrinelli Foundation, Corton, 29–31 May 1990.

Grant, W. (1995) *Pressure Groups, Politics and Democracy in Britain*, 2nd edn, Hemel Hempstead: Harvester Wheatsheaf.

Gray, V. and Lowery, D. (1995) 'Reconceptualising PAC Formation: It's Not a Collective Action Problem, and it May Be an Arms Race', paper prepared for presentation to the annual meeting of the American Political Science Association, Chicago, 30 August–3 September 1995.

Greenwood, J. (1988) *The Market and the State: the Pharmaceutical Representative and General Medical Practice*, PhD thesis, University of Nottingham.

Greenwood, J. (ed.) (1995a) *European Casebook on Business Alliances*, Hemel Hempstead: Prentice Hall.

Greenwood, J. (1995b) 'The Pharmaceutical Industry: A European Business Alliance That Works', in J. Greenwood (ed.), *European Casebook on Business Alliances*, Hemel Hempstead: Prentice Hall, pp. 38–48.

Greenwood, J. (1995c) 'Tourism: How well Served, and Organised, is the 'World's Largest Industry' in Europe?', in J. Greenwood (ed.), *European Casebook on Business Alliances*, Hemel Hempstead: Prentice Hall, pp. 128–142.

Greenwood, J. (1997) *Representing Interests in the European Union*, London: Macmillan.

Greenwood, J. and Aspinwall, M. (eds), (1997) *Collective Action in the European Union: Interests and the new politics of associability*, London: Routledge.

Greenwood, J. and Cram, L. (1996) 'European Level Business Collective Action: The Study Agenda Ahead', *Journal of Common Market Studies*, vol. 34, no. 3, September, pp. 449–63.

Greenwood, J., Grote, J. and Ronit, K. (eds.) (1992) *Organized Interests and the European Community*, London: Sage.

Greenwood, J. and Ronit, K. (1994) 'Interest Groups in the European Community: Newly Emerging Dynamics and Firms' *West European Politics*, vol. 17, pp. 31–52.

Greenwood, J. and Stancich, L. (1997) 'British Business: Managing Complexity', in D. Baker and D. Seawright (eds), *Britain For and Against Europe*, Oxford: Oxford University Press.

Greenwood, J., Strangward, L. and Stancich, L. (1999) 'The Capacities of Euro Groups in the Integration Process', *Political Studies*, 4, 7, 1, March, pp. 127–138.

Grieco, J. (1990) *Cooperation among Nations: Europe, America and Non-Tariff Barriers to Trade,* Cornell, Ithaca: Cornell University Press.

Grimaldi, H.E. (1996) 'El SEBRAE crece en Argentina', *Gazeta Mercantil Latinoamericana. Suplemento Especial*, vol. 1, no. 37, December 1996, pp. 15–21.

Gruen, F.H. (1990) 'Economic Development and Agriculture since 1945', in D.B. Williams (ed.), *Agriculture in the Australian Economy*, 3rd edn, Sydney: Sydney University Press/Oxford University Press, pp. 19–26.

Grunberg, L (1996) 'The IPE of multinational corporations', in D.N. Balaam, and M. Veseth (eds), *Introduction to International Political Economy*, New Jersey: Prentice Hall, pp. 338–359

Gustavo del Castillo, V. (1995) 'Private Sector Trade Advisory Groups in North America: A Comparative Perspective', in V. Gustavo del Castillo and C. Gustavo Vega, *The Politics of Free Trade in North America* Ottawa, Ontario: Centre for Trade Policy and Law, Carleton University, pp. 21–50.

Haas, E.B. (1958) *The Uniting of Europe: Political, Economic and Social Forces 1950–57,* Stanford: Stanford University Press.

Hague, R. and Harrop, M. (1987) *Comparative Government and Politics. An Introduction,* London: Macmillan.

Hall, P. (1986) *Governing the Economy: the Politics of State Intervention in Britain and France,* Cambridge: Polity Press.

Hancher, L. (1990) *Government, Law and the Pharmaceutical Industry in the UK and France,* Oxford: Clarendon Press.

Harding, A. (1985) 'Unemployment Policy: A Case Study in Agenda Management' *Australian Journal of Public Administration*, vol. 44, no. 3, September, pp. 224–246.

Harris, S., Crawford, J., Gruen, F. and Honan, N. (1974) *The Principles of Rural Policy in Australia: A Discussion Paper.* Canberra: AGPS.

Harris, S. (1990) 'Agricultural Trade and Agricultural Trade Policy', in D.B. Williams (ed.), *Agriculture in the Australian Economy*, 3rd edn, Sydney: Sydney University Press/Oxford University Press.

Hartridge, D and Subramanian, A (1989) 'Intellectual Property Rights: the issues in GATT', *Vanderbilt Journal of International Law*, vol. 22, no. 4, pp. 893–910.

Haufler, V (1993) 'Crossing the Boundary between Public and Private: International Regimes and Non State Actors', in V. Rittberger (eds), *Regime Theory and International Relations*, Oxford: Clarendon Press, pp. 94–111.

Haufler, V (1998) Private Sector International Regimes: An Assessment, *Polibus*, vol. 4, no. 1, pp 14–17.

Hayes, J. (1989) 'Who Sets the Standards?' *Forbes Magazine*, April 17, pp. 111–12.

Hayward, J. (1995) 'Organized Interests and Public Policies', in J. Hayward, and E. Page (eds), *Governing the New Europe*, Cambridge: Polity Press, pp. 224–256.

Heath, J. (1997) Interview with Dr Jonathan Heath, economist, Mexico City, 22 May.

Heinz, J.P., Laumann, E.O., Nelson, R.L. and Salisbury, R.H. (1993) *The Hollow Core: Private Interests in National Policy Making*, Cambridge, Mass.: Harvard University Press.

Held, D. (1991) 'Democracy, the Nation-State and the Global System', in D. Held (ed.), *Political Theory Today*, Cambridge: Polity Press, pp. 197–235.

Held, D. (1991) 'Democracy, the nation-state and the global system' *Economy and Society*, vol. 20, pp. 138–72.

Held, D. (1995) *Democracy and the Global Order* , London: Polity Press.

Hendriks, G. (1987) 'The Politics of Food: The Case of FR Germany', *Food Policy*, vol. 12, no. 1, February, pp. 35–45.

Herzenberg, S. (1996) 'Calling Maggie's Bluff: The NAFTA Labor Agreement and the Development of an Alternative to Neoliberalism', *Canadian-American Public Policy*, no. 28, December, pp. 1–39.

Higgott, R. (1994) 'APEC: A Sceptical View', in A. Mack and J. Ravenhill (eds), *Pacific Cooperation: Building Economic and Security Regimes in the Asia Pacific Region*, St. Leonards, New South Wales: Allen & Unwin, pp. 66–97.

Higgott, R. (1991) 'The Politics of Australia's International Economic Relations: Adjustment and Two-Level Games', *Australian Journal of Political Science*, vol. 26, no. 1, March, pp. 2–28.

Higgott, R. and Stubbs, R. (1995) 'Competing Conceptions of Economic Regionalism: APEC versus EAEC in the Asia Pacific', *Review of International Political Economy*, vol. 2, Summer, pp. 516–35.

Hillman, J.S. (1991) *Technical Barriers to Agricultural Trade*, Boulder, CO: Westview Press.

Hinsley, F.H. (1963) *Power and the Pursuit of Peace*, Cambridge: Cambridge University Press.

Hirst, P. and Thompson, G. (1996) *Globalization in Question*, Cambridge: Polity Press.

Hix, S. (1994) 'The Study of the European Community: The Challenge to Comparative Politics', *West European Politics*, vol. 17, no. 1, January, pp. 1–30.

Hoberg, G. (1997) 'Governing the Environment: Comparing Canada and the United States', in K. Banting, G. Hoberg and R. Simeon (eds), *Degrees of Freedom: Canada and the United States in a Changing World*. Montreal: McGill-Queen's University Press, pp. 341–385.

Hoekman, B. and Kostecki, M. (1995) *The Political Economy of the World Trading System: From GATT to WTO*, Oxford, Oxford University Press.

Höhne, G. and Rose, H. (1969) 'Internationale Handelskammer', in G. Höhne and H. Rose (eds), *Handbuch der Internationalen Organisationen*, Berlin: Dietz, pp. 643–646.

Hollingsworth, J.R. and Boyer, R. (1997) 'Coordination of Economic Actors and Social systmes of Production', in J.R. Hollingsworth and R. Boyer (eds) *Contemporary Capitalism: The Embeddedness of Institutions*, Cambridge Cambridge University Press, pp. 1–47.

Holsti, K.J. (1985) *The Dividing Discipline: Hegemony and Diversity in International Relations Theory*, London: Unwin Hyman.

Horridge, M., Pearce, D. and Walker, A. (1990) 'World Agricultural Trade Reform: Implications for Australia', *Economic Record*, vol. 66, no. 194, September, pp. 235–48.

Howlett, M. (1997) 'Sustainable Development: Environmental Policy', in A.F. Johnson and A. Stritch (eds), *Canadian Public Policy: Globalization and Political Parties*. Toronto: Copp Clark Ltd., pp. 99–121.

Huber, E.R. (1958) *Selbstverwaltung der Wirtschaft*, Stuttgart: Kohlhammer.

Hulme, D. (1996) 'Asia Takes Charge of the APEC Train', *Asian Business*, January 1996, p. 34.

Hülsemeyer, A. (1996) 'International Commercial Terms (InCoTerms)' in T. Plümper, *Lexikon der Internationalen Wirtschaftsbeziehungen*, München: Oldenbourg, pp. 161–2.

Hurrell, A. (1995) 'Explaining the Resurgence of Regionalism in World Politics', *Review of International Studies*, vol. 21, no. 4, pp. 331–58.

IAC (1987) *Assistance to Agricultural and Manufacturing Industries*, Canberra: Industries Assistance Commission, Information Paper.

ICC (1996) *The Annual Report of the International Chamber of Commerce 1995*.

ICC (1996) ICC Information pages in the World Wide Web (http://www1.usa1.com/~ibnet/index.html)

ICC (1991) *The Annual Report of the International Chamber of Commerce 1990*.

Inglehart, R., Nevitte, N. and Basáñez, M. (1996) *The North American Trajectory: Cultural, Economic, and Political Ties Among the United States, Canada, and Mexico*, New York: Aldine de Gruyter.

Inter-Federal Advisory Committee (IFAC) *Report to the Secretary of Commerce on the EC Approach to Standards, Testing and Certification*, May 1991, Washington, DC.

International Maritime Organization (1995) *A Summary of IMO Conventions*, London: IMO.

Izvestija, 27 June 1995.

Jacek, H. (1986) 'Pluralist and Corportatist Intermediation, Activities of Business Interest Associations, and Corporate Profits: Some Evidence from Canada', *Comparative Politics*, vol. 18, no. 4, July 1986, pp. 419–37.

Jacek, H. (1987) 'Business Interest Associations as Private Interest Governments', in W. Grant (ed.), *Business Interests, Organizational Development and Private Interest Government: An International Comparative Study of the Food Processing Industry*, Berlin: Walter de Gruyter.

Jacek, H. (1994) 'Public Policy and NAFTA: The Role of Organized Business Interests and the Labor Movement', *Canadian-American Public Policy*, no. 19 October, pp. 1–33.

Jacek, H. (1995) 'The American Organization of Firms', in J. Greenwood (ed.), *European Casebook on Business Alliances*, Hemel Hempstead: Prentice Hall, pp. 197–207.

Jacek, H. (1997) 'The New World of Interest Group Politics in Ontario', in G. White (ed.), *The Government and Politics of Ontario*, 5th edn, Toronto: University of Toronto Press, pp. 307–27.

Jack, A. (1995) 'Business ally means business – International Chamber of Commerce chief plans to raise the body's profile', *Financial Times*, 18 November 1995.

Jacquemin, A. and Wright, D. (1994) 'Corporate Strategies and European Challenges post 1992', in S. Bulmer and A. Scott (eds), *Economic and Political*

Integration in Europe: Internal Dynamics and Global Context, Oxford: Blackwell, pp. 218–31.

Japanese Standards Association (JSA) (1994) 'Outlook of Industrial Standardization in Japan'.

Jarrett, F.G. (1990) 'Rural Research Organisation and Policies', in D.B. Williams (ed.), *Agriculture in the Australian Economy*, 3rd edn, Sydney: Sydney University Press/Oxford University Press, pp. 82–96.

Jimenez, J.C. (1997) Subdirector de Analisis Financiero, Asociacion Mexicana Bancaria , interview conducted 26/08/97, Mexico City.

Johnson, D.G. (1991) *World Agriculture in Disarray*, 2nd edn, London: MacMillan.

Johnson, N. (1973) *Government in the Federal Republic of Germany: The Executive at Work*, New York: Pergamon Press.

Johnson, P.M. and Beaulieu, A. (1996) *The Environment and NAFTA: Understanding and Implementing the New Continental Law*, Washington: Island Press.

Jones, R.S. (1989) 'Political Economy of Japan's Agricultural Policies', *The World Economy*, vol. 12, no. 1, March. pp. 29–38

Jordan, G., Maloney, W.A. and McLaughlin, A.M. (1994) 'Characterizing Agricultural Policy-Making', *Public Administration*, vol. 72, Winter, pp. 505–26.

Kantz, Paul (1997) 'NAFTA Is About Foreign Relations, Not Jobs', *The New York Times*. New York, 16 July 1997, p. A16.

Keeley, J.F. (1983) 'Cast in Concrete for All Time? The Negotiation of the Auto Pact', *Candian Journal of Political Science*, XVI:2 (June) pp. 281–98.

Kelley, D.R. (ed.) (1980) *Soviet Politics in the Brezhnev Era*, New York: Praeger.

Kenis, P. and Schneider, V. (1996) *Organisation und Netzwerk. Institutionelle Steuerung in Wirtschaft und Politik*, Frankfurt/M: Campus.

Keohane, R.O. (1984) *After Hegemony: Cooperation and Discord in the World Political Economy*, Princeton: Princeton University Press.

Keohane, R.O. (1989) *International Institutions and State Power*, Boulder, CO: Westview Press.

Keohane, R.O. (1993) 'The Analysis of International Regimes: Towards a European – American Research Program' in Rittberger, V. (eds), *Regime Theory and International Relations*, Oxford, Clarendon Press, pp. 23–48.

Keohane, R.O. and Nye, J.S. (eds) (1972) *Transnational Relations and World Politics*, Cambridge, Mass.: Harvard University Press.

Keohane, R.O. and Nye, J.S. (1977) *Power and Interdependence: World Politics in Transition*, Boston: Little, Brown.

Kindleberger, C. (1983) 'Standards as Public, Collective and Private Goods', *Kyklos*, vol. 36, no. 3, pp. 377–95.

Kingdon, J. (1984) *Agendas, Alternatives and Public Policies*, Glenview, Illinois: Scott Foresman.

Knorr, K. (1977) 'Economic Interdependence and National Security', in K. Knorr and F.N. Trager (eds), *Economic Issues and National Security*, Kansas: Regents Press of Kansas/National Security Education Programme, pp. 1–18.

Knorr, K. and Trager, F.N. (eds) (1977) *Economic Issues and National Security*, Kansas: Regents Press of Kansas/National Security Education Programme.

Kohler-Koch, B. (1996a) 'Catching up with change: the transformation of governance in the European Union', *Journal of European Public Policy*, vol. 3, pp. 359–80.

Kohler-Koch, B. (1996b) 'Die Gestaltungsmacht organisierter Interessen', in M. Jachtenfuchs and B. Kohler-Koch (eds), *Europäische Integration*, Opladen: Leske & Budrich.

Kolk, A. (1996) *Forests in International Environmental Politics: International Organisations, NGOs and the Brazilian Amazon*, Utrecht, International Books.

Kopinak, K. (1993) 'The Maquiladorization of the Mexican Economy', in R. Grinspun and M.A. Cameron (eds), *The Political Economy of North American Free Trade* Montreal: McGill-Queen's University Press, pp. 141–61.

Kosacoff, B. and Bezchinsky, G. (1994) 'Nuevas estrategias de las empresas transnacionales en la Argentina', *Revista de la CEPAL*, 52, April.

Kozul-Wright, R. (1995) 'Transnational Corporations and the Nation State', in J. Michie and J. Grieve Smith (eds), *Managing the Global Economy*, Oxford: Oxford University Press, pp. 135–71.

Krasheninnikov, Y. (ed.) (1993) *Liberalizm v Rossii*, Moscow: Agentstvo 'Znak'.

Krasner, S.D. (1979) 'The Tokyo Round: Particularistic Interests and Prospects for Stability in the Global Trading System', *International Studies Quarterly*, vol. 23, no. 4, December, pp. 491–531.

Krasner, S.D. (ed.) (1983) *International Regimes*, Ithaca: Cornell University Press.

Krasner, S.D. (1983a) 'Structural Causes and Regime Consequences: Regimes as Intervening Variable', in S.D. Krasner (ed.), (1983) *International Regimes*, Ithaca: Cornell University Press, pp. 1–21.

Krasner, S.D. (1991) 'Global Communications and National Power: Life on the Pareto Fronteir' *World Politics*, vol. 43, pp. 336–66.

Krasner, S.D. (1994) 'International Political Economy: Abiding Discord', *Review of International Political Economy*, vol. 1, no. 1, Spring, pp. 13–9.

Kriesi, H. and Farago, P. (1989) 'The Regional Differentiation of Business Interest Associations in Switzerland', in W. Coleman and H. Jacek (eds), *Regionalism, Business Interests and Public Policy*, London: Sage Publications, pp. 153–72.

Lachica, E. (1997) 'NAFTA shifts textile trade: Canada and Mexico gain U.S. market share at Asia's expense', *The Globe and Mail*, Toronto: 16 July 1997, p. B8.

Landmarks Publications (1997) *European Public Affairs Directory 1998*, 8th edn, Brussels: Landmarks.

Lanzalaco, L. (1990) 'Pininfarina President of the Confederation of Industry and the Problems of Business Interest Associations', in R.Y. Nanetti and R. Catanzaro (eds), *Politics in Italy: A Reader*, vol. IV, London: Pinter, pp. 102–23.

Lanzalaco, L. (1992) 'Coping with Heterogeneity: Peak Associations of Business within and across Western European Nations', in J.Greenwood, J.R. Grote and K. Ronit (eds), *Organized Interests and the European Community*, London: Sage, pp. 173–205.

Lanzalaco, L. (1993) 'Interest Groups in Italy: from Pressure Activity to Policy Networks', in J. J. Richardson (ed.), *Pressure Groups*, Oxford: Oxford University Press, pp.113–130.

Lanzalaco, L. (1995) 'Constructing Political Unity by Combining Organizations: UNICE as a European Peak Association', in J. Greenwood (ed.), *European Casebook on Business Alliances*, Hemel Hempstead: Prentice Hall, pp. 259–70.

Lanzalaco, L. and Schmitter, P. (1992) 'Europe's Internal Market, Business Associability and the Labour Movement', in M. Regini (ed.), *The Future of Labour Movements*, London: Sage, pp. 188–216.

Lapina, N. (1993) *Rossijskoye predprinimatelstvo. Opyt sociologicheskogo analiza*, Moscow: Institute Nauchkoi Informatzic, 1993.

LatinFinance (1997) *Mexico: Building for Growth*, LatinFinance Government Relations Supplement, September 1997.

Lattimore, R., Ross, B. and Sandrey, R. (1988) *'Agricultural Policy Reforms in New Zealand'*, Paper Presented to the 20th International Conference of Agricultural Economists, Buenos Aires, 24–26 August, Mimeo.

Lazlovich, M. (1993) 'The American Tradition: Federalism in the United States', in M. Burgess and A-G. Gagnon (eds), *Comparative Federalism and Federation: Competing Traditions and Future Directions*, Toronto: University of Toronto Press, pp. 187–202.

Lecraw, D. (1987) 'Japanese Standards – a barrier to trade?', in H. Landis Gabel (ed.), *Product Standardization and Competitive Strategy*, North Holland, Amsterdam.

Lee Tsao, Y. (1994) 'The ASEAN Free Trade Area: The Search for a Common Prosperity', *Asian-Pacific Economic Literature*, vol. 8, May 1994, pp. 1–7.

Lenin, V.I. (1967) *Imperialism, the Highest Stage of Capitalism*, New York: International Publishers.

Levy, M.A., Young, O.R. and Zürn, M. (1996) 'The Study of International Regimes', in Young, O. (ed), *The International Political Economy and International Institutions*, Vol II, Cheltenham: Edward Elgar, pp. 503–57.

Lewin, L. (1994) 'The Rise and Decline of Corporatism: The Case of Sweden', *European Journal of Political Research*, vol. 26, no. 1, pp. 59–80.

Lewis, P. (1990) 'Rural Population and Workforce', in D.B. Williams (ed.), *Agriculture in the Australian Economy*, 3rd edn, Sydney: Sydney University Press/Oxford University Press, pp. 201–14.

Ley-Borras, R. (1997) 'Forecasts and Decisions on Economic Pacts in Mexico', *The Annals of the American Academy of Political and Social Science*, vol. 550, March 1997, pp. 85–95.

Lindert, P.H. (1991) 'Historical Patterns of Agricultural Policy', in C.P. Timmer (ed.), *Agriculture and the State*, Ithaca: Cornell University Press, pp. 29–83.

Lloyd, A.G. (1987) 'The Australia–New Zealand Farm Problem and the Appropriate Role for Government', *Australian Economic Review*, vol. 79, Spring, pp. 3–20.

Lopes, F. (1996) 'La columna vertebral del MERCOSUR', *Gazeta Mercantil Latinoamericana. Suplemento Especial*, vol. 1, no. 37, December 1996, pp. 15–21.

Luna, Jose de (1996), Director de Asuntos Internacionales, Comision Nacional Bancaria y de Valores, interview conducted 10 September 1996, Mexico City.

Magliulo, B. (1980) *Les Chambres de Commerce et d'Industrie*, Paris: Press Universitaires de France.

Mahler, V.A. (1991) 'Domestic and International Sources of Trade Policy: The Case of Agriculture in the European Community and the United States' *Polity*, vol. 24, no. 1, Fall, pp. 27–47.

Majone, G. (no date) *'Independence vs Accountability? Non-Majoritarian Institutions and Democratic Control in Europe'* European University Institute: Florence, Mimeo.

Majone, G. (1989) *Evidence, Argument and Persuasion in the Policy Process*, New Haven: Yale University Press.

Mansbach, R.W., Ferguson, Y.H. and Lampert, D. (1976) *The Web of World Politics: Non State Actors in the Global System*, Englewood Cliffs: Prentice Hall.

Martin, W. (1990) 'Rural Policy', in C. Jennett and R. Stewart (eds.), *Hawke and Australian Public Policy: Consensus and Restructuring*, South Melbourne: Macmillan Australia, pp. 155–79.

Martinelli, A. (ed) (1991) *International Markets and Global Firms. A Comparative Study of Organized Business in the Chemical Industry*, London: Sage.

Martinelli, A. and Treu, T. (1984) 'Employers' Associations in Italy', in J.P. Windmuller and A. Gladstone (eds), *Employers' Associations and Industrial Relations: A Comparative Study*, Oxford: Clarendon Press, pp. 264–93.

Mazza, S., ANSI President, Testimony Before the House Subcommittee on Technology, Environment and Aviation, 101 Congress, Second Session, 22 September 1994.

McDonald, B.J. (1990) 'Agricultural Negotiations in the Uruguay Round' *The World Economy*, vol. 13, no. 3, September. pp. 299–327.

McDowell, S.D. (1994) 'India, the LDCs, and GATT Negotiations on Trade and Investment in Services', in R. Stubbs, and G. Underhill. (eds), *Political Economy and the Changing Global Order*, London: Macmillan, pp. 497–510.

Méndez, A. (1996) 'El gobierno promete que protestará', *La Voz del Interior*, 24 December 1996.

Méndez, A. (1996) 'Preocupan promociones de Brasil a la producción de automóviles', *La Voz del Interior*, 17 December 1996.

Middlemas, K. (1979) *Politics in Industrial Society*, London: Deutsch.

Middleton, I. (1993) 'A Number of Hats', *Seatrade Review*, December, pp. 6–7.

Milgrom P.R., North, D.C. and Weingast, B.R. (1990) 'The Role of Institutions in the Revival of Trade: The Law Merchant, Private Judges, and the Champagne Fairs' *Economics and Politics*, 2, pp. 1–23.

Millman, G.J. (1995) *The Vandals' Crown: How Rebel Currency Traders Overthrew the World's Central Banks*, New York: Free Press.

Milner, H. (1991) 'The Assumption of Anarchy in International Relations Theory: a Critique', *Review of International Studies*, 17:1, January, pp. 67–85.

Milner, H. (1988) *Resisting Protectionism: Global Industries and the Politics of International Trade*, Princeton: Princeton University Press.

Miner, W.M. and Hathaway, D.E. (1992) 'World Agriculture in Crisis: Reforming Government Policies', in W.M. Miner and D.E. Hathaway (eds), *World Agricultural Trade: Building a Consensus*, Halifax: Institute for Research on Public Policy.

Moody-O'Grady, K. (1994) 'Dispute Settlement Provisions in the NAFTA and the CAFTA: Progress or Protectionism', *The Fletcher Forum of World Affairs*, Winter/Spring, pp. 121–34.

Moran, M. (1991) *The Politics of the Financial Services Revolution*, London: Macmillan.

Moravcsik, A. (1993) 'Preferences and Power in the European Community: A Liberal Intergovernmentalist Approach', *Journal of Common Market Studies*, vol. 31, pp. 473–524.

Morgenthau, H.J. (1956) *Politics among Nations: the Struggle for Power and Peace*, New York: Alfred Knopf.

Morrison, C.E., (1994) 'The Future of APEC: Institutional and Structural Issues', *Analysis*, vol. 6, no. 1, Special Issue 'APEC at the Crossroads'.

Morse, E.L. (1976) *Modernization and the Transformation of International Relations*, New York: Free Press.

Murphy, C. and Tooze, R. (eds) (1991) *The New International Political Economy*, Boulder: Lynne Rienner.

Naishul, V. (1982) 'Liberalism è economicheskye reforme', *Mirovaya economica i meshdunarodniye otnosheniya*, no. 8, pp. 69–81.

Nassif, A.A. (1994) 'The Mexican Dual Transition: State, Unionism and the Political System', in M.L. Cook and H.C. Katz (eds.), *Regional Integration and Industrial Relations in North America*. Ithaca, New York: Institute of Collective Bargaining, New York State School of Industrial and Labor Relations, Cornell University, pp. 132–41.

Nejamkis, G. (1995) 'Las trabas que el mercado ampliado le pone a las empresas', *Suplemento Gazeta Mercantil*, 15 December 1995.

Nejamkis, G. (1996) 'Malta argentina para Kaiser', *Gazeta Mercantil Latinoamericana*, vol. 1, no. 42, 26 January 1996–1 February 1996.

Newton, A. (1990) 'Innovations in the Administration of Primary Industry Statutory Authorities', in A. Kouzmin and K. Scott (eds), *Dynamics in Australian Public Sector Management: Selected Essays*, Melbourne: Macmillan Australia, pp. 120–36.

Nezavisimaja Gazeta, 23 July 1992.

Nezavisimaja Gazeta, 19 April 1995.

Nofal, M.B. (1996) 'Acuerdo Automotriz: ¿Realismo negociador, paso hacia adelante en la armonización o retroceso en la integración?', *Revista Pulso*, SOCMA, May.

North, D. (1990) 'Institutions and their Consequences for Economic Performance' in K. Cook, and M. Levi (eds), *The Limits of Rationality*, Chicago: University of Chicago Press, pp. 383–401.

O'Brien, R. (1995) 'North American Integration and International Relations Theory', in the *Canadian Journal of Political Science*, vol. xxviii; no. 4, December, pp. 693–724.

O'Brien, R. (1997) '*Complex Multilateralism: The Global Economic Institutions – Global Social Movement Nexus*', Paper prepared for presentation to the 'Non State Actors in the Global System' conference, University of Warwick, 31 October–1 November 1997.

O'Brien, R. (1997) *Subsidy Regulation and State Transformation in North America, the GATT and the EU*, Basingstoke: Macmillan.

O'Brien, R. et al. (1998) *Complex Multilateralism: The Global Economic Institution Global Social Movement Nexus*, Report prepared for the Global Economic Institutions and Global Social Movements Workshop, London, 29 February 1998.

Ockwell, A. (1990) 'The Economic Structure of Australian Agriculture', in D.B. Williams (ed.), *Agriculture in the Australian Economy* (3rd edn), Sydney: Sydney UniversityPress/Oxford University Press, pp. 27–49.

OECD (1990) *OECD Economic Outlook 47, June (Supplement: Progress of Structural Reform)*, Paris: OECD.

Olson, M. (1965) *The Logic of Collective Action: Public Goods and the Theory of Groups*, Cambridge, Mass: Harvard University Press.

Olson, M. (1982) *The Rise and Decline of Nations. Economic Growth, Stagflation and Rigidities*. New Haven: Yale University Press.

Olson, M. (1993) 'The Logic of Collective Action', in J. Richardson (ed.), *Pressure Groups*, Oxford: Oxford University Press, pp. 23–37.

Ons, C. (1994) 'La promoción de la complementación económica entre empresas de la región', *Integración Latinoamericana*, vol. 19, no. 197, INTAL, January–February.

Owen, R. and Sutcliffe, B. (eds.) (1972) *Studies in the Theory of Imperialism*, London: Longman.

Pacific Business Forum, (1995) Report: *The Osaka Action Plan: Roadmap to Realising the APEC Vision*, Singapore: APEC Secretariat.

Pacific Business Forum, (1994) Report: *A Business Blueprint for APEC: Strategies for Growth and Common Prosperity*, Singapore: APEC Secretariat.

Pedler, R. and van Schendelen, M.P.C.M. (eds.) (1994) *Lobbying the European Union: Companies, Trade Associations and Issue Groups*, Aldershot: Dartmouth.

Pei-Heng, C. (1981) *Non-Governmental Organizations at the United Nations: Identity, Role, and Function*, New York: Praeger.

Pelkmans, J. (1982) 'The Assignment of Public Functions in Economic Integration', *Journal of Common Market Studies*, vol. 25, pp. 249–69.

Peregudov, S. (1997) *Business Interest Groups and the State in the CIS*, Paper delivered at the International Political Science Association World Congress, Seoul, 17– 21 August 1997.

Peston, R. (1993) 'Eurotunnel seeks help from French', *Financial Times*, 21 August.

Petit, M. (1985) *Determinants of Agricultural Policies in the United States and the European Community*, Washington: International Food Policy Research Institute, Research Report No. 51.

Pijnenburg, B. (1996) *'EU Lobbying by Ad Hoc Coalitions: an exploratory case study'*, Paper prepared for presentation to the Annual Meeting of the Western Political Science Association, San Francisco, 14–16 March 1996.

Pitigalini, F. (1934) *The Italian Corporate State*, NY: Macmillan.

Platzer, H-W. (1995) 'Internationale Handelskammer', in U. Andersen, and W. Woyke, (Hrsg.) *Handwörterbuch Internationale Organisationen*, Opladen: Leske und Budrich (2. Auflage), pp. 188–191.

Porter, T. (1997) *Private International Goverance and Inter-state Regimes: The Case of the Chemical and Steel Industries*, Paper delivered at the International Studies Association, Toronto, March 1997.

Princen, T. and Finger, M. (1994) *Environmental NGOs in World Politics*, London: Routledge.

Putnam, R. (1988) 'Diplomacy and domestic politics: the logic of two-level games' *International Organization*, vol. 42, pp. 427–60.

Randle, W.P. (1996) Assistant General Counsel and Foreign Bank Secretary, Canadian Banking Association, interview conducted 18 March 1996, Toronto, Ontario.

Rausser, G.C. (1990) 'The Political Economy of Agriculture in the United States', in H. Michelmann; J. Stabler and G. Storey (eds), *The Political Economy of Agricultural Trade and Policy*, Boulder: Westview Press, pp. 57–91.

Ravenhill, J. (1995) 'Economic Cooperation in Southeast Asia: Changing Incentives', *Asian Survey*, vol. 35, September.

Reich, R.B. (1997) *Locked in the Cabinet*. New York: Alfred A. Knopf.

Reichman, J.H. (1989) Intellectual Property in International Trade: Opportunities and Risks of a GATT connection, *Vanderbilt Journal of International Law*, vol. 22, no. 4, pp. 747–891.

'Report to Secretary of Commerce of the (IFAC) Federal Advisory Committee on the EC Common Approach to Standards, Testing and Certification in 1992', Washington DC, 1991.

Rieger, H.C. (1991) *ASEAN Economic Cooperation Handbook*, Singapore: ISEAS.

Risse-Kappen, T. (1995a) 'Exploring the Nature of the Beast: International Relations Theory and Comparative Policy Analysis Meet the European Union' *Journal of Common Market Studies*, vol. 34, pp. 53–80.

Risse-Kappen, T. (1995b) *Bringing Transnational Relations Back In*, New York: Cambridge University Press.

Rittberger, V. (1995) *Regime Theory and International Relations*, Oxford University Press.

Roberts, I. and Whish-Wilson, P. (1993) 'The US Export Enhancement Program and the Australian Wheat Industry', *Agriculture and Resources Quarterly*, vol. 5, no. 2, June, pp. 228–41.

Robinson, I. (1994) 'How Will the North American Free Trade Agreement Affect Worker Rights in North America?', in M.L. Cook and H.C. Katz (eds.), *Regional Integration and Industrial Relations in North America*. Ithaca, New York: Institute of Collective Bargaining, New York State School of Industrial and Labor Relations, Cornell University, pp. 105–31

Robinson, I. (1995) '*The NAFTA Labour Accord in Canada: Experience, Prospects, and Alternatives*', Symposium on NAFTA at Age One: A Blueprint for Hemispheric Integration? vol. 10, no. 2, *Connecticut Journal of International Law*. Spring, pp. 475–531.

Ronit, K. (1995) 'European Actions of Organized Shipping: National and Global Constraints', in J. Greenwood (ed.), *European Business Alliances*, Hemel Hempstead: Prentice Hall, pp. 184–96.

Rose, R. (1993) *Lesson Drawing in Public Policy: A Guide to Learning Across Time and Space*. Chathman, New Jersey: Chathman House Publishers, Inc.

Rosenau, J.N. (1980) *The Study of Global Interdependence: Essays on the Transnationalization of World Affairs*, London: Frances Pinter.

Rosenau, J.N. (1986) *The Study of Global Interdependence*, London: Frances Pinter.

Rosenau, J.N. (1990) *Turbulence in World Politics: A Theory of Change and Continuity*. Princeton, NJ: Princeton University Press.

Rosenau, J.N. and Czempiel, E-O. (eds) (1992) *Governance without Government: Order and Change in World Politics*. Cambridge: Cambridge University Press.

Sajem, M.C. (1995) '*Sectores Industriales en Argentina y Brasil. Situación actual y perspectivas frente a la formación de un Área de Libre Comercio en América del Sur*', Mimeo: Cordoba.

Salgado, A. (1997) 'Participacion foranea de 53.1% en el sistema bancario azteca', *El Financiero*, 25 September 1997.

Sally, R. (1994) 'Multinational Enterprises, Political Economy, and Institutional Theory: Domestic Embeddedness in the Context of Internationalization', *Review of International Political Economy*, vol. 1, no. 1, Spring, pp. 161–92.

Scharpf, F.W. (1988) 'The Joint-Decision Trap: Lessons from German Federalism and European Integration', *Public Administration*, vol. 66, Autumn, pp. 239–78.

Scharpf, F.W. (1989) 'Decision Rules, Decision Styles and Policy Choices', *Journal of Theoretical Politics*, vol. 1, pp. 149–76.

Scharpf, F.W. (1991) 'Political Institutions, Decision Styles and Policy Choices', in R. Czada, and A. Windhoff-Heritier (eds), *Political Choice: Institutions, Rules, and the Limits of Rationality*, Boulder, CO: Westview Press, pp. 53–86.

Schendelen, M. van (ed.) (1994) *National Public and Private EC Lobbying*, Aldershot: Dartmouth.

Schmidt, S.C. (1991) 'Agricultural Self-Sufficiency in Developed Countries', in F.J. Ruppel and E.D. Kellogg (eds), *National and Regional Self-Sufficiency: Implications for International Agriculture*, Boulder: Lynne Rienner Publishers.

Schmitter, P. (1974) 'Still the Century of Corporatism?', *Review of Politics*, vol. 36, no. 1, pp. 85–131.

Schmitter, P.C. (1986) *Experimenting with the Scale of Culture, Production and Governance in Western Europe*, Firenze, European University Institute, May, mimeo, second version.

Schmitter, P.C. (1988) 'Corporative democracy: oxymoronic, Just plain moronic? Or a promising way out the present impasse?', mimeo, Stanford: Stanford University Press, March.

Schmitter, P.C. (1996) *Corporatism Meets the Globalized Economy: Is There going to Be a Predictable Winner or Looser?*, Paper presented at the panel on 'International Relations' of the International Conference on 'Technology, Environment, Economy and Society in a World Context', Fondazione Enrico Mattei, Milano, 24–26 October 1996.

Schmitter, P.C. (1997) 'The Emerging Europolity and Its Impacts Upon National Systems of Production', in J.R. Hollingsworth and R. Boyer (eds), *Contemporary Capitalism: The Embeddedness of Institutions*, Cambridge: Cambridge University Press.

Schmitter, P.C. and Lanzalaco, L. (1988) 'L'organizzazione degli interessi imprenditoriali a livello regionale', *Stato e mercato*, no. 22, April 1988, pp. 63–96.

Schmitter, P. and Lanzalaco, L. (1989) 'Regions and the Organization of Business Interests', in W. Coleman and H. Jacek (eds), *Regionalism, Business Interests and Public Policy*, London: Sage, pp. 201–30.

Schmitter, P.C. and Scharpf, F.W. (1985) 'Experimenting with Scale: Further Thoughts on an (un)common frame of reference', mimeo.

Schmitter, P.C. and Streeck, W. (1981) '*The Organization of Business Interests, A Research Design to Study the Associative Action of Business in the Advanced Industrial Societies of Western Europe*', Discussion Paper of the International Institute of Management-Labour Market Policies Division IIM/LMP 1981/13, Berlin: Wissenschaftszentrum.

Schmitz, A. (1988) 'GATT and Agriculture: The Role of Special Interest Groups' *American Journal of Agricultural Economics*, vol. 70, no. 5, December, pp. 994–1005.

Schneider, V. (1994) 'Multinationals in Transition: Global Technical Integration and the Role of Corporate Telecommunication Networks', in J. Summerton (ed.), *Large Technical Systems in Change*, Boulder, CO: Westview, pp. 71–91.

Schuknecht, L. (1991) 'The Political Economy of EC Protectionism: National Protectionism Based on Article 115, Treaty of Rome', *Public Choice*, vol. 72, pp. 37–50.

Schultz, S. (1996) 'Regionalisation of World Trade: Dead End or Way Out?' in M.P. van Dijk and S. Sideri (eds), *Multilateralism versus Regionalism: Trade Issues After the Uruguay Round*, London: Frank Cass, pp. 20–39.

Schwartz, H.M. (1994), *States versus Markets: History, Geography, and the Development of the International Political Economy*, New York: St Martin's Press.

Segodnja, 7 July 1995.

Segodnja, 14 July 1995.

Seiper, E. (1982) *Rationalising Rustic Regulation*, St Leonards, NSW: Centre for Independent Studies.

Sell, S. (1997) '*The Agent-Structure Debate: Corporate Actors, Intellectual Property and the WTO*', Paper prepared for presentation to the 'Non-State Actors and Authority in the Global System' conference, University of Warwick, 31 October–1 November 1997.

Siglioccoli, A. (1994) 'Las Multinacionales apuntan a la industria de los alimentos', *Clarín-Suplemento Económico*, 18 September 1994.

Siglioccoli, A. (1995) 'La alimentación invirtió US$ 3500 millones en instalaciones fabriles' *El Economista*, 24 November 1995.

Simandjuntak, D. (1994) 'Regionalism and Its Implications for the Asia-Pacific', *The Indonesian Quarterly*, vol. 22, no. 4, pp. 355–66.

Simeon, R. and Robinson, I. (1991) *State, Society and the Development of Canadian Federalism*, Toronto: University of Toronto Press.

Simon, M. (1995) 'Is APEC Irrelevant?', *Far Eastern Economic Review*, 23 March 1995, p. 35.

Sinclair, T.J. (1994) 'Passing Judgement: Credit Rating Processes as Regulatory Mechanisms of Governance in the Emerging World Order', *Review of International Political Economy*, vol. 1, no. 1, Spring, pp. 133–159.

Singleton, R. (1996) 'Knowledge and Technology: The Basis of Wealth and Power', in Balaam, D.N and Veseth, M. (1996) *Introduction to International Political Economy*, New Jersey: Prentice Hall, pp. 195–214.

Skogstad, G. (1987a) *The Politics of Agricultural Policy-Making in Canada*, Toronto: University of Toronto Press.

Skogstadt, G. (1987b) 'Federalism and Agricultural Policy', in H.M. Bakvis and W.M. Chandler (eds), *Federalism and the Role of the State*, Toronto: University of Toronto Press, pp. 188–215.

Smith, M.P. (1996) 'Beyond Clientelism: Agricultural Networks in Ireland and the European Union', *West European Politics*, vol. 19, pp. 583–609.

Solé, C. (1989) 'Regionalism and the Organization of Business Interests in the Spanish Textile Industry', in W. Coleman and H. Jacek (eds), *Regionalism, Business Interests and Public Policy*, London: Sage, pp. 113–26.

Solomon, S.G. (ed.) (1983) *Pluralism in the Soviet Union*, London: Macmillan.

Sosa, D.V. (1996) 'Continúan llegando capitales externos', *Gazeta Mercantil Latinoamericana. Suplemento Especial*, vol. 1, no. 37, December 1996, pp. 15–21.

Stern, A. (1994) *Lobbying in Europe After Maastricht: How to Keep Abreast and Wield Influence in the European Union*, Brussels: Club de Bruxelles.

Stewart, W. H. (1984) *Concepts of Federalism*, Lanham, Maryland: University Press of America.

Stigler, G. (1974) 'Free Riders and Collective Action: An Appendix to Theories of Economic Regulation', *Bell Journal of Economics and Management Science*, vol. 5, pp. 359–65.

Stoeckel, A. (1985) *Intersectoral Effects of the CAP: Growth, Trade and Unemployment*. Bureau of Agricultural Economics, Occasional Paper No. 95, Canberra: AGPS.

Stone, D. (1997) 'Think Tanks as Global Actors', paper prepared for presentation to the 'Non State Actors in the Global System' conference, University of Warwick, 31 December–1 November 1997.

Stopford, J. and Strange S. with Henley, J. (1991) *Rival States, Rival Firms*, Cambridge: Cambridge University Press.

Straits Times, The (1994) 'APEC: Stage set for Consensus on Direction', 13 November 1994, p. 1

Strange, S. (1971) *Sterling and British Policy: A Political Study of an International Currency in Decline*, London: Oxford University Press.

Strange, S. (1976) *International Monetary Relations*, vol. II of A. Shonfield ed. *International Economic Relations of the Western World 1959–1971*, Oxford: Oxford University Press.

Strange, S. (1979) 'The Management of Surplus Capacity: Or How Does Theory Stand Up to Protectionism 1970s Style?', *International Organization*, vol. 33, no. 3, Summer, pp. 303–34.

Strange, S. (1983) 'Cave! Hic Dragones: a Critique of Regime Analysis', in S.D. Krasner (ed.), (1983) *International Regimes*, Ithaca: Cornell University Press, pp. 337–354.

Strange, S. (1986) *Casino Capitalism*, Oxford: Blackwell.

Strange, S. (1994) 'Rethinking Structural Change in the International Political Economy: States, Firms and Diplomacy', in Stubbs R. and Underhill G. (eds), *Political Economy and the Changing Global Order*, London, Macmillan pp. 103–15.

Strange, S. (1994), 'Wake Up Krasner! the World *has* Changed', *Review of International Political Economy*, vol. 1, no. 2, Summer, pp. 209–219.

Strange, S. (1994) 'Who Governs? Networks of Power in World Society', *Hitotsubashi Journal of Law and Politics*, Special Issue, June, pp. 5–17.

Strange, S. (1995a) 'Political Economy and International Relations', in K. Booth, and S. Smith (eds), *International Relations Theory Today*, Cambridge: Polity Press, pp. 154–74.

Strange, S. (1995b) 'What Future the State?', *Daedalus*, vol. 124, no. 2, Spring, pp. 55–74.

Strange, S. (1996) *The Retreat of the State: the diffusion of power in the world economy*, Cambridge: Cambridge University Press.

Stratta, I. (1996) 'Fuerte expansión del área alimenticia', *Gazeta Mercantil Latinoamericana. Suplemento Especial*, vol. 1, no. 37, December 1996, pp. 15–21.

Strawbridge, G.M. (No date) *'The New Approach to Technical Harmonization and Standards'* British Standards Institute: 2.

Streeck, W. (1988) *'Interest Variety and Organizing Capacity: Two Class Logics of Collective Action?'*, Paper presented at the International Conference on 'Political Institutions and Interest Intermediation', University of Konstanz, Germany, 20–21 April.

Streeck, W. (1989) *'The Social Dimension of the European Economy'*, Paper presented to the Andrew Shonfield Association, Florence, Italy, September.

Streek, W. (1989) 'The Territorial Organization of Interest and the Logics of Associative Action: The Case of *Handwerk* Organization in West Germany', in

W. Coleman and H. Jacek (eds), *Regionalism, Business Intersts and Public Policy*, London: Sage, pp. 59–94.

Streeck, W. (1992) *Social Institutions and Economic Perforamce: Studies of Industrial Relations In Advanced Capitalist Economies*, London and Newbury Park, CA: Sage.

Streeck, W. and Schmitter, P. (1991) 'From National Corporatism to Transnational Pluralism: Organized Interests in the Single European Market', *Politics and Society*, vol. 19, pp. 133–64.

Streeck, W. and Schmitter, P. (1985) 'Community, Market, State – and associations? The prospective contribution of interest governance to social order', in W. Streeck and P. Schmitter (eds), *Private Interest Government. Beyond Market and State*, Beverly Hills: Sage, pp. 1–29.

Streeck, W. and Schmitter, P. (eds) (1985) *Private Interest Government. Beyond Market and State*, London: Sage.

Stubbs, R. (1994) 'The Political Economy of the Asia-Pacific Region', in R. Stubbs and G.R.D. Underhill (eds), *Political Economy and the Changing Global Order*, London: Macmillan, pp. 366–71.

Stubbs, R. (1995) 'Asia-Pacific Regionalization and the Global Economy: A Third Form of Capitalism?' *Asian Survey*, vol. 35, September, pp. 793–95.

Stubbs, R. and Underhill, G.R.D. (1994a), 'Global Issues in Historical Perspective', in R. Stubbs, and G.R.D. Underhill (eds), (1994), *Political Economy and the Changing Global Order*, London: Macmillan, pp. 145–62.

Stubbs, R. and Underhill, G.R.D. (eds) (1994) *Political Economy and the Changing Global Order*, London: Macmillan.

Tangeman, M. (1995) 'Mexico: the once, and future, banking crises', *Institutional Investor*, November 1995.

Terry, C., Jones, R. and Braddock, R. (1988) *Australian Microeconomic Policies*, 3rd edn, Sydney: Prentice Hall.

Thambipollai, P. (1994) 'Continuity and Change in ASEAN: The Politics of Regional Cooperation in South East Asia', in Axline, pp. 105–35.

Thorburn, H. (1985) *Interest Groups in the Canadian Federal System*, The Collected Research Studies/Royal Commission on the Economic Union and development Prospects for Canada, vol. 69, Toronto: University of Toronto Press.

Thorelli, H. (1986) 'Networks: Between Markets and Hierarchies', *Strategic Management Journal*, vol. 7, no. 1, pp. 37–51.

Todesca, J.A. (1996) *La necesidad de una política industrial en la Argentina*, SOCMA-Sociedad Macri, Buenos Aires.

Toner, G. and Conway, T. (1996) 'Environmental Policy', in G.B. Doern, L.A. Pal and B.W. Tomlin (eds), (1996) *Border Crossings: The Internationalization of Canadian Public Policy*, Toronto: Oxford University Press, pp. 108–44.

Tracy, M. (1990) 'The Political Economy of Agriculture in the European Community', in H. Michelmann; J. Stabler and G. Storey (eds), *The Political Economy of Agricultural Trade and Policy*, Boulder: Westview Press, pp. 9–34.

Traxler, F. and Schmitter, P.C. (1994) 'Prospective Thoughts on Regional Integration, Interest Politics and Policy Formation in the European Community/Union', Paper prepared for presentation to the XVth World Congress of the International Political Science Association, Berlin, 20–24 August 1994.

Trebbeck, D. (1990) 'Farmer Organisations', in D.B. Williams (ed.), *Agriculture in the Australian Economy*, 3rd edn, Sydney: Sydney University Press/Oxford University Press, pp. 127–43.

Troughton, M.J. (1985) 'Industrialisation of US and Canadian Agriculture', *Journal of Geography*, vol. 84, pp. 255–64.

Tyers, R. (1991) 'On the Neglect of Dynamics, Risk and Market Insulation in the Analysis of Uruguay Round Food Trade Reforms', *Australian Journal of Agricultural Economics*, vol. 35, no. 3, December, pp. 295–313.

Tyers, R. and Anderson, K. (1992) *Disarray in World Food Markets: A Quantitative Assessment*, Cambridge: Cambridge University Press.

Underhill, G.R.D. (1990) 'Industrial Crisis and International Regimes: France, the EEC, and International Trade in Textiles, 1974–1984', *Millennium: Journal of International Studies*, vol. 19, no. 2, Summer, pp. 185–206.

Underhill, G.R.D. (1994) 'Conceptualising the Changing Global Order', in R. Stubbs and G.R.D. Underhill (eds), *Political Economy and the Changing Global Order*, London: Macmillan, pp. 17–44.

Underhill, G.R.D. (1997), 'Private Markets and Public Responsibility in Global System: Conflict and Co-operation in Transnational Banking and Securities Regulation', in G.R.D. Underhill (ed.), *The New World Order in International Finance*, London: Macmillan, pp. 17–49.

Underhill, G. R. D. (1998) *Industrial Crisis and the Open Economy*, London: Macmillan.

Union of International Associations (UIA) (ed.) (1996) 'International Chamber of Commerce (ICC)', in UIA, *International Organizations and Biographies* (CD-Rom), #B14901391920 – NGOB, Brussels.

Union of International Associations (ed.) (1994) *Yearbook of International Organizations 1994/1995, Vol. 1*, Organization Descriptions and Cross-References, 30th edn, Munich: K.G. Saur.

US Congress (1994) Hearings Before the House Subcommittee on Technology, Environment and Aviation, 101 Congress, Second Session, September 22, 1994.

US Congress (1989) Hearings Before the Subcommittee on Europe and the Middle East, and on International Economic Policy and Trade, Committee on Foreign Affairs, House of Representatives, 'Europe 1992: Economic Integration Plan' 101st Congress, 23 February, 23 March, 5–13 April, 10–11 May 1989.

US Congress (1966) Hearings Before the Ad Hoc Subcommittee of the House Committee on Science and Astronautics, 'International Commercial Standards Activities', 89 Congress, 1966.

US Congress Office of Technology Assessment, (1992) *Global Standards: Building Blocks for the Future*, Washington DC.

Valdez, A. (1987) 'Agriculture in the Uruguay Round: Interests of the Developing Countries', *World Bank Economic Review*, vol. 1, pp. 571–93.

Valle, A. del (1997) CEO of Banco Internacional and President of the ABM, speech given to the 60th Banking Convention, Cancun, Quintana Roo, March 7/8, 1997.

Vera, T. and Bizzozero, L. (1993) 'La dimensión sectorial de la integración en el Mercosur', *Integración Latinoamericana*, vol. 18, no. 196, INTAL, December 1993.

Vines, D. (1997) *'Open Regionalism'*, Paper prepared for presentation to the 'Non State Actors in the Global System' conference, University of Warwick, 31 October–1 November 1997

Viotti, P.R. and Kauppi, M.V. (1987) *International Relations Theory: Realism, Pluralism, Globalism*, New York: Macmillan.

Wallerstein, I. (1974) *The Modern World-System*, New York: Academic Press.

Wallerstein, I. (1979) *The Capitalist World-Economy*, Cambridge: Cambridge University Press.

Walter, A. (1997) *Globalization and Corporate Power: who is setting the rules on international direct investment?*, paper prepared for presentation to the 'Non State Actors in the Global System' conference, University of Warwick, 31 October–1 November 1997.

Walters, P.G. and Toyne, B. (1989) 'Product Modification and Standardization in International Markets', *Columbia Journal of World Business*, vol. 24, Winter, pp. 37–44.

Waltz, K. (1959) *Man, the State, and War*, New York: Columbia University Press.

Waltz, K. (1979) *Theory of International Politics*, Reading, Mass.: Addison-Wesley.

Watson, A. (1979) 'Rural Policies', in A. Patience and B. Head (eds), *From Whitlam to Fraser: Reform and Reaction in Australian Politics*, Melbourne: Oxford University Press, pp. 157–72.

Westell, D. (1994) 'Ottawa to throw green at green: Strategy earmarks over $200 million to study, promote environment industry', *The Globe and Mail*, Toronto: September 23, p. B4.

Willetts, P. (1982) *Pressure Groups in the Global System*, London: Pinter.

Willetts, P. (1990) 'Transactions, Networks and Systems', in A.J.R. Groom and P. Taylor (eds), *Frameworks for International Co-operation*, London: Frances Pinter, pp. 255–84.

Williams, M. (1997) 'International Organisations and the Environmental Social Movement', paper prepared for the conference Non-state Actors and Authority in the Global System Governance, University of Warwick, 31 October–1 November 1997.

Williamson, O.E. (1991) 'Comparative Economic Organization: The Analysis of Discrete Structural Alternatives', *Administrative Science Quarterly*, vol. 36, pp. 269–96.

Winham, G.R. and H.A. Grant (1995) 'NAFTA: An Overview', in D. Barry, M.O. Dickerson and J.D. Gaisford (eds.), *Toward a North American Community? Canada, the United States, and Mexico*. Boulder, CO: Westview Press, pp. 15–31.

Winters, L.A. (1990) 'Digging for Victory: Agricultural Policy and National Security', *The World Economy*, vol. 13, no. 2, June, pp. 170–90.

Witzke, H. von (1986) 'Endogenous Supranational Policy Decisions: The Common Agricultural Policy of the European Community', *Public Choice*, vol. 48, pp. 157–74.

Wolman, H. (1988) 'Understanding Recent Trends in Central-Local Relations: Centralisation in Great Britain and Decentralisation in the United States', *European Journal of Political Research*, vol. 16, pp. 425–35.

Wonder, B. and Fisher, B. (1990) 'Agriculture in the Economy', in D.B. Williams (ed.), *Agriculture in the Australian Economy*, 3rd edn, Sydney: Sydney University Press/Oxford University Press, pp. 50–67.

Woods, L.T. (1993) *Asia-Pacific Diplomacy: Nongovernmental Organisations and International Relations,* Vancouver: University of British Columbia Press.

Woods, L.T. (1991) 'Non-governmental Organisations and Pacific Cooperation: Back to the Future?', *The Pacific Review,* vol. 4, no. 4, pp. 312–21.

Yarbrough, B.V. and Yarbrough, R.M. (1990), 'International institutions and the new economics of organization', *International Organization,* vol. 44, no. 2, Spring, pp. 235–59.

Young, A.R. (1995) 'Participation and Policy Making in the European Community: Mediating between Contending Interests', Paper prepared for presentation to the Fourth biennial International Conference of the European Community Studies Association, Charleston, South Carolina, 11–14 May 1995.

Young, O. (1989) *International Cooperation: Building Regimes for Natural Resources and the Environment,* Ithaca: Cornell University Press.

Zito, A. (1995) 'Integrating the Environment into the European Union: the History of the Controversial Carbon Tax', in C. Rhodes and S. Mazey (eds), *State of the EU,* vol. iii, Boulder, CO: Lynne Rienner, pp. 431–48.

Index